JESUS IN AN AGE OF CONTROVERSY

Douglas Groothuis

Doug Groothuis
Jude 3

HARVEST HOUSE PUBLISHERS
Eugene, Oregon 97402

Cover by Left Coast Design, Portland Oregon.

JESUS IN AN AGE OF CONTROVERSY
Copyright © 1996 by Harvest House Publishers
Eugene, Oregon 97402

Library of Congress Cataloging-in-Publication Data

Groothuis, Douglas R., 1957–
    [Revealing the New Age Jesus]
    Who is this man Jesus? / Douglas Groothuis.
        p.   cm.
    Originally published: Revealing the New Age Jesus. Downers Grove,
Ill. : InterVarsity Press, c1990.
    Includes bibliographical references and index.
    ISBN 1-56507-497-1 (alk. paper)
    1. Jesus Christ—New Age movement interpretations—Controversial literature.
2. Jesus Christ—History of doctrines—20th century.   3. New Age movement—
Controversial literature.   4. Jesus Christ—Person and offices.   I. Title.
[BT304.93.G76   1996]
232—dc20   96-3673
                                                                   CIP

Printed in the United States of America.

96 97 98 99 00 01 02 /BF/ 10 9 8 7 6 5 4 3 2 1

Dedicated to Rebecca Merrill Groothuis,
whose intellectual insights, spiritual wisdom,
and faithful companionship
mean more to me than words can say.

Jesus in An Age of Controversy is an expanded, updated, and extensively revised version of *Revealing the New Age Jesus,* which was published in 1990. Given the recent controversies over Jesus, I believe this material is more needed today than it was six years ago. Chapters 2 and 16 are entirely new and all the other chapters have been reworked and augmented considerably.

My thanks go to Terry Glaspey at Harvest House for his editorial wisdom in revising this book to make it more readable and attractive, and to the whole Harvest House team for their professionalism and efficiency.

Thanks go also to Gordon Lewis, Craig Blomberg, and James Sire, who made helpful comments on portions of the manuscript. Any defects that remain are my responsibility.

As always, I appreciate the prayers and moral support of Paul and Jean Merrill and Lillian Groothuis Dunn. Rebecca Merrill Groothuis, my wife, remains my best editor, best friend, and indispensable partner in ministry.

Contents

1

WHO DO YOU SAY THAT I AM?

JESUS OF NAZARETH. No other name has inspired greater devotion, evoked greater reverence, or ignited greater controversy.

For 2000 years, the controversy over Christ has continued to rage without letup. Today, everyone has an opinion about Jesus, and these opinions range from the traditional to the novel to the heretical. For many, Jesus is merely the expression of one's desires and imagination. A *Life* magazine article on differing views of Jesus stated that "We see Jesus as many different people—dutiful son, ascetic, sage, martyr—depending on our personal needs. . . . We see Jesus in our own image."[1] This is true psychologically; we tend to see what we want to see about the world, Jesus included. But is this the end of the story? Or is it a challenge to look past our prejudices for the truth?

What of the objective reality of Jesus? The *Life* article says that the various views of Jesus help us to know him and understand him. This cannot be true, because many views of Jesus contradict each other. He cannot be both a New

Age guru and the Lord of the universe. The earnest seeker of truth should move beyond a subjective image of Jesus toward an objective knowledge of who he really is.

Was Jesus a Party Animal?

Some people seem to rejoice in their heretical pronouncements about Jesus and thrill to the fact that they offend the religious sensibilities of the unenlightened. In the last few years a group of maverick scholars have been making headlines by debunking the Jesus of traditional faith. The Jesus Seminar delights in shocking the public. Seminar founder Robert Funk claims that:

> What we need is a new fiction that takes as its starting point the central event in the Judaeo-Christian drama and reconciles the [Messiah] with a new story that reaches beyond old beginnings and endings. In sum, we need a new narrative of Jesus, a new Gospel, if you will, that places Jesus differently in the grand scheme, the epic story.[2]

Leif Vaage, a professor at Emmanuel College, declares that Jesus was most likely "a party animal, somewhat shiftless, and disrespectful of the fifth commandment: Honor your father and mother."[3] This inflammatory remark intentionally draws attention to the Seminar and its "new and improved" Jesus—a "fictional" Jesus who somehow better fits our times.

The goal of the Jesus Seminar is nothing less than the creation of a new image of Jesus—a Jesus who is not divine, performed no miracles, never wanted to found a religion, and did not rise from the dead. The "new fiction" of which Funk speaks is a Jesus for today, not yesterday—a Jesus fashioned by the experts. This, of course, goes against the biblical pronouncement that "Jesus Christ is the same yesterday and today and forever" (Hebrews 13:8). The Jesus of the Seminar has been reduced to a sage who uttered scattered words of wisdom intended to challenge the thinking of his audience. Funk says, "Jesus was a subversive sage. His witticisms tended to undermine the everyday view of things."[4] Then, somehow, the mysterious wise man was transformed by his misinformed followers into the divine Son of God.

Which Jesus?

The crucial question remains, "Which Jesus is the real one?" In his book on the Sermon on the Mount, the popular New Thought teacher Emmet Fox notes that whatever you make of him, "Jesus Christ is easily the most important figure that has ever appeared in the history of mankind."[5] Fox continues, "There can hardly, therefore, be a more important understanding than to inquire into the question of what Jesus really did stand for."[6]

Jesus himself, according to the biblical Gospels, displayed considerable skill in eliciting the opinion of others toward him.

> When Jesus came to the region of Caesarea Philippi, he asked his disciples, "Who do people say the Son of Man is?" They replied, "Some say John the Baptist; others say Elijah; and still others, Jeremiah or one of the prophets." "But what about you?" he asked. "Who do you say I am?" Simon

Peter answered, "You are the Christ, the Son of the living God" (Matthew 16:13-16).

On the other hand, some claim that Jesus was a spiritual master who should serve as an example for our enlightenment. Author F. Forrester Church states that:

Jesus was one deeply in touch with what [Ralph Waldo] Emerson called the "over soul." He thought Jesus divine precisely to the extent that we are divine. The difference being: Jesus recognized it, and most of the rest of us don't.[7]

In other words, Jesus is merely one among a host of spiritual masters, gurus, prophets, and teachers who can point us toward the divinity in our midst. As Stephen Mitchell says, Jesus "was one of the world's great teachers, perhaps the greatest poet among them, and a brother to all the awakened ones," which includes the mystics of all religions.[8] Such a Jesus is not worshiped or served, but respected as a God-conscious master, a herald of the New Age.

Several years ago, controversy raged over *The Last Temptation of Christ,* a film depicting Jesus as a kind of New Ager—a struggling, imperfect man trying to find the God hidden within himself. The motion picture, adapted from Nikos Kazantzakis's novel of the same name, served as a theological lightning rod, attracting both bitter condemnation and enthusiastic praise.

In the film, Jesus is tormented over his divine calling. He admits, "I am a liar, I am a hypocrite, I am afraid of everything. . . . Lucifer is inside of me"[9]; he barely resists his "last temptation" to leave the cross and his calling in pursuit of sexual gratification. Jesus also proclaims that "everything's part of God"—a remark that caused one reviewer to speak of this Jesus as "a recent graduate of the Shirley MacLaine School of Theology."[10] After handling some dirt and stones, Jesus announces, "This is my body too,"[11] thus deifying the cosmos in New Age fashion.

The film begins with a disclaimer by director Martin Scorsese, stating, "This film is not based on the Gospels but is a fictional exploration of the eternal spiritual conflict." This did not dissuade many Christians from staging demonstrations, denouncing it as blasphemy, and promising to boycott the film and everything else associated with Universal Studios.

Others defended the film's right of artistic exploration and decried the religious intolerance of fussy fundamentalists. A review in a New Age-oriented journal called *Gnosis* attacked the fundamentalist "fetish of monotheism—the belief that there is only one true image of God."[12] The reviewer applauded the film's recasting of the traditional Jesus and suggested that those who held orthodox views may have "been dupes of a two thousand year old coverup."[13] For him Jesus was a Gnostic, "like all the great explorers and discoverers of the spirit."[14]

Writers such as Elaine Pagels claim that the Jesus of the New Testament is an incomplete, sanitized version of the original Jesus who was a Gnostic mystic. They claim that ancient documents discovered in Egypt reveal the real Jesus— a Jesus who claimed to discover a divine spark within himself and who helped others do the same. The Gnostic Jesus rejected the Hebrew Scriptures, disparaged the physical world, and did not die on a cross to reconcile people to a

holy God. Many claim that the rediscovery of this Jesus—
and the rejection of the biblical portrait of Jesus—is the key
to spiritual enlightenment.

Others spin intriguing tales about the "lost years" Jesus
spent as a world traveler to India, Egypt, and other exotic
environs. The Jesus of the Gospels is deemed only one
small part of the Jesus story. The records documenting his
eastward journeys have been suppressed by the church, we
are told.

The Dead Sea Scrolls have provided fodder for various
religious speculations about Jesus. Many claim that these recently discovered ancient texts overthrow the biblical view
of Jesus and establish him as an Essene mystic with essentially New Age beliefs. Barbara Thiering's controversial
book *Jesus and the Riddle of the Dead Sea Scrolls* (1992) has
startled many by claiming that the scrolls speak of Jesus and
his disciples in code language. Once decoded, the scrolls
tell us that Jesus was not a miracle-worker, and that he married and had children. He did not ascend into heaven but
died an uneventful death in Rome at an old age.

The supernatural realm is also bursting with opinions on
Jesus. A host of channelers and mediums tell us that there is
no fundamental difference between us and Christ. Jesus was
a spiritual model, but not the only way to God. Marianne
Williamson, a teacher of the channeled document *A Course
in Miracles* (1975), assures us that we are all part of the Christ
spirit. Famous medium Edgar Cayce believed that Jesus
taught reincarnation and was himself reincarnated 30 times
before he became the Christ. Transmissions from extraterrestrials also compete for our attention, claiming a perspective on Jesus not available to the earthbound.

Popular authors such as David Spangler and Matthew Fox want to expand our ideas about Jesus to include "the Cosmic Christ," who is at the heart of all religions and manifested in nature. We must leave our narrow, parochial views of Jesus. The Cosmic Christ is the key to our spiritual liberation, they claim. But how do we view Jesus?

The Jesus of the Opinion Polls

Recent Gallup polls reveal that a large majority of the American public highly esteems Jesus in one way or another, and few—New Age or otherwise—actively oppose him. Although Bertrand Russell spurned the character of Jesus by saying, "I do not grant either the superlative wisdom or the superlative goodness of Christ as depicted in the Gospels,"[15] and Friedrich Nietzsche vigorously denounced the biblical Christ,[16] few today would be so militant. Gallup remarks, "Research indicates that our image of Christ—while a bit murky in spots—is overwhelmingly favorable."[17]

When asked if Jesus was God or just another religious leader like Mohammed or Buddha, 70 percent of Americans surveyed affirmed that he was God. When asked, "In your own life, how important is the belief that Christ was fully God and fully human?" 81 percent responded that this belief was either "very important" (58 percent) or "fairly important" (23 percent).[18] Some 91 percent believe that Jesus existed as a historical figure.[19] After reviewing an impressive array of statistics regarding Americans' evaluation of Jesus, Gallup concludes that "virtually all Americans are, in some measure, drawn to the person of Christ."[20]

But who is the Christ to whom they are drawn? Gallup observed that few were conversant with even the most basic biblical material. Only 42 percent of respondents knew that Jesus preached the Sermon on the Mount; only 46 percent could name the first four books in the New Testament; and only 70 percent knew that Jesus was born in Bethlehem.[21]

The lack of knowledge also betrays a lack of commitment. Gallup says that "probing more deeply through surveys indicates that even if religion is an important force in our lives it is not the center of our lives. It does not have primacy. Interest may be high, but commitment is often low."[22]

Finding the Real Jesus

This book will seriously consider various reports about Jesus Christ. Our aim is to find the real Jesus and to respond according to his identity. The volume of conflicting opinions on Jesus should not drive us to despair. A willingness to go wherever the facts, logic, and common sense lead is the right way to approach the issue of Jesus Christ. One should not underestimate the value of a patient but passionate investigation of ultimate concerns.

Despite the fact that everyone wants to claim Jesus as his or her own, he is not a ventriloquist's dummy who gladly mouths whatever anyone likes. Religious opinions are legion; thoughtful and reasoned convictions on ultimate matters are far fewer. Our goal is to discover the objective truth about Jesus of Nazareth because, as the Theosophical Society's motto puts it, "There is no religion higher than truth."

Therefore, in the following chapters we will concentrate on the controversy over Christ by comparing rival *truth claims* about his identity and teaching. We do well to remember Blaise Pascal's warning, which remains timely though written three centuries ago: "Truth is so obscure in these times, and falsehood so established, that, unless we love the truth, we cannot know it."[23] Or, as Jesus expressed it in the Sermon on the Mount:

Ask and it will be given to you; seek and you will find; knock and the door will be opened to you. For everyone who asks receives; he who seeks finds; and to him who knocks, the door will be opened (Matthew 7:7,8).

Although our study will marshal logical arguments and sift through historical evidence, it will not be a merely academic exercise. What is at stake is of far greater consequence than scoring theological points or winning debates. If the Jesus of the New Testament is the true Jesus, several cutting conclusions irresistibly follow. First, to trust and obey this Jesus means eternal life beginning here and now and continuing forever. In the Gospel of John, Jesus prays to the Father: "Now this is eternal life: that they may know you, the only true God, and Jesus Christ, whom you have sent" (John 17:3). Second, to reject this Jesus means missing Incarnate Life itself and forfeiting one's own life eternally. As Jesus told his opposition, "If you do not believe that I am the one I claim to be, you will indeed die in your sins" (John 8:24).

The Jesus of the Gospels warned his disciples that spiritual counterfeits would arise. Speaking of false prophets dressed as wolves in sheep's clothing, he warned:

Not everyone who says to me, "Lord, Lord," will enter the kingdom of heaven, but only he who does the will of my Father who is in heaven. Many will say to me on that day, "Lord, Lord, did we not prophesy in your name, and in your name drive out demons and perform many miracles?" Then I will tell them plainly, "I never knew you. Away from me, you evildoers!" (Matthew 7:21-23).

An awareness of the weightiness of the issue does not tell us which Jesus is authentic, but it does underscore the importance of our conclusions. Because of what there is to gain and what there is to lose, anyone interested in Jesus should be willing to consider seriously the biblical witness to Jesus.

2

THE DEMOTED DEITY OF THE JESUS SEMINAR

ACADEMICS ARE NOT usually known for theatrics, but for scholarship. The ivory tower looks down on Hollywood's endless antics of self-promotion, glamour, and propaganda. Or so we thought. A group of New Testament scholars calling themselves the Jesus Seminar has recently flooded the media with controversial views of Jesus. The group was formed in 1985 with the express purpose of educating the uneducated Christian concerning what "scholarship" could tell us of the New Testament and Jesus. As Seminar member John Dominic Crossan put it, the "search for the historical Jesus has started to reach out beyond scholarship and not just into the pew and pulpit, but into the popular press and onto the television screen as well."[1]

The real Jesus, they assure us, is not the Jesus of traditional piety, but a countercultural figure whom the church must learn to take seriously. Robert Funk, the mastermind and leading advocate of the Seminar, says, "We want to liberate Jesus. The only Jesus most people want is the mythic one. They don't want the real Jesus. They want one they can worship. The cultic Jesus."[2] Roy Hoover, another prominent member of the Seminar, cuttingly remarks that its mission is to "rescue Jesus from the spin doctors" who composed the Gospels.[3] The Seminar's methods of determining the real Jesus—let alone their conclusions—have sometimes scandalized both scholars and people in the pews.

Before we consider the character of this group and their aims, we should consider their color-coded translation of the Gospels. The members of the Seminar meet twice a year to record their opinions on the words of Jesus. The group at first included approximately 200 members, but dwindled to 74 at the publication of *The Five Gospels* (1993). They went through the four biblical Gospels and the Gospel of Thomas and tried to determine the authenticity of each of Jesus' sayings. Each member voted by using colored beads to indicate the likelihood of a particular saying being authentic. The votes were then tallied and weighted to determine how to color-code each saying of Jesus.[4] Unlike a traditional red-letter edition, where the words of Jesus are marked in red, the Jesus Seminar used four colors to highlight Jesus' words, with each color corresponding to the likelihood that Jesus really said what is claimed for him. A member of the Jesus Seminar popularly summarized the choice of colors like this:

red: That's Jesus!
pink: Sure sounds like Jesus.
gray: Well, maybe.
black: There's been some mistake.[5]

Crossan notes that "there was a deliberate decision to play to the media. We thought colors would be more photogenic."[6] The result of these iconoclastic efforts was a book provocatively entitled *The Five Gospels*. The "fifth gospel" is the Gospel of Thomas—mostly a collection of pithy and mysterious sayings quite unlike the canonical Gospels of the New Testament. (We will assess this document in chapters 5 and 6.) *The Five Gospels* gives a new, breezy, and sometimes irreverent translation (which the Seminar pretentiously calls the Scholars Version) of the canonical Gospels and the Gospel of Thomas, along with commentary and an introduction explaining the Jesus Seminar's rationale. Luke Timothy Johnson notes that while the translation claims to be more in touch with the ancient sources than other translations, this is not always so. In some cases "the colloquial and slangy seem to be chosen for their own sake—and reflect the deliberate insouciance and irreverence of the Seminar's press conferences. The result is not always greater accuracy."[7] One rendering of Jesus' teaching may surprise many: "You scholars and Pharisees, you impostors. Damn you! You slam the door of Heaven's domain in people's faces" (Matthew 23:13). As D.A. Carson comments, "Somehow this does not sound like the Jesus who simultaneously denounces and weeps over the city."[8]

According to the Jesus Seminar, the vast majority of the Gospel of John is a mistake; it has no red markings, one pink, and only a few gray patches. The one pink passage (John 4:43) is translated: "A prophet gets no respect on his own turf."[9] Only one saying in Mark is colored red: "Pay the emperor what belongs to the emperor, and God what belongs to God!" (Mark 12:17). Overall, 82 percent of Jesus' words in Matthew, Mark, Luke, and John are judged as inauthentic.[10] Only 15 sayings of Jesus are red-lettered, all of which are short, pungent remarks such as "turn the other cheek" (Matthew 5:39; Luke 6:29) and "congratulations you poor" (Luke 6:20), or parables such as the Good Samaritan (Luke 10:30-35) and the shrewd manager (Luke 16:1-8).

What, then, is left of the Jesus of historical Christianity after the color-coding? Precious little survives the death by coloration. The Seminar repeatedly silences Jesus: He did not claim to be the Messiah or God Incarnate; he did not speak of his second coming; he did not promise to forgive sins; and he did not preach the Sermon on the Mount. This diminished Jesus is akin to a wandering sage who utters memorable one-liners, disturbs the status quo, supports politically correct causes, is only faintly religious, and not even very Jewish. Somehow, Jesus was radically misinterpreted by the Gospel writers, who promoted him to the status of Lord and Savior when he himself had no such designs. Seminar member Arthur Dewey quips, "There is more of David Letterman in the historical Jesus than Pat Robertson."[11]

Although *The Five Gospels* gives us a rather secular Jesus, one well-known member of the Seminar pictures Jesus a bit differently. Marcus Borg's book *Meeting Jesus Again for the First Time* (1994) employs the same skeptical approach to the Gospels used in *The Five Gospels,* but comes up with a Jesus more akin to the New Age view.[12] Having dispensed with the resurrection of Jesus as a literal, historical truth, Borg sees Jesus not as "the exclusive revelation of God" but as "one of many mediators of the sacred" who help us connect with the spiritual reality within us and around us.[13] After rejecting much of the Gospels as unhistorical, Borg selects certain elements from the Gospels and places them into a religious framework he derived from non-Western religions and the general categories of cultural anthropology.[14]

Borg's Jesus is not the orthodox Jesus of his Lutheran youth, but a spirit-person who, like many other mystics and shamans, experiences the sacred through a non-ordinary state of consciousness.[15] Borg's sense of the sacred is not a supernatural reality, but a dimension within us and around us that is not normally perceived.[16] For him, Jesus serves as a model for perceiving this reality and being transformed by it. He is not God's only Son:

> The notion that God's only son came to this planet to offer his life as a sacrifice for the sins of the world, and that God could not forgive us without that having happened, and that we are saved by believing this story, is simply incredible. . . . To many people it simply makes no sense.[17]

The results of the Jesus Seminar concur with Borg's assessment and dismissal of the Jesus of the New Testament. We need to take a hard look at the Seminar and its methods; for if we find that the Seminar's conclusions simply make no sense, then it becomes easier to embrace the Jesus that the Seminar rejects.[18]

The Seminar and Its Members

Who are the people that make up the Jesus Seminar and why should we believe them? They describe themselves as scholars who have no theological or denominational axes to grind, and whose purpose is to stimulate fresh thinking about the historical Jesus. Unlike most scholars who have been analyzing, criticizing, and defending the New Testament for hundreds of years, the Seminar members are intent on taking their conclusions directly to the people through popular media. They are not content to stay hidden in the academy. They want—and are getting—spotlights, headlines, and airtime. At the first meeting of the Seminar in 1985, Robert Funk said, "The religious establishment has not allowed the intelligence of high scholarship to pass through pastors and priests to a hungry laity." Worse yet, he says, television evangelists have "preyed on the ignorance of the uninformed." The Seminar, however, offers "liberty for . . . millions" otherwise deceived.[19]

The Seminar's radical pronouncements on Jesus were bound to attract media attention and spark controversy. The orthodox beliefs of the masses—no matter how ardently defended or earnestly applied to real life—usually do not make for sensational stories. That masses of people—including noted scholars—confess the Jesus of the Gospels is just old news. Enter the Jesus Seminar. Johnson's assessment invites a full quotation:

> It wanted coverage! It sought coverage! It understood deadlines! It invited media response! Best of all, it provided colored beads, the closest thing (outside the Vatican) that religion ever provided to an actual election, *plus* provocative statements crafted into usable sound bites! As a bonus, it dealt not with hard-to-cover issues like sin and grace, but with a *personality,* the founding figure himself, Jesus. And to bring it all home, it promised, vote by vote, statement by statement, the shape of a scandalous attack on the foundations of Christianity. The conscious crafting of the Jesus Seminar into a media darling could not but be embraced by a segment of the media starved for a chance to do real news.[20]

The hungry media sometimes swallowed the Seminar's statements without sufficiently digesting them. Hype often overwhelmed thought, and controversy replaced reasonable conversation. This was especially true when the media pitted the supposedly objective "scholars" of the Seminar against the fuming fundamentalists who were threatened by this ever-so-reasonable attack on their faith. It was the fundies versus the scholars—which was no contest. Funk declared that *The Five Gospels* "should be helpful to anyone who is looking for a different approach to biblical material, based on hard historical evidence."[21] He assumes that the traditional views lack evidence and must rely only on blind faith. Throughout the introduction to *The Five Gospels,* the "scholars" are depicted as objective, neutral, and intellectually disciplined seekers of truth who dare to challenge the church establishment, which is ignorant, dogmatic, and anti-intellectual. It is assumed that no credible biblical scholar would either disagree with the Seminar or identify with the Christian church.

Although the members of the Seminar present themselves as representative of the entire scholarly community, this is far from true. They are only a small subset of New Testament scholars, and, as scholarly critics have pointed out, do not represent the broader world of New Testament scholarship. Although 74 scholars contributed to the final work of *The Five Gospels,* there are 6900 members of the Society of Biblical Literature, at least half of whom are New Testament experts.[22] The two leading academic organizations for biblical study, the Society of Biblical Literature and the Society for the Study of the New Testament, have no official association with the Jesus Seminar.[23] The Seminar is funded by the Weststar Institute, which drew its participants very selectively. As Johnson observes, although the Seminar does boast some scholars of high reputation, "the roster of fellows by no means represents the cream of New Testament scholarship in this country."[24]

New Testament scholar Craig Blomberg notes that 36 of the 74 members received their graduate degrees from or teach at one of the three "most liberal departments of New Testament studies anywhere"—Harvard, Claremont, and Vanderbilt.[25] European scholars are also excluded. Moreover, 40 of the participants "are relative unknowns" who are not academically established.[26] New Testament professor Richard Hays puts it strongly: "In fact—let it be said clearly—most professional biblical scholars are profoundly skeptical of the methods and conclusions of this academic splinter group." Although there are credentialed and respected scholars in the group, "their attempt to present these views as 'the assured results of critical scholarship' is—one must say it—reprehensible deception."[27]

What Are Their Assumptions?

Of course, the fact that the members of the Jesus Seminar bill themselves as spokespeople for the academic community does not mean that their views are wrong. It simply indicates that the issues are more involved than their narrow categories allow. The introduction to *The Five Gospels* lays out "seven pillars of scholarly wisdom," which are the assumptions on which the book is based.

The first pillar is the distinction between "the historical Jesus, to be uncovered by historical excavation, and the Christ of faith encapsulated in the first creeds."[28] This assumption severs faith from history and claims that orthodox Christian doctrine is not justified by the Gospels

and the rest of the New Testament. The Jesus Seminar repeatedly asserts that scholars cannot believe in historical
Christian doctrines and remain real scholars. This, however, is much disputed by large numbers of academically
trained Christians who teach and publish in the area of New
Testament studies. If the seminar had selected its members
primarily from the Institute of Biblical Research and the
Evangelical Theological Society, the results would have
been drastically different. However, the Seminar does not
admit to there being credible scholars outside its guild.[29]

Blomberg argues that many evangelicals use all the
tools of historical research and remain convinced that the
Gospels are historically reliable and even inspired by the
Holy Spirit. They try to discern how each Gospel writer
gathered and arranged his material and for what purposes.
Evangelicals can agree with the Seminar that the four
Gospels are a complex product of tradition and editorial
arrangement. This, however, does not imply that these writings fail to reflect the affirmations found in the classic
Christian creeds.[30] Conservative biblical scholars also grant
that some of the words of Jesus in standard red-letter New
Testaments may not be the exact, literal words of Jesus. This
is no threat to the Gospels' trustworthiness, however, since
a good paraphrase communicates the same meaning as the
original utterance—especially if the paraphrase is written
under the inspiration of the Holy Spirit.[31]

The second pillar of the Seminar is that Matthew, Mark,
and Luke "are much closer to the historical Jesus than the
Fourth Gospel [John], which presents a 'spiritual' Jesus."[32]
Before addressing this in detail in the next chapter, we
should note that an emphasis on some spiritual teaching
not mentioned in the other Gospels does not invalidate

John's Gospel. John may well have been privy to information not available to the other writers, or he may have emphasized certain teachings for a particular purpose for his original audience. John's unique angle also helps explain apparent contradictions between his Gospel and the other three.[33] Moreover, the Gospel of John is rich with historical details that have been corroborated by other sources. The Seminar unjustifiably assumes that John's heavily theological emphasis negates historical accuracy. Of course, this does not follow logically. If some of Jesus' teachings were heavily theological, then an accurate record of them would be also.

Pillar three states that the Gospel of Mark was written before the other canonical Gospels.[34] This is affirmed by most—but not all—evangelical scholars. If Mark is taken to be historically reliable, then this view does not necessarily lead to the Seminar's radical conclusions. We will explore this in the next chapter.

The fourth pillar claims that Luke and Matthew both depended on a common source for the material they have in common, but which is not found in Mark. This hypothetical source is called Q (which stands for the German word *Quelle*, meaning "source").[35] Again, numerous scholars hold this theory without questioning the trustworthiness of Luke and Matthew, because they take Q and the Gospel writers' other sources as historically credible.

Pillar five claims that modern biblical scholarship has dispensed with a Jesus who spoke of a final judgment and the end of the world. These scholars see Jesus not as a prophet of judgment but as a witty subversive who had no views on such theological matters. The Seminar again presents its views as being in the mainstream when, in reality, many in the scholarly community believe that Jesus spoke as a prophet warning of God's ultimate judgment. Furthermore, if we can establish that the Gospels are historically trustworthy, it is artificial to edit out Jesus' pronouncements concerning his second coming and the end of the world. Ben Witherington, along with many other New Testament scholars, argues that Jesus' sense of historical culmination and divine judgment are basic aspects of his character and message.[36]

The sixth pillar seeks to separate the written culture of our day from the oral culture of Jesus' time. The upshot is that we should not expect an ancient oral culture to have preserved very much of the real words and actions of Jesus by the time the material was finally written down as a Gospel. "The Jesus whom historians seek will be found in those fragments of tradition that bear the imprint of orality: short, provocative, memorable, oft-repeated phrases, sentences, and stories."[37] In other words, the Jesus of the Gospels is largely an amplified Jesus: The Gospel writers added various layers of detail on top of the original short, pithy statements that had been memorized. This assumption rips Jesus' words out of their contexts in the Gospel accounts, and attempts to ferret out the supposed aphorisms or witticisms originally uttered by Jesus. Besides being enormously speculative, this archaeological enterprise falsely assumes that oral cultures were incapable of preserving large amounts of detailed material and ignores the substantial evidence for the careful preservation of oral material within ancient Judaism. This will be taken up in the next chapter.

The most telling and controversial of all the Seminar's pillars listed is the insistence that material in the Gospels be considered guilty of unhistorical fabrication until proven innocent (by the "scholars"). This is because "the gospels are now assumed to be narratives in which the memory of Jesus is embellished by mythic elements that express the church's faith in him, and by plausible fictions that enhance the telling of the gospel story for first-century listeners."[38] Once more, the Seminar asserts its own views and not those of New Testament scholarship in general, which are far less pessimistic about the nature of the Gospels. As Carson says, "There is substantial literature on the 'burden of proof' argument, and less and less of it aligns with such skepticism."[39] This "guilty until proven innocent" method is wrongheaded for at least two main reasons.

First, if historians were to adopt such extreme skepticism regarding ancient sources, it would rob us of any certain knowledge of the remote past. Blomberg comments that historians of the ancient world generally "assume that if writers prove trustworthy where they can be tested, they are given the benefit of the doubt where they cannot be tested."[40] As we will discover in the next chapter, there is plenty of extrabiblical evidence confirming many New Testament accounts and no hard evidence that decisively refutes them.

Second, the Seminar's skepticism presupposes a naturalistic view of the universe that excludes any supernatural intervention in principle. Naturalism claims that everything in the universe can be explained on the basis of thoroughly natural occurrences that function according to uniform laws of nature, plus nothing. Once this titanic assumption is in place, any statement or action of Jesus in the Gospels that involves the supernatural must be deemed a mythic or fictional embellishment, for the supernatural cannot possibly intrude on the natural realm. The naturalist net will catch no supernatural fish.

As Gregory Boyd has pointed out, this assumption puts the naturalistic students of the New Testament in a strange situation. They want a hard, historical, factual view of Jesus, or so they claim. Yet because they deny the supernatural, they must reject the actual accounts of Jesus in the Gospels—which overflow with the supernatural—as unhistorical. "This means that the view of Jesus these scholars decide on will be arrived at *in spite of* what the New Testament says, not *because* of what it says."[41]

The naturalistic critics must rely entirely upon the supposition that there was a source Q, from which the Gospels of Matthew and Luke were partially drawn, and that the earliest layer of material in Q was entirely nonsupernatural, although Q itself as a whole contains supernatural references.[42] They must also assume that this early layer of Q was meant to exclude the supernatural. This does not follow logically. If there were such an earlier layer, its main purpose could have been to record Jesus' sayings without making any commentary one way or the other on his supernatural actions. To say that its purpose was to show that Jesus' ministry was entirely non-supernatural is to commit the fallacy of arguing from silence. Even more, the Seminar must assume that any supernatural accounts incorporated in other supposed layers of Q and by Matthew and Luke (and the rest of the Gospels) are inauthentic.

Boyd's comment is on target: "Historical theories should be built upon the foundation of what is *present* in concrete evidence that is available; not in what is absent in *hypothetical* evidence that is altogether *unavailable*."[43] All that is left for these naturalistic critics is to "guess what is behind this veil of myth and guess at how this veil of myth got there in the first place."[44] Instead of accepting the Gospel accounts as they stand, the critics are forced to suppose hypothetical nonsupernatural documents, of which no one has seen a single copy. As C. S. Lewis perceptively remarked a generation ago,

> [The higher critics] ask me to believe they can read be-
> tween the lines of the old texts; the evidence is their obvi-
> ous inability to read (in any sense worth discussing) the
> lines themselves. They claim to see fern-seed and can't see
> an elephant ten yards away in broad daylight.[45]

Those refusing to read the lines themselves must account
for the existence of four very ancient documents with which
they thoroughly disagree. They must come up with conjectures
on how the thoroughly natural events of Jesus' life ever came to
be recorded in Gospels so riddled with supernatural elements.
This project can become quite complex, with the probability of
every particular conjecture depending on the probability of
other conjectures. The more complex it all becomes, the more
unlikely it all becomes.

When each speculative hypothesis is linked with all the
others the overall probability becomes even lower than the
probability of each speculation.[46] For instance, if each of
four hypotheses has a probability of 70% (which is quite
generous) the probability of all four hypotheses being true
is only twenty-four percent![47] This estimate itself is generous
since more than four hypotheses are needed to explain
away the supernatural in the Gospels. It ends up taking
more faith to believe in the Seminar's naturalized Jesus
than to believe the Gospels themselves.

Questioning Naturalism

For the vast majority (93 percent) of Americans who believe
in "God or a universal spirit,"[48] the assumption of naturalism
should carry no weight at all. The 76 percent who believe that
"God is a heavenly father who can be reached by prayers"[49]

should have no trouble believing that a prayer-hearing God could act in human affairs. The reports of such supernatural interaction in the Gospels should be taken seriously, not rejected without a second thought—especially if they pass the basic tests of historicity, as we will discuss in the next chapter.[50]

The Seminar presents no arguments in favor of naturalism; it is simply assumed to be the only intellectually credible option. The closest the Seminar comes to making a case is to invoke scientific discoveries that supposedly invalidate supernatural belief. "The Christ of creed and dogma . . . can no longer command the assent of those who have seen the heavens through Galileo's telescope. Copernicus, Kepler, and Galileo have dismantled the mythological abodes of the gods and Satan, and bequeathed us secular heavens."[51]

Ironically, Copernicus, Kepler, and Galileo were all theists and not naturalists! Nor does the Bible claim that "gods and Satan" live in outer space! There are no "gods" but only one God (1 Corinthians 8:4-6). Satan and demons (if that is what was meant by "gods") are spiritual beings, not extraterrestrial physical beings. The Seminar maintains that "historical reason" debunks the Bible in the same way these astronomers debunked previous cosmologies. This reflects a naive view of science; it assumes that science must always conflict with core Christian claims and that, in such a conflict, science must always win. In reality, scientific evidence can be marshaled in support of Christian truth claims. One need not avoid science to have Christian faith. Well-respected members of the scientific and philosophical communities are becoming increasing vocal in defense of the existence of God.[52]

Physicists and philosophers persuasively argue that the universe sprang into existence at the Big Bang. Either it all came from nothing, without a cause, or something outside the universe called it into being. Divine creation is surely more reasonable than chance origination because, as the ancients knew, "from nothing, nothing comes." We know this universe to be a cosmos, not a chaos. From the farthest star to the cells in our own bodies, we find evidence of order, regularity, and design. Our earth and its atmosphere are fine-tuned to support life in numerous ways. It is impossible to conceive that chance could have created creatures such as us. The Designer has left his fingerprints everywhere. Our sense of conscience that binds us to a higher moral authority reveals that God's law is inscribed on our hearts. Morality is more than the movement of atoms in the brain. Our Creator and Designer is also our Lawgiver.

I have only sketched a few arguments for the existence of God.[53] Suffice it to say that scores of intellectuals in science and philosophy have ardently and powerfully defended these and other claims. Two recent volumes, *God and the Philosophers* (1994)[54] and *Philosophers Who Believe* (1993),[55] chronicle the Christian faith of leading philosophers such as Richard Swinburne, Alvin Plantinga, and others. The American Scientific Affiliation, which publishes *Perspectives on Faith and Science,* is a professional organization of hundreds of working scientists who are also Christians. The Jesus Seminar has done nothing to refute the theistic beliefs of these leading Christian intellectuals. Therefore, much of the Seminar's case for a thoroughly natural Jesus demoted of deity simply evaporates for lack of evidence.

Was Jesus Neither Jewish nor Christian?

Given its summary rejection of the supernatural, the Seminar must reconstruct a new image of Jesus that goes beyond

what is claimed by the Gospels themselves. Having decon-
structed the historical view of Jesus, they feel free to construct an entirely foreign one. In selecting which of Jesus'
sayings are authentic and which are not, they rely heavily on
very questionable principles. I will limit my comments to
one of the principles they have used unreasonably to pluck
many words out of Jesus' mouth.

This principle is known as the criterion of dissimilarity:
A saying of Jesus is deemed authentic if it differs from both
the Jewish tradition of the time and the views of the early
Christian church. When used as one of several criteria, the
dissimilarity criterion is helpful in establishing the authentic words of Jesus based on what is unique to his teaching.
The problem comes when it is used negatively to eliminate
Jesus' words that agree with the current Jewish tradition or
the later beliefs of the earlier church.

First of all, when used negatively, the dissimilarity criterion
detaches Jesus from his Jewish environment and his identity as
a Jew. Of all the bad names Jesus is called in the Gospels (such
as "glutton," "blasphemer," "prince of the demons," etc.),
"Gentile" is never one of them. The Gospels record his respect
for the Hebrew Scriptures (Matthew 5:17-20; John 10:35) and
his observance of Jewish ceremonies. Most New Testament
scholars currently emphasize the importance of recognizing
Jesus' Jewishness in order to understand him.[56] A completely
negative use of the dissimilarity criterion, however, strips Jesus
of his Jewish identity as an ardent monotheist and interpreter
of God's word found in the Hebrew Scriptures.

Secondly, the negative misuse of the dissimilarity criterion assumes that Jesus had no influence on his early
disciples which was, in turn, transferred into the life of the
Christian church. For instance, the Seminar claims that

Jesus probably did not say that the bread of the Last Supper was his body (Matthew 26:28; Mark 14:22; Luke 22:19), because communion was practiced in the early church, which the Seminar assumes created the practice instead of simply following Jesus' command. The early followers of Jesus became known as Christians (or imitators of Christ) in Antioch precisely because they followed in Jesus' footsteps (Acts 11:26). Ancient non-Christian writers also tell us that Jesus' followers took on this name.[57] It is simply incredible to say that Jesus had little influence on the movement that bore his name and that this movement felt free to improvise wildly about the one they worshiped and for whom they sometimes died. It renders Jesus a cultural nonentity who inspired no one to follow him. The notion that only the idiosyncratic is the authentic is not a trustworthy principle for any historical investigation. Would we expect that Churchill would not sound English and not influence later British statesmen?[58] Churchill's uniqueness is found within his English identity, not in spite of it. The same is true for Jesus.[59]

Despite their reckless revisionism, the Seminar warns: "Beware of finding a Jesus entirely congenial to you."[60] (This, of course, is precisely what they have done themselves.) They assume that the Jesus "of creed and dogma" is somehow congenial to Christians. This is light-years from the truth. Jesus remains the great disturber who challenges his followers to heed his hard words and put their lives on the line for him. One reading of the Sermon on the Mount brings this home. Christians claim to find forgiveness and eternal life through this Jesus, but they do not find a placid, mediocre, and superficial life. After all, Jesus said things like, "Blessed are you when people insult you, persecute you and falsely say all kinds of evil against you because of me"

(Matthew 5:11), and, "Anyone who does not take his cross and follow me is not worthy of me" (Matthew 10:38). I am a follower of Jesus who takes the Gospels to be historically true, but these sayings are not "entirely congenial to me"— or to anyone else who takes them to be true.

The Jesus of the Jesus Seminar, on the other hand, is a domesticated and manageable Jesus. His "wisdom" fits the sensibilities of liberal academics, who are more interested in politics than theology. He issues no threats of hell and makes no promises of heaven. Nor does he affirm his own deity. As Ben Witherington concludes, the Seminar "probably tells us more about the various members of the Jesus Seminar than about Jesus. Perhaps they wish to see themselves as sages offering countercultural wisdom."[61]

For all the Seminar's claims to historical accuracy, this view of Jesus cannot explain the most basic aspects of Christian history. First, how could such a Jesus ever get himself crucified? As Witherington states:

> The seminar [suggests] that Jesus was not a controversialist, never initiated debates or controversies, and was passive until someone questioned or criticized him or his followers. He was not a prophet or a radical reformer. He is presented as a person who never spoke for himself or claimed to play any decisive role in God's final plans for humankind, never claimed to be the Messiah.[62]

In light of this innocuous identity, one must ask how such a Jesus could have sparked enough controversy for anyone to nail him to a Roman cross. Even the most liberal scholars admit that Jesus was crucified, and ancient non-Christian sources attest to this as well.[63] According to Hays, "The Jesus constructed by the Jesus Seminar is a talking head, whose teachings bear no intelligible relation to his death on a cross."[64] Why was Jesus executed? The Gospel's answer—that Jesus offended both the Roman and Jewish establishment because of his controversial claims—has not been refuted by the Seminar and remains the most satisfying option available.

Another principal problem haunts the Seminar. How could a nontheological, nonsupernatural, and nonmessianic Jesus be the source of a Christian movement that so fundamentally misunderstood him? Why would Christianity enshrine such a twisted image of its founder in its primary documents (the Gospels)? The demoted Jesus cannot account for the explosion of Christian evangelism and literature in the ancient world. If the Seminar supposes that later writers remade Jesus the sage into a supernatural Messiah as a kind of posthumous gift, it is imperative that they spell out why misrepresenting the founder of one's religion should be considered as a fitting practice for his followers. The Seminar claims that the Gospels misrepresent Christ in the name of Christ. How could this have happened so quickly after Jesus' days on earth? The Seminar's historical reconstructions leave the historical question of the nature and growth of the earlier church without an adequate explanation.[65]

The historical question of the New Testament Jesus remains to be answered in adequate detail. We have found the Jesus of the Jesus Seminar to lack credibility, but what of the Jesus of the Gospels and the rest of the New Testament? Can we depend on these ancient sources to tell us about the real Jesus?

3

THE NEW TESTAMENT WITNESS TO JESUS

WHAT DO THE New Testament books contribute to our understanding of Jesus of Nazareth? Does the orthodox view of Jesus rest upon a blind faith in the biblical record—"the Bible says it, I believe it, that settles it"—or are there solid reasons to believe these documents are factually and verifiably true?

Although some Christians have disdained reason as opposed to faith, the New Testament itself repeatedly appeals to historical evidence to substantiate its claims. The biblical writers call for faith, but it is a faith based on knowable facts. When the apostle Paul defended Christianity before King Agrippa and Festus, he exclaimed, "What I am saying is true and reasonable." Paul went on to say that the events of Jesus' life that he described were historical facts: "The king is familiar with these things, and I can speak freely to him. I am convinced that none of this has escaped his notice, *because it was not done in a corner*" (Acts 26:26, emphasis added).

Christianity is an inseparable mixture of timeless truths and temporal events. Without the Jesus of the New

Testament, historic Christianity shatters into a thousand pieces. We should remember that if the New Testament account of Jesus passes important historical tests, any rival view of Jesus based on other extrabiblical materials will inherit the burden of proof. For example, *The Original Jesus* (1995) by Elmar R. Gruber and Holger Kersten advances the notion that Jesus was originally a Buddhist whose teachings were later distorted.[1] In order to defend this view, they must discredit the New Testament testimony to Jesus since these documents know nothing of Buddhism. Let us, therefore, look at the nature of the New Testament itself, to see if the Jesus it presents can be trusted as the Jesus who actually is. To do this, we will consider the integrity, veracity, and authenticity of the Gospels, Acts, and some of Paul's writings.[2]

The Integrity of the New Testament

The integrity of the documents concerns the accuracy of the *transmission* of the texts through history, the journey from then to now. It can be broken down into the number, type, and age of the extant manuscripts of the New Testament. The greater the number of manuscripts and the closer their age to the date of the original writing, the greater will be the integrity of the document.

Since 1976, the scholarly world has had at its disposal at least 5366 handwritten manuscripts in the Greek language alone.[3] The number has steadily increased during the last few decades as archaeologists uncover more records of the world's most copied and collected books. The manuscripts range from small fragments to complete New Testaments. They can be divided into four types.

First, papyrus fragments are small portions of ancient papyrus scrolls. The oldest of 88 known fragments[4] contains portions of John and dates from approximately A.D. 125.[5] The Chester Beatty Papyri are much larger, containing much of our New Testament and dating from about A.D. 200.[6] Second, the important uncial—so-called because of the formal Greek script in which the manuscripts are written—number 274 (usually not entire New Testaments).[7] These date from the fourth to the tenth centuries A.D.[8] Codex Vaticanus (B) is dated from approximately A.D. 350 and contains most of the Bible and other documents.[9] Third, 2795 manuscripts[10] from the ninth to the fifteenth centuries are written in a less formal Greek script called minuscules.[11] Fourth, lectionaries are manuscripts of church service books, the majority of which consist of only passages from the Gospels. Some contain other New Testament books. These date from the ninth century and number 2209.[12]

Besides these ancient Greek manuscripts, there are 8000 copies of the Latin Vulgate translation, originally done by Jerome (382-405), and other manuscripts of varying dates in Syriac, Coptic, and other languages.[13]

We should consider this arresting point: The New Testament is better attested by ancient manuscripts than any other piece of ancient literature. Positive evidence for its integrity consists of the number, quality, and age of the manuscripts. There now exists no original document (autograph) for any ancient work; therefore, scholars seek to compare manuscripts to determine the original text. This is known as textual criticism (or analysis).

With the relatively early dates of the New Testament manuscripts, their plentiful number, and frequently high quality, scholars believe they can restore the original texts with a very high degree of accuracy. They readily trust the integrity of many ancient documents that have fewer manuscripts and a much greater time gap between the earliest extant manuscripts and the original writing than the New Testament. For instance, Caesar's *The Gallic Wars* dates from 100-44 B.C. The earliest copy is from A.D. 900, with a time gap of 1000 years. Furthermore, there are only ten copies.[14] In discussing the identity of Jesus, a cover story in *Time* granted that "existing copies of the New Testament are far older and more numerous than those of any other ancient body of literature."[15]

Because of the large number of New Testament texts, certain variations are found between texts. This is evidenced in English translations of the Bible, where an alternative reading is listed in the margin or at the bottom of the page. But it should be remembered that these variants are few and far between and usually do not affect the meaning of any given sentence.

Cornelius Hagerty helps explain this:

> The more manuscripts discovered the more error, but most of them are such things as omissions of lines, changes in spelling, and transpositions of words, due to carelessness of copyists. They do not affect the meaning of the text. Copyists do not make the same mistakes, and their errors may be corrected by comparing manuscripts.[16]

The very existence of variants in early manuscripts witnesses to the fact that the respective documents were not products of an artificial homogenization; that is, they were not intentionally and illegitimately standardized. This underscores the reliability of the manuscripts. The existence of early variants argues against any contrived tampering with the material. Small, inconsequential deviations in copying are evidence of human error, not deception.[17]

Stephen Neill and Tom Wright comment that the paucity of significant textual variants is "astonishing." They conclude:

> Anyone who reads the New Testament in any one of half a dozen recent Greek editions, or in any modern translation, can feel confident that, though there may be uncertainties in detail, in almost everything of importance he is close indeed to the text of the New Testament books as they were originally written.[18]

If we have given sufficient reason to trust the basic integrity of the New Testament concerning its textual attestation and accuracy of transmission, we still need to consider the authenticity and veracity of the material, lest our texts be nothing more than faithfully preserved falsehoods.[19]

The Veracity of the Gospels and Acts

The New Testament receives high marks for the relatively short time gap between the dates of the earliest extant manuscripts and the dates of the original writing of the manuscripts. But another time gap must be considered: that between the event and the recording of those events. Of course, generally speaking, the smaller the time gap the better for ensuring historical accuracy. Rather than discussing every New Testament book, we will center on the

Gospels, Acts, and several of the apostle Paul's letters.[20] The issue is this: When were these documents written, and was the time gap so long as to disqualify them as reliable historical reports?

One sure way to fix the outer limit of the age of the Gospels is to cite postapostolic church fathers who quote from or refer to these sources. Since we know when the church fathers wrote, we can be assured that the Gospels predate them. This is called external documentary evidence.

Polycarp, who was the mentor to Irenaeus and disciple of the apostle John—cites several New Testament passages in a short section of his letter to the Philippians, written about A.D. 110. The entire letter goes on to quote from or refer to all four Gospels, the book of Acts, and 13 other New Testament books. We can be sure that these books were in circulation by A.D. 110.[21]

Ignatius wrote seven short letters in approximately A.D. 108, in which he quotes or refers to every Gospel, Acts, and 19 other New Testament books.[22] Matthew, Mark, and Luke are mentioned by Clement, writing from Rome in about A.D. 96. He also refers to eight other books of the New Testament.[23]

By virtue of these three ancient documents, we can conclude that at least 25 of the 27 books of the New Testament were in circulation by about the year 100.[24] This method of dating very conservatively fixes an outer limit: The books cannot be dated after about A.D. 100. But they could very likely be dated considerably earlier, as we will soon see.[25]

Most modern scholars believe that Mark was written before Matthew and Luke, because it seems the latter two quite often refer to material in Mark, using it as one of their primary sources.[26] We also know that Luke was written sometime before Acts because the author of Acts speaks of his "former book," in which he wrote about "all that Jesus began to do and to teach" (Acts 1:1). This "former book" is, in all likelihood, Luke's Gospel. Therefore, if we can date Acts, we can date Luke sometime before it. We can also infer that Mark and Matthew precede Luke, because it appears that Luke relies on Mark and Matthew as sources of information (see Luke 1:1-4, where he mentions previously existing documents about Jesus).[27]

Acts is a history of the early apostolic church in action. As such, it is loaded with historical detail. In light of this, four separate considerations argue for an early date for Acts.[28]

First, although much of Acts concerns activities around Jerusalem, it does not record the fall of Jerusalem in A.D. 70, when Roman armies obliterated it. (This event is assuredly dated by the Jewish historian Josephus.) This was a profoundly important event in the ancient world and signified the end of a distinct Jewish state. If the author of Acts wrote after A.D. 70, it seems improbable that he would have omitted this great catastrophe.

Furthermore, the Gospels depict Jesus as repeatedly predicting the fall of Jerusalem because of its rejection of the Messiah (Luke 13:22-35, etc.). Would the author of the Gospel of Luke, if writing after A.D. 70, not mention *this* fulfillment of prophecy, especially when the Gospel of Luke itself records Jesus' life as a fulfillment of various prophecies?

Second, Acts does not mention Nero's intense persecution of Christians in the mid-sixties. In fact, Acts' general attitude toward Rome is favorable. Other persecutions are recorded, such as Stephen's martyrdom (Acts 7) and the subsequent persecution of the church in Jerusalem (Acts 8), so it would seem odd for the writer to leave Nero unscathed if the document were composed after these persecutions. This seems about as likely as an African Christian historian writing in 1996 on the history of the church in Uganda without mentioning the savage persecution by Idi Amin in the 1970s.

Third, the martyrdoms of James (in A.D. 61) and Peter (in A.D. 65) are not referred to in Acts. It would be highly unusual for these deaths to be left out if the book were written after this time because James and Peter are key players in the book of Acts.

Fourth, the writer does not give us the outcome of Paul's trial (28:30). This is probably because it was still not known at the time Acts was written. If Paul were martyred in A.D. 64, as is commonly held, this would argue for Acts being written before that.[29]

Given these four factors, we can make a reasonable case that the original composition of Acts was in the early sixties A.D. This would make Luke, Mark, and Matthew even earlier—perhaps as early as the mid-forties or mid-fifties, just one or two decades after the death of Jesus.[30]

Our argument does not necessarily commit the logical fallacy of the argument from silence; it is, rather, an argument appealing to what appears to be conspicuous absence. We have said that *if* Acts were older than A.D. 70, *then* we would expect to see several important factors that are, in fact, absent. This *conspicuous absence* argues for an earlier date.[31] More positively, the material we find *present* in Acts fits very well with it being written in the early sixties A.D.

The dating of Acts and the Gospels is hotly contested, and absolute certainty is unavailable. William F. Albright, the distinguished archaeologist and biblical scholar, affirmed that "every book of the New Testament was written by a baptized Jew between the forties and the eighties of the first century A.D. (very probably sometime between about A.D. 50 and 75)."[32]

Even if we argue that the Synoptic Gospels are somewhat older, the time gap need not discourage those seeking accurate information on Jesus. F.F. Bruce, who dates Mark "at around A.D. 64 or 65, Luke shortly before 70, and Matthew shortly after 70,"[33] has noted that "the time elapsing between the evangelistic events and the writing of most of the New Testament books [including all the Gospels] was, from the standpoint of historical research, satisfactorily short."[34]

It is often assumed that the synoptic Gospels depended, to some degree, on previously written (and now unavailable) material about the life of Jesus. Luke seems to state this openly when he speaks of the many others who "have undertaken to draw up an account of the things that have been fulfilled among us" (Luke 1:1). This can also be inferred with Mark and Matthew.[35]

Bruce also notes that the "written sources of our Synoptic Gospels are not later than c. A.D. 60." He believes that some of these sources may even be rooted in notes taken as Jesus himself was speaking.[36] This concept is important in dealing with the common objection that the Gospel writers made up false stories about Jesus. Bruce continues:

> It can have been by no means as easy as some writers seem to think to invent words and deeds of Jesus in those early

years, when so many of His disciples were about, who could
remember what had and had not happened.[37]

Bruce also notes that the earlier Christians were careful
to distinguish the words of Jesus and their own conclusions
or judgments, as did Paul (see 1 Corinthians 7).[38] Furthermore, since Christianity began amidst hostility and controversy, "the disciples could not afford to risk inaccuracies
(not to speak of willful manipulations of the facts), which
would at once be exposed by those who would be only too
glad to do so."[39] This clearly contradicts the notions of the
Jesus Seminar and other liberal scholars that the early
church freely created stories about Jesus.

Paul Barnett observes that "it is instructive to compare
the literary evidence for Jesus with that of other famous
men of antiquity."[40] Tiberius, the Roman emperor during
whose lifetime Jesus died, was born in 42 B.C. and reigned
from A.D. 14-37. One account of his earlier military exploits
dates at A.D. 30, but the major accounts are much later, with
Tacitus writing about A.D. 110, Suetonius about A.D. 120,
and Dio Cassius about A.D. 220.[41]

Barnett also notes that "the major outlines of Alexander [the Great's] career are not doubted despite a period
exceeding four hundred years separating the man and
the chief source of information on him."[42] If we date the
Gospels very circumspectly at no earlier than A.D. 90 (and
they are probably much earlier), we have a time span of
fewer than 60 years.

Since John's Gospel seems independent of Matthew,
Mark, and Luke, the dating of Acts does not bear on its date
of composition in the manner explained above. It is often

dated last of the four Gospels at sometime near A.D. 90 because of several reasons, one being a reference by Clement of Alexandria (recorded by Eusebius) that John wrote to supplement the writings of the other Gospels.[43] Irenaeus also comments that John wrote after the first three Gospels.[44] Many have argued that John's developed theology is an indication of a later date because such theological sophistication takes time to develop and because he uses language and concepts not available to earlier writers.

The latter argument loses its punch, though, when we consider that Paul's letter to the Romans is dated in the A.D. 50s and is every bit as theologically "developed" as John.[45] Robust theology may appear quickly, especially if one is taught by Jesus himself. The Dead Sea Scrolls, which are dated before the time of Christ, use some terminology similar to John, so this kind of language was functioning in Palestine earlier than was once thought. Moreover, the words by Clement and Irenaeus that John was written last need not necessarily mean it was written in the 90s, especially if the Synoptic Gospels were written as early as we have just argued. Therefore, John could be dated earlier, although it is granted that this is at present a minority viewpoint.

Even if we date John at around A.D. 90, this is fewer than 60 years removed from the events themselves—a time gap much shorter than that of most classical literature. Many scholars date John in the 90s, while trusting its historical accuracy because of apostolic authorship and corroboration with ancient history.

Yet, some readers may still be troubled by the time period, however long it may have been, separating the life of Jesus and the first written records we now possess. Was there sufficient time for historical distortions? In an age of instant news via magazine, newspaper, and television, the idea of a time gap of several decades between the life of Jesus and the dating of our Gospels may be disturbing. Yet, besides the veracity of available written sources used by the Gospel writers, this ignores another key fact: the importance of oral tradition in the ancient Near East. Although the Jews were "people of the book," written resources were far less available than they are today. Consequently, memorization of religious teaching was fundamental to instruction. If people could not easily write it down or tape it, they had to memorize it. The idea of oral tradition goes beyond "hearsay." It was an integral part of the historical memory of the people.

The Jesus of the Gospels is certainly an unforgettable figure. The events of his ministry were indelibly etched on his disciples' minds as the records relate, and it is highly likely that his disciples memorized large amounts of his teachings. Memorization was widespread and impressive in ancient rabbinical circles (with many rabbis memorizing the entire Old Testament!).[46] As Blomberg has noted, "The gospels depict Jesus as . . . a teacher of wisdom and phrase over 90% of his sayings in forms which would have been easy to remember, using figures and styles of speech much like that found in Hebrew poetry."[47] If we add to this that Jesus spoke the Word of God with a prophet's authority, presented himself as the Savior and impelled his disciples to learn and teach his message, there appears a strong dynamic for faithfully remembering his words and deeds.[48]

So even if we date all the Gospels quite late (which I find no good reason for doing), and thus weaken our case for their traditional authenticity, the gap does not increase so measurably as to render their testimony unreliable. Historians have indeed noted that longer time gaps are required for legendary material to take firm hold. The Jesus Seminar to the contrary, oral cultures emphasized the memorization of sizable amounts of material.

The noted historian of Roman times, A.N. Sherwin-White, observes that the sources for Roman and Greek history are often at least one or two generations removed from the events they relate; yet this does not prevent historians from confidently consulting the material. White argues that the works of the Greek historian Herodotus equip us to test the rate of legendary accumulation. They show that even two generations is not enough of a time span to allow legendary tendencies to destroy primary facts. When White consults the Gospels, he finds that if the Gospel stories were to contain legends, the rate of legendary development would have to have been "unbelievable" in its rapidity. The Gospels were written too soon after the events to allow for this process of distortion.[49]

In all likelihood the Gospels were circulated when some of Jesus' contemporaries were still living (or at least many of the second generation would have heard about him from eyewitnesses). In this kind of situation, legendary frosting is difficult to apply. The memory of the events would be too close at hand for sugary embellishments.

J. B. Phillips, the celebrated modern translator of the Bible, finds the Gospels and mythological tales to be entirely different:

> I have read, in Greek and Latin, scores of myths, but I did not find the slightest flavour of myth here. There is no

hysteria, no careful working for effect, and no attempt at collusion. These are not embroidered tales. The material is cut to the bone.[50]

He further speaks of the "almost childlike candour and simplicity" of the accounts and affirms that "no man could ever have invented such a character as Jesus." A "real Event" must lie behind the Gospels.[51]

External Confirmation of Veracity

The veracity or truthfulness of documents can also be checked by looking for confirmation of their historical content from external sources. This is often called the external test of reliability. This is such a vast subject that we can only touch on it, noting that the New Testament documents have been substantially confirmed by archaeology and other ancient writings. (We should also remember that the New Testament is better attested than any other piece of ancient literature, so we might better speak of the New Testament confirming other accounts.)

Various archaeological discoveries harmonize with historical details found in the Gospels. For instance, the discovery of the bones of Yohan Ben Ha'galgol shed light on the method of crucifixion recorded in the Gospels. In 1968 an ancient Jewish burial site was accidentally unearthed. In it were 15 stone ossuaries holding the bones of 35 Jews who were killed in the fall of Jerusalem in A.D. 70. One ossuary identified its victim as Yohan, whose feet were pierced by a long nail still attached to some wood. Nails had also pierced his wrist, and the puncture showed that he had moved up and down on the cross while struggling for breath. His legs had also been broken. After describing the above in much more detail, Gary Habermas concludes, "In this case the crucifixion process recorded in the Gospels has been largely corroborated by this new discovery."[52] Archaeological findings have also corroborated the pool of Bethesda (cf. John 5:2), discovered in 1888[53]; the existence of Pontius Pilate, mentioned on a fragment of a Latin plaque[54]; the greatness of the temple during Jesus' time[55]; the kind of tomb Jesus was buried in, many of which have been unearthed in Palestine[56]; and many other items. These findings do not in themselves prove that everything the Gospels say is true, but they harmonize well with the Gospel accounts.

Luke's writings were scrupulously scrutinized by the renowned archaeologist Sir William Ramsay, who began his investigation assuming that Acts was a basically unreliable document written in the middle of the second century. His studied conclusion was far different: "Luke is a historian of the first rank.... In short this author should be placed along with the very greatest of historians."[57] Archaeology also gives us material on censuses that fits in some detail with Luke's mention of a Roman census.[58]

John's Gospel, once thought by many as too theological to be of much historical worth, has more recently received respect as precise history. After discussing John's knowledge of the buildings and landscapes of ancient Palestine, Barnett comments that "the archaeology evidence is that the author had minute local knowledge which, however, he discloses in quite inconspicuous ways."[59] Again, this observation goes against the Jesus Seminar's negative assessment of John as a historical theology.

Added to the external archaeology evidence are significant references to Jesus found in the writings of Jewish and Roman historians, early church fathers, and others. Habermas collected 110 separate facts about Jesus from these sources that agree with the New Testament accounts.[60]

The Authenticity of the Gospels: Who Wrote Them?

We now move from a consideration of the veracity or truthfulness of the events recorded in the Gospels and Acts (in light of their date of composition) to the question of *authenticity*: the identity and qualifications of the persons who recorded the events.

Determining the authorship of any document involves both internal and external criteria. We look at the document itself to ascertain its author, and we look to outside attestation of the authorship. For instance, it is not impossible to determine who wrote an unsigned editorial in the local newspaper. We can look at the writing style of the document itself (internal evidence), and we can gather external evidence (by calling the newspaper, comparing the writing to signed editorials, and so on).

Concerning external criteria of authenticity, the unanimous tradition of Christianity has been that Matthew wrote Matthew, Mark wrote Mark, Luke wrote Luke, and John wrote John. Although tradition can certainly be wrong, the burden of proof seems to be on those who would dispute this claim. Hagerty explains this in legal terms:

Prescription is a process by which a right is acquired through long use. It is important for a lawyer to show a court on which side of a case lies the burden of proof. Now it is an undisputed fact that Matthew, Mark, Luke and John have been credited with being the authors of the Gospels since the last quarter of the second century. . . . The burden of proof is definitely on any modern scholar who contradicts this ancient tradition.[61]

During the first quarter of the fourth century, the church historian Eusebius in his *Ecclesiastical History*[62] quotes from the writings of Bishop Papias of Hierapolis (c. A.D. 70-140) who wrote a treatise in five books on the sayings of the apostles and other contemporaries of Christ. The quotation mentions that Mark, the interpreter of Peter, wrote a record of Christ. It also mentions that Matthew recorded the sayings of Jesus.[63]

Irenaeus explicitly names the authors of all four Gospels, explains the occasion for their being written, and quotes from them (and almost all the books of the New Testament) extensively.[64] In *Against Heresies* (A.D. 180), he speaks of these writings that are "the ground and pillar of our faith," saying that:

Matthew . . . issued a Gospel among the Hebrews. . . . Mark, the disciple and interpreter of Peter, did also hand down to us in writing what had been preached by Peter. Luke also, the companion of Paul, recorded in a book the Gospel preached by him. Afterward, John, the disciple of the Lord, who had leaned on His breast, did himself publish a Gospel during his residence at Ephesus in Asia.[65]

Even before Irenaeus, Justin Martyr (A.D. 100-165), in his *First Apology*, speaks this way concerning the Lord's Supper:

> For the Apostles *in their memoirs composed by them which are called gospels,* have delivered unto us what was enjoined upon them: that Jesus took bread, and when He had given thanks said "This do ye in remembrance of me."[66]

Justin Martyr also speaks of "the memoirs of the apostles" when recounting Jesus' baptism and subsequent temptation by the devil.[67]

An ancient Latin manuscript called the Muratorian Fragment, dating from about A.D. 190, also mentions "the third book of the gospel: according to Luke" which was written by a "physician whom Paul had taken along with him as a legal expert." The document also states that Luke wrote "in accordance with [Paul's] opinion."[68] The text also mentions "the fourth gospel" which "is by John, one of the disciples."[69]

The testimony of other writers such as Origen (A.D. 185-254), Clement of Alexandria (A.D. 150-215), and Tertullian (A.D. 155-220) agrees with the attributions given by Irenaeus.[70] Hagerty also notes, "It cannot be too strongly emphasized that the scholars of the early centuries had access to sources of information that later scholars and critics did not."[71]

If external criteria point toward traditional authorship, what of internal matters? Do the Gospels themselves betray their authorship?

The Gospels do not openly reveal their authors, but various internal factors fit well with the external evidence. We have already argued in general for early dates for the Gospels. The dating of Matthew, Mark, and Luke as before, or even shortly after, A.D. 70 certainly leaves open the possibility of them being penned by these men.

Certain features of the Gospel of Matthew fit with the predilections of a diligent tax collector, especially an attention to detail that matches "the methodical arrangement of this Gospel."[72] Although Mark and Luke record the dispute over paying taxes, Matthew uses a more precise Greek term for a state coin, something a tax collector would notice.[73] Also noticeable is his frequent reference to money, an interest in large amounts (18:24; 25:15), and a general interest in statistics (e.g., 1:17).[74]

Only Matthew records the call of the tax collector to be a disciple. Mark and Luke refer to him as Levi but in the lists of apostles call him Matthew. The Gospel of Matthew consistently refers to him as Matthew, which could indicate that "the name Matthew came to have greater significance than the name Levi from the time of his dramatic call to follow Jesus."[75]

The internal evidence for Matthew's authorship is not, in itself, overwhelming; but nothing in the Gospel excludes it, and much external evidence encourages it.[76]

With the Gospel of Mark we find no explicit reference to authorship, but neither do we find anything in the Gospel which is incompatible with Mark—"the disciple and interpreter of Peter," as Irenaeus put it—being the author. The Gospel's dramatic style mirrors the rather flamboyant and dramatic character of Peter himself as evidenced in all four Gospels. New Testament scholar C.H. Dodd also noted the similarity between the outlines of the life of Christ given in Peter's sermons in Acts (10:34-43) and the chronology of the Gospel of Mark, thus giving more evidence to a connection with the apostle Peter.[77] Mark is the only Gospel that refers to a rather strange detail of the passion story: a young man wearing nothing but a linen cloth who escaped being captured when he ran away naked, leaving his garment behind (Mark 14:51,52). Many have taken this to be a veiled (or unveiled, actually) reference to Mark himself.[78] There is also good reason to identify Mark with the John Mark referred to in several other New Testament texts.[79]

The writer of Luke speaks in the first person, as does the writer of Acts, which is written as a continuation of Luke. Both books are addressed to Theophilus, have common concerns and similar style. The author of Luke does not directly identify himself, but he was a companion of Paul, as several "we" passages in Acts reveal (16:10-17; 20:5-15; 21:1-18; 27:1–28:16). Paul mentions his "dear friend Luke, the doctor" (Colossians 4:14) and Luke his "fellow worker" (Philemon 24), so Luke is the likeliest candidate, which fits well with the strong external evidence.

The Gospel of John claims to be written by a disciple of Jesus. After describing the death of Jesus, the text reads, "The man who saw it has given testimony, and his testimony is true. He knows that he tells the truth, and he testifies so that you also may believe" (19:35). It also says, "This is the disciple who testifies to these things and who wrote them down. We know that his testimony is true" (21:24). The "we" here very likely refers not to a group of authors but to the disciples whom John often refers to as "we" (see 1:14; 2:11).[80] Though the disciple does not explicitly identify himself, his references to "the disciple whom Jesus loved," taken together with several other references, identifies him as John.[81] (The three letters of John show such a strong stylistic resemblance to the Gospel of John that they, too, can be considered penned by the apostle.)

Our survey finds good external and internal reasons to view the Gospels as written by their traditional authors. The significance of this is that each author was in a position to flesh out the historical facts about Jesus. Matthew and John were disciples themselves, so their testimony has the ring of eyewitnesses. Luke very likely was not an eyewitness but inspected the records carefully (Luke 1:1-4) and has traditionally been viewed as the companion of Paul who, although also not an eyewitness to the earthly Jesus, is, as we will see, a reliable source of information as well. Mark may or may not have been an eyewitness, but it is very likely that his Gospel bears the stamp of the apostle Peter himself.[82] Although we cannot range over the vast amount of historical claims made in the Gospels, it must be noted that they bear the marks of historicity. They are plentiful in references to politics, geography, specific individuals, and the minutiae of history. The fact that they contain theological message is not a sufficient reason to jettison their historical reliability. The New Testament can be "full of faith and full of fact."[83] As David Wells has noted:

> It is consistent with the practice of historical research in other fields to assume the New Testament record is innocent in respect to the accuracy of its portrayal of Jesus until proven guilty. . . . It is true that the Gospels were written in the context of faith, but that does not mean that they are thereby distorted.[84]

R.T. France asks, "How much worthwhile biography has ever been written by authors who did not have a deep personal motivation for writing?"[85] Yet this motivation need not exclude historical integrity. Some of the most compelling and historically accurate accounts of the Nazi Holocaust have been written by Jewish writers, such as Elie Weisel, who experienced its horrors. These writers intimate participation in their subject matter, and their emotional involvement does not invalidate their historical reports. The same is true for the Gospel writers.

This is all the more compelling when we realize that the writers of the Gospels had no ulterior motives for dishonesty: This was no get-rich-quick scheme, and Christian discipleship often meant persecution by unresponsive Jews and threatened political forces.

We just noted John's declaration that he preserved the truth about Jesus in order that his readers would believe that truth. Even the skeptical Will Durant in his multivolume series *The Story of Civilization* says that

> despite the prejudices and theological preconceptions of the evangelists, they record many incidents that mere inventors would have concealed—the competition of the apostles for high places in the Kingdom, their flight after Jesus' arrest, Peter's denial, the failure of Christ to work miracles in Galilee, the references of some auditors to his possible insanity, his early uncertainty as to his mission, his confessions of ignorance as to the future, his moments of bitterness, his despairing cry on the cross; no one reading these scenes can doubt the reality of the figure behind them.[86]

Do the Gospels Contradict Each Other?

Our case for the trustworthiness of the Gospels has been steadily building, but some people will object that the four different accounts of Jesus contradict each other, thus vitiating their force as historical. So Joseph Campbell says, "We just don't know much about Jesus. All we know are four contradictory texts that purport to tell us what he said and did."[87]

To answer this would involve a careful look at the relationships between four separate and substantial texts. Yet a few general remarks help refute the objections of Campbell and others. The very fact that we have four distinct accounts actually strengthens the evidence for Jesus. We are not dependent on merely one witness, neither do the accounts evidence a contrived uniformity.

Each Gospel was written by a different author, at a different time, with a different style, and with a different audience in mind. Each, of course, had to be selective in his choice of material. Many supposed contradictions evaporate quite quickly by keeping this in mind. Two newspapers, for instance, may write up the last game of the World Series somewhat differently without contradicting each other. If John records a miracle not mentioned by Matthew, Mark, and Luke, this is no contradiction, but rather an addition. If Matthew omits something in Mark, it is no contradiction, but a deletion. One account may also paraphrase an event somewhat differently without actually contradicting another account. In most cases a little historical snooping can resolve apparent contradictions. A good "harmony of the Gospels" gives a composite picture of all four accounts.

Simply consulting the notes of The New International Version Study Bible is very helpful in working with apparent contradictions, as is the book *The Historical Reliability of the Gospels* (1987) by Craig Blomberg.[88]

Paul As a Witness to Jesus

But we have another witness who presents very early material on Jesus: Paul of Tarsus. Almost all biblical scholars accept that Paul wrote Romans, 1 and 2 Corinthians, Galatians, Philippians, 1 Thessalonians, and Philemon. Although a strong case can be made that he wrote all the letters of the New Testament attributed to him,[89] we will limit our discussion primarily to these seven letters.

We have already seen the evidence for the *integrity* of the New Testament, and even the most liberal scholars grant that Paul authored the above books, so we are assured of their *authenticity* as well. But what of their *veracity*?

Scholars agree that Paul died by about A.D. 65, so all his letters predate this. F.F. Bruce estimates that all of Paul's letters were written between A.D. 48 and 60.[90] The very early dating of these letters witnesses to their veracity, as does their very character as letters. Historians relish personal letters as primary source material, especially if they contain trivia and lots of details, are written in an unpolished style, and were originally for a small audience. Paul's letters fulfill most, if not all of these requirements, and thus evidence historical reliability.[91]

In several places Paul refers to hymns and creeds (Philippians 2:6-11; Colossians 1:15-20; Ephesians 2:14-16;

1 Timothy 3:16), which scholars believe predate his writings because they betray features of Hebrew poetry and thought forms, and they translate easily into Aramaic—the language in which they would have been spoken in the very early church.[92]

These creeds and hymns lend veracity to Paul's writings for two reasons. First, they reveal a view of Jesus that predates Paul's writings, taking us even closer to the life of Jesus himself. The majority of scholars date them from A.D. 33 to 48.[93] Second, they evidence an emphasis on the death, resurrection, and deity of Jesus from an early date. These ideas were not grafted onto a nonsupernatural Jesus by the later church. These creeds and hymns represent the "rich Christological content"[94] of the young church's confessions and worship. They cannot be arranged in order from earlier, more simple views, to later, more complex and imaginative ones. Their theology is consistently rich and developed from the beginning.[95]

New Testament writers such as Peter (1 Peter 3:18-22), the authors of Hebrews (Hebrews 1:13) and John (John 1:1-18) repeat various other hymnic and creedal material as well. Even if there is some debate as to which passages reflect earlier hymns and creeds, their existence and frequency has been positively established, and this more firmly anchors the historicity of the record of Jesus.

The early dates for Paul's writings and the primitive nature of these hymns and creeds also weakens the contention of many that Paul departed from the original spirit of Jesus and invented a Christianity (or Paulinism) of his own design.[96] Although Paul claimed to receive direct revelation from the risen Christ, he is in full agreement with the

Gospel accounts of Jesus (whether he knew of these or not). Paul's emphasis is on the glorified Christ (as we will explore in chapter 15), but he by no means ignores the earthly life or teachings of Jesus. For Paul, the outline of Jesus' earthly ministry was a given that he naturally incorporated into his letters. About Jesus, Paul declares: He descended from Abraham (Galatians 3:16); he was a descendant of David (Romans 1:3); he was born of a woman (Galatians 4:4); he lived under the law (Galatians 4:4); he was humble (Philippians 2:6-7); he did not please himself, but was insulted (Romans 15:3); he instituted the Lord's Supper (1 Corinthians 11:23); he was betrayed (1 Corinthians 11:23); he was killed by Jews of Judea (1 Thessalonians 2:14,15); he was buried and rose again (1 Corinthians 15:4-8).[97]

Paul's teaching also deeply reflects the ethics of Jesus at many points, concerning the Lord's Supper (1 Corinthians 11:23-25; cf. Mark 14:22-25), divorce and remarriage (1 Corinthians 7:10,11; cf. Mark 10:1-12), practical ethics (Romans 12:9–13:10; cf. Matthew 5-7), and other issues. F.F. Bruce puts this in perspective:

> The outline of the gospel story . . . in the writings of Paul agrees with the outlines which we find elsewhere in the New Testament, and in the four gospels in particular. Paul himself is at pains to point out that the gospel which he preached was one and the same gospel as that preached by the other apostles (1 Corinthians 15:11), a striking claim, considering that Paul was neither a companion of Christ in the days of his flesh nor of the original apostles, and that he vigorously asserts his independence of these (Galatians 1-2).[98]

In our inspection of the New Testament witness to Jesus, we have found it to pass the crucial tests of integrity, authenticity, and veracity.[99] For those who have a sense of historical evidence, these factors should lead to respect for the New Testament record of Jesus. We have good reason to trust its testimony as reliable.

The burden of proof would be on anyone marshaling a historical case against the evidence of the New Testament that Jesus of Nazareth is the only Christ.

4

JESUS AND THE NEW SPIRITUALITY

SPIRITUALITY IS IN style. Bestselling books such as *Care of the Soul* (1992) by Thomas Moore and *The Seven Spiritual Laws of Success* (1994) by Deepak Chopra have led the way for the rediscovery of the soul in popular culture. As Americans lament the violence in our streets, the corruption in our courts, the hollowness of materialism, racial strife, and the moral rot eating away at every level of culture, they are turning to spiritual interests in an effort to find a foundation for self and society. What spirituality will carry us successfully into the third millennium? Faced with graying hair, wrinkling skin, an increasing number of doctor visits, and offspring with religious questions, many baby boomers are turning toward an exploration of the spiritual world. A recent *Newsweek* poll found that 58 percent of Americans claim they "need to experience spiritual growth," and one-third say they have had a mystical or religious experience.[1]

The title of a recent article in *Psychology Today* captured the mood of many: "Desperately Seeking Spirituality."[2] This quest for the sacred, sometimes called "the new spirituality," often bypasses the traditional spiritual direction in favor of the eclectic and the unorthodox. The *Psychology Today* article explained and praised practices and beliefs that are entirely outside traditional Christianity, and which usually are associated with aspects of New Age thinking such as Zen meditation, parapsychology, and goddess religion.

Although those experimenting with the new spirituality may shun the term "New Age" for various reasons, the worldview at the heart of much of the resurgent interest in spirituality fits with what many critics label as "New Age." Shirley MacLaine's books may no longer be bestsellers, but many of the ideas she championed in the late 1980s have found their way into the mainstream culture. This is evident in Deepak Chopra's book *The Seven Spiritual Laws of Success.*

Chopra promises us the moon. If we master his principles, we will gain the "ability to create unlimited wealth with effortless ease, and to experience success in every endeavor."[3] The basis for such optimism is that "we are divinity in disguise, and the gods and goddesses in embryo that are contained within us seek to be fully materialized."[4] Chopra's seven spiritual laws assume that we are one with the universal field of energy (an impersonal deity), and that we find spiritual liberation by learning how to release the divine power within ourselves. Chopra is restating the philosophy of his spiritual mentor, Maharishi Mahesh Yogi, who founded Transcendental Meditation—a system of Hindu yoga designed for secular Westerners. This is classic New Age teaching: everything is one (monism); everything is divine (pantheism); we are divine (self-deification); and we have unlimited potential to shape our destiny apart from any Creator who stands over us as Lord.[5]

Similarly, Thomas Moore's approach in *The Care of the Soul* emphasizes the sacredness of the soul, its connection to the world soul (*anima mundi*),[6] and rejects set moral categories in favor of balancing the light and the dark sides of the self.[7] In rejecting the idea of sin, Moore says that the story of Jesus being crucified between two thieves may be "an elevation of thieving," and goes on to cite Oscar Wilde's notion that Christ "regarded sin and suffering as being in themselves beautiful holy things and modes of perfection."[8] Moore teaches we can find spiritual wisdom in all the world's scriptures, so long as we reject any literal understanding of the Bible or an objective sense of truth.[9] Given the uniqueness of each soul, he argues that a polytheistic approach to the sacred is in order, so long as all are deemed sacred and somehow connected to the world soul.[10]

Moore's sense of the soul draws from a variety of sources and is offered as a generic spirituality, free from the confines of organized religion.[11] Likewise, although his beliefs are essentially Hindu, Chopra outlines spiritual principles for anyone, irrespective of one's religious background. This approach typifies the new spirituality: one can construct a spirituality according to personal preference without concern for religious authority. This smorgasbord mentality often leads to confused and contradictory beliefs.[12] For instance, Pastor Leith Anderson encountered a young man who said he believed in Reformed theology, the inerrancy of Scripture, and reincarnation. When the pastor challenged him that Christianity logically cannot be squared with reincarnation, the man was unfazed. He preferred to believe in all three, even though they are irreconcilable.[13]

This new spirituality, while contradicting Christian essentials, often enlists Jesus as a model or master. Jesus is mixed in with a variety of beliefs that oppose what the New Testament says he taught. The spiritual ideas of Chopra, Moore, and many others are so prevalent that many people apply them to their thinking about Jesus. In assorted New Age circles, Jesus is often praised as a herald of the New Age. This "New Age" of self-realization, love, and world peace will break forth when humans reclaim a lost divinity and manifest their latent potential for the healing of our beleaguered planet. Social and planetary transformation will be triggered through inner transformation and the release of evolutionary energies that bubble below the surface of ordinary consciousness. A few choice beings have blazed the path to this New Age. Jesus is often proclaimed as one of these trailblazers.

A New Jesus?

In an article capturing the essence of the New Age Jesus, New Age writer John White[14] presents Jesus as the West's most familiar example of "Cosmic Consciousness"—a state of awareness attuned to the oneness of being and universal energy, which releases vibrant evolutionary forces. White says, "Jesus' unique place in history is based upon his unprecedented realization of the higher intelligence, the divinity, the Ground of Being incarnated in him."[15]

White is but one voice in a growing chorus of New Age writers, teachers, and prophets who insist that the Jesus of biblical orthodoxy is the product of misunderstanding and spiritual immaturity. White strives to free Jesus from the shackles of orthodoxy and to rediscover his true teachings and identity.

According to White, Jesus taught that sin is not the transgression of God's moral law for which we deserve punishment. It is simply "missing the mark" by not hitting the bull's-eye of the God within us. The antidote to this error is not found in seeking forgiveness from God but in changing one's consciousness. "God does not condemn us for our sins," White insists. "Rather, we condemn ourselves *by* our sins. And thus forgiveness by God is not necessary; it is there always as unconditional love, the instant we turn in our hearts and minds to God."[16] This, in essence, means turning our minds back to our identity as God.

When Jesus called people to "repent," White alleges this has nothing to do with sorrow over sin, but everything to do with going "beyond or higher than the ordinary mental state." This "means transcending self-centered ego and becoming God-centered, God-realized."[17] To go beyond our self-imposed limitations is "to become experientially aware" that "all is God and there is only God." This change of mind gives us the mind of Jesus when he said, "I and the Father are one."[18]

Jesus is lauded as the great illuminator, the archetype of higher awareness, an inspiring example of self-discovery. The historical man Jesus of Nazareth is distinguished from "the Christ." According to White, "Christ, the Christos, the Messiah, is an eternal transpersonal condition of being to which *we must all someday come.* Jesus did not say that this higher state of consciousness realized in him was his alone for all time."[19] Moreover, Jesus does not bid us to worship him but to follow him on the path of enlightenment "*as if we were Jesus himself.*"[20]

For White, "the significance of the incarnation and resurrection is not that Jesus was human like us but rather that *we are gods like him or at least have the potential to be.*"[21] He believes it is more accurate to say "Christ was Jesus" than "Jesus was the Christ," because that "allows for *other* Christs—you and me."[22] Jesus is not "the sole path to cosmic consciousness," but one of many "evolutionary forerunners of a new Earth and a new Humanity" including Buddha, Krishna, Lao Tze, Moses, and Mohammed. All taught that "*thou shalt evolve to a higher state of being and ultimately return to the godhead which is your very self.*"[23]

White's affirmations resist orthodoxy at every point, and his portrait of Jesus is echoed by many others in the New Age fold, whether their roots be in Gnosticism, Essenism, the theosophical movement, the Mind Sciences, Eastern religions, Western occultism, channeling, or elsewhere. According to such thinking, Jesus is not the unique, unrepeatable, and unsurpassable incarnation of a personal God, but a manifestation of a universal state of consciousness that anyone can attain through proper techniques. Jesus came into the world as an example of God-realization, not to reconcile sinful humanity with a holy God through his vicarious sacrifice on the cross. For White, Jesus does not deliver anyone from a literal hell, because hell is simply a state of mind that denies one's transcendent identity as God. Conversely, heaven is the consciousness of one's union of identity with God.[24] We should never fling ourselves at Jesus' nail-pierced feet in worshipful abandon; rather, we should stand tall and salute one who has attained what we too shall one day possess as Christed beings, much as an aspiring and gifted commissioned officer salutes a five-star general.

The real Jesus, many claim, would stand against present "orthodox" perversions of his message as narrow-minded,

dogmatic, and exclusivistic. New Age author Michael
Grosso relates that John White wrote him a note that stated
the outrage of Christians over *The Last Temptation of Christ* is
"a lot of noise by immature/juvenile Christians who want to
keep Jesus on a pedestal rather than grow up and relate to
him as an elder brother."[25]

The New Age Jesus Revealed

It is not possible to present *the* New Age view of Jesus because there is a diversity of views. It might be better, though,
to refer to this diversity as a *family* of related views, all sharing the same bloodline despite certain idiosyncrasies. The
various New Age views of Jesus tend to share eight common
approaches.

1. Jesus is revered or respected as a highly spiritually
evolved being who serves as an example for our own spiritual evolution. Jesus is called a master, guru, yogi, adept,
avatar, shaman, and way-shower, among other terms of
metaphysical endearment. Jesus' miracles are often accepted as manifestations of his mastery of divine energy or
his ability to tap into the Christ power.

2. The individual, personal, historical Jesus is separated
from the universal, impersonal, eternal Christ or Christ
Consciousness, which Jesus embodied but did not monopo-
lize. Jesus is regarded as a Christ who did not corner the
market on the expansive Christ Consciousness. David Spangler says that "the Christ is not the province of a single individual," although Jesus "focused the universal life/growth
quality we call the Christ."[26] In *What Do We Mean When We*

Say God? (1990), Kathy Korpi says that Jesus "channeled the Christ spirit and the Christ spirit is a very strong spirit, a spirit of healing." She adds that if "every person on this planet could share that feeling simultaneously for one second, this planet would be healed."[27]

This same idea of separating Jesus from a universal energy he tapped into is captured in different terminology in a book of daily spiritual readings called *The Tao of Jesus* (1994) by John Beverly Butcher. Butcher's selections are largely taken from non-Christian sources, including Gnostic and Taoist literature. For him, Jesus is not the fullness of God in human form (Colossians 2:9), but a person through whom the Tao (the impersonal Life Force) is manifested. However, the Tao is also manifested through Lao-Tzu, Socrates, Carl Jung, Joseph Campbell, Matthew Fox, Starhawk (a witch), and others.[28] Butcher emphasizes the Tao far more than he emphasizes Jesus.

3. The orthodox understanding of Jesus as the supreme and final revelation of God is dismissed as illegitimate. Jesus is not seen as the one and only Christ that ever was, is, or will be. This is viewed as too limiting and provincial. God cannot be so narrow as to restrict divine incarnation to one revelator. In a book on the "lost years and unknown travels" of Jesus, Janet Bock states, "For many, the position that Jesus was the only 'Son of God' . . . is, in effect, a limiting of the power of God, a shackling of divinity to one physical form for all eternity."[29] In his popular book *Living Buddha, Living Christ* (1995), Buddhist monk Thich Nhat Hanh asserts that Jesus and Buddha are equally enlightened masters from whom we have much to learn. His private altar contains images of Jesus and Buddha, both of whom he claims as his

"spiritual ancestors."[30] For Hanh, Jesus is no more exalted than Buddha. Stephen Mitchell likewise puts Jesus on the same level as other spiritual teachers when he says that "we can recognize that Jesus speaks in harmony with the supreme teachings of all the great religions: the Upanishads, the Tao Te Ching, the Buddhist sutras, the Zen and Sufi and Hasidic Masters."[31]

4. Jesus' death on the cross (if recognized at all) is not accepted as having any ethical significance for salvation. The crucifixion is either denied as a historical event or reinterpreted to exclude the idea that Jesus suffered *as the Christ* to pay the just penalty for human sin. For instance, Hanh claims that the Christian practice of communion does not focus on the death of Christ to atone for sin. Rather, if we eat the bread and drink the beverage "deeply, we touch the sun, the clouds, the earth, and everything in the cosmos. We touch life, and we touch the Kingdom of God."[32] Hahn empties a Christian practice of its significance and reinterprets it to refer to our mystical connection to the universe.

5. Jesus' resurrection from the dead is not viewed as a physical and historical fact demonstrating his victory over sin, death, and Satan; rather, if recognized at all, it is understood as a spiritual triumph not unique to Jesus. There are many other "ascended masters." Although he considers Jesus a spiritual teacher, Hanh denies the importance of the resurrection, saying that making belief in the resurrection a requirement for being a Christian "may discourage some people from looking into the life of Jesus."[33] Similarly, Marcus Borg, a member of the Jesus Seminar with New Age leanings, says, "I believe in the resurrection of Jesus. But I doubt that it involved anything happening to his corpse."[34]

For him, Jesus can be a "mediator of the sacred," without being resurrected Lord.[35]

6. Jesus' "second coming" is not judged to be a literal, physical, and visible return in the clouds at the end of the age (Acts 1:8), but a stage in the evolutionary advancement of the race when the Christic energies escape the confines of ignorance. Soli, an "off-planet being" channeled through Neville Rowe, tells his clients, "You are God, You are, each and every one, part of the Second Coming."[36] Some New Age figures may claim to embody this energy more perfectly than others and so better personify the second coming. The historic Christian understanding of the second coming and a final judgment is deemed as being too severe, final, and divisive.

7. Exotic, extrabiblical documents are regarded as authentic sources for information about the life of Jesus not found in the canonical Scriptures. Although the Bible may be selectively studied and paid due respect, it is routinely eclipsed by alien sources that reveal a Jesus foreign to the Bible, yet quite at home in New Age quarters. The quest for this "lost Christianity" follows several routes which, nevertheless, converge at key points.

Historically based claims may appeal to ancient Gnostic texts discovered in 1945 at Nag Hammadi, Egypt, as the original message of a Gnostic hierarchy. Neo-Gnostics of various stripes argue that the genuine Jesus came not to rescue us from our sins, but to stir us to discover and rekindle the divine spark within. Commenting on a text from the Gnostic Gospel of Thomas that has Jesus saying, "He who drinks from my mouth will become as I am, and I shall be he," noted scholar of world religions and mythology Joseph Campbell declares:

Now, that is exactly Buddhism. We are all manifestations of Buddha consciousness, or Christ consciousness, only we do not know it. The word "Buddha" means "the one who waked up." We are all to do that—to wake up to the Christ or Buddha consciousness within us. That is blasphemy in the normal way of Christian thinking, but it is the very essence of Christian Gnosticism and of the Thomas Gospel.[37]

Another brand of historical revisionism spotlights a Tibetan document published at the turn of the century by a Russian journalist that purports to tell of "the lost years of Jesus" (between ages 13 and 29), which he spent studying, teaching, and traveling in the mystic East. Elizabeth Clare Prophet, the leader of Church Universal and Triumphant, hails the discovery as "an historical breakthrough that will shake the foundations of modern Christendom."[38]

Claiming to base their interpretation on the Dead Sea Scrolls or additional documents, other revisionists uncover "an Essene Jesus" who drastically differs from the figure who dominates the Gospels. New Age celebrity Shirley MacLaine typifies this approach by saying, "Christ was a member of the Essene Brotherhood, which, among other things, believed in reincarnation."[39] She goes so far as to identify Jesus as a proto-New Ager by saying that "Jesus and the Essenes, with their teachings on love and light and cosmic laws along with the Golden Rule of karma, sound very much like metaphysical seekers in the New Age today."[40]

Other revelations of a nonhistorical sort emanate from assorted channelers who extract information about—or even ostensibly from—Jesus through their entities, spirit guides, and ascended masters, or from less personal sources such as the Akashic Records or the collective unconscious. An increasingly popular three-volume work called *A Course in Miracles,* popularized by Marianne Williamson, presents itself as nothing less than a transcript of a postmortem message from Jesus himself.

8. Historic orthodox doctrine is rejected and replaced by an esoteric interpretation of biblical texts that yields unorthodox results. "Esoteric" refers to a hidden, secret, or arcane meaning. For instance, John White interprets being "born again" as "dying to the past and the old sense of self through a change in consciousness,"[41] rather than receiving forgiveness of sin and new life through faith in Jesus as Lord and Savior.

Christianity is deemed a mere rigid shell of "exoteric" (or external) religion disconnected from the inner or "esoteric" core of spiritual reality. For Christianity to be salvaged and rehabilitated for this New Age, it must be reinterpreted esoterically. According to White, "*Exoteric* Judeao-Christianity must reawaken to the truth preserved in its *esoteric* tradition."[42] He laments the casting of esoteric pearls before exoteric swine:

> The institutional church tells us that Jesus was the only Son of God, that he incarnated as a human to die on the cross as a penalty for our sins, and thereby save the world. But that is a sad caricature, a pale reflection of the true story.[43]

Although he does not use the term *esoteric,* Joseph Campbell esoterically recasts a classical Christian doctrine when he digs for the mythological core of the ascension of Jesus. He says:

> If you read "Jesus ascended into heaven" in terms of its metaphoric connotation, you see that he has gone inward—not into outer space but into inner space, to the place from which all being comes, into the consciousness that is the source of all things, the kingdom of heaven within.[44]

In other words, Jesus did not ascend to the "right hand of the Father" in cosmic triumph, but descended into the divine depths of the collective soul.

With such a background of interpretation, New Agers can selectively approve certain (reinterpreted) biblical texts in reference to Jesus, such as, "the kingdom of God is within you" (Luke 17:21), "'I have said you are gods'" (John 10:34), which they take to refer to all enlightened beings as well as Jesus.[45] These verses are believed to endorse the divinity and unlimited potential of all persons. Stephen Mitchell rejects the idea that the gospel is Christ's offer of forgiveness of sins and reconciliation with God. Instead, he claims that the gospel is "that the love we all long for in our innermost heart is already present, beyond longing."[46] He reaches this conclusion only through extensive reinterpretation of New Testament passages and by rejecting many verses he claims are not authentic.

Many people are yearning for a new spirituality, for something beyond the traditional views of Jesus. Which Jesus can refresh and restore the human soul? The remainder of this book addresses the controversies born of these desires for a new Jesus.

5

JESUS AND SECRET KNOWLEDGE: GNOSTICISM

POPULAR OPINION OFTEN comes from obscure sources. The more obscure and mysterious the sources, the more intriguing and entrancing they become. Until recently, the teachings of an obscure sect called the Gnostics was primarily the concern of the specialized scholar or the occultist. Yet Gnosticism has influenced a revised portrait of Jesus as an Illuminator who serves as a guide for others' awakening.

Many essentially Gnostic notions received wide attention through the authority of Joseph Campbell in the television series and bestselling book *The Power of Myth* (1988). In discussing the idea that "God was in Christ," Campbell affirms that "the basic Gnostic and Buddhist idea is that it is true of you and me as well." Jesus was an enlightened example who "realized in himself that he and what he called the Father were one, and he lived out of that knowledge of the Christhood of his nature." According to Campbell, anyone can live out his or her Christ nature. Campbell noted that a priest who heard him make this point in a lecture called it "blasphemy."[1]

Elaine Pagels, a scholar of Gnosticism, also finds parallels between Gnostic texts and the Buddhism presented in Thich Nhat Hanh's book *Living Buddha, Living Christ* (1995). "Voyaging from the gnostic Christian texts to the work of Thich Nhat Hanh, I feel I am in familiar territory" because Hanh, like the Gnostics, saw "Jesus as one through whom the divine was manifested, and through whose example and teaching they could hope for similar enlightenment."[2] The implication from Pagels' observations is that both views may have intuited the same spiritual reality—a reality that opposes the views of orthodox Christians.[3]

Gnosticism refers to a related body of teachings stressing the acquisition of "gnosis," or secret, inner knowledge. The knowledge sought is not strictly intellectual, but mystical; not merely a detached knowledge of or about something, but a knowing by experience or participation. This gnosis is the inner and esoteric mystical knowledge of ultimate reality. Gnosis reveals the spark of divinity within, which Gnostics think is obscured by ignorance, convention, and mere outer (exoteric) religiosity.

Gnosis is not the possession of the masses, but of the Gnostics—the Knowers—who are privy to its benefits. While the orthodox may exult in the exoteric religious trappings that stress dogmatic *belief* and prescribed behavior, the Gnostic few pierce through the surface to the esoteric spiritual *knowledge* of God. The Gnostics claim the orthodox mistake the shell for the core; the orthodox claim the Gnostics dive past the true core into a nonexistent one of their own invention.

To make sense this ancient dispute requires that in this and the next chapter we examine Gnosticism's perennial allure, expose its philosophical foundations, size up its historical claims, and bring it before the Jesus of the New Testament.

Gnosticism: Ancient and Modern

Gnosticism is experiencing something of a revival, despite its historical status within Christianity as a vanquished heresy. The publication *Gnosis,* which bills itself as a "journal of western inner traditions," began publication in 1985 and has become a popular magazine. *Gnosis* regularly runs articles on Gnosticism and Gnostic themes. The editor, Jay Kinney, dabbled in "Eastern mysticism, yoga and assorted gurus" before he returned to a Christianity "far more esoteric than the midwestern Methodist church in which he was raised."[4]

Some have even created institutional forms of this ancient religion. In Palo Alto, priestess Bishop Rosamonde Miller officiates at the weekly gatherings of Ecclesia Gnostica Mysteriorum (Church of Gnostic Mysteries), as she has done for the last 11 years. The chapel holds 40 to 60 participants each Sunday and includes Gnostic readings in its liturgy.[5] Miller says she knows of 12 organizationally unrelated Gnostic churches throughout the world.[6] Stephen Hoeller, a frequent contributor to *Gnosis,* who since 1967 has been a bishop of Ecclesia Gnostica in Los Angeles, notes that "gnostic churches . . . have sprung up in recent years in increasing numbers."[7]

These exotic-sounding enclaves of the esoteric are minute when compared to historic Christian denominations. The appeal of Gnosticism is not so much organizational as it is intellectual. Gnosticism in its various forms has often appealed to the alienated intellectuals who yearn for spiritual experience outside the bounds of the ordinary. Historian Patrick Henry observes that "the appeal of Gnosticism . . . is the appeal to a person's sense of superiority to the world. It is not I who am the victim of the Fall, or original sin, but the world itself. We come trailing clouds of glory—into a polluted environment."[8]

The Swiss psychiatrist Carl Jung, a constant source of inspiration for the New Age, did much to introduce Gnosticism to the modern world by viewing it as kind of ancient depth psychology. According to Stephen Hoeller, an interpreter of Jung and author of *The Gnostic Jung*:

> It was Jung's contention that Christianity and Western culture have suffered grievously because of the repression of the Gnostic approach to religion, and it was his hope that in time this approach would be reincorporated in our culture, our Western spirituality.[9]

In his *Psychological Types* (1921), Jung praised "the intellectual content of Gnosis" as "vastly superior" to the orthodox church. He also affirmed that "in light of our present mental development [Gnosticism] has not lost but considerably gained in value."[10] In 1916, after experiencing some bizarre paranormal events, Jung wrote in three nights a mystical tract called *The Seven Sermons to the Dead*. He ascribed this writing to Basilides, a Gnostic teacher of the second century in Alexandria. In his autobiography Jung states:

I can say that I have never lost touch with my initial experiences. All my works, all my creative activity, has come from those initial fantasies and dreams. . . . Everything that I accomplished in later life was already contained in them, although at first only in the form of emotions and images.[11]

A variety of esoterically oriented groups have roots in Gnostic soil. Madame Helene P. Blavatsky, who founded Theosophy in 1875, viewed the Gnostics as precursors of modern occult movements and hailed them for preserving an inner teaching lost to orthodoxy.[12] Theosophy and its various and varying spin-offs, such as Rudolph Steiner's Anthroposophy, Alice Bailey's Arcane School, the I Am movement, and the Church Universal and Triumphant all draw water from this same well, as do various other esoteric groups like the Rosicrucians. These organizations share an emphasis on esoteric teaching, the hidden divinity of humanity, and contact with nonmaterial higher beings called masters or adepts.

A New Age-oriented journal gets into the heart of the revived Gnostic-orthodox debate, claiming that the "Gnostic Gospels . . . were written around the same time as the gospels of the New Testament but . . . were purposely left out."[13] The review refers to Nag Hammadi, one of the most significant archaeological finds of the twentieth century—a discovery seen by some as overthrowing the orthodox view of Jesus and Christianity forever.

Gold in the Jar

In December of 1945, while digging for soil to fertilize his crops, an Arab peasant named Muhammed 'Ali found a red earthenware jar near Nag Hammadi, a city in upper Egypt. His fear of uncorking an evil spirit was shortly overcome by the hope of finding gold within. His find has been for hundreds of scholars far more precious than gold. Inside the jar were 13 leather-bound papyrus books (codices), dating from approximately A.D. 350. Although several of the texts were burned or thrown out, 52 texts were eventually recovered through many years of intrigue involving illegal sales, violence, smuggling, and academic rivalry.[14]

Some of the texts found near Nag Hammadi were first published singly or in small collections, but the complete collection was not made available in a popular format in English until 1977. It was released as *The Nag Hammadi Library* and was reissued in revised form in 1988.

These documents are thought by some to have been the property of a monastery that existed near the middle of the fourth century. The arid climate of Egypt preserved these long-lost texts from corruption. Their burial protected them from confiscation. The collection contains several kinds of documents, most of which are recognized as Gnostic. Although many of the documents had been referred to and denounced in the writings of early church theologians such as Justin Martyr and Irenaeus, most of the texts themselves had been thought to be extinct. So, as Elaine Pagels put it in her bestselling book *The Gnostic Gospels* (1979), "Now for the first time, we have the opportunity to find out about the earliest Christian heresy; for the first time, the heretics can speak for themselves."[15]

Pagels's book, winner of the National Book Critics Circle Award, arguably did more than any other effort to ingratiate the Gnostics to modern Americans. She made them accessible and even likable. Her scholarly expertise (she was one of the first to translate the Nag Hammadi texts from Coptic into English), coupled with her ability to relate an ancient religion to contemporary concerns, made for a compelling combination in the minds of many. Her central thesis was simple: Gnosticism should be considered at least as legitimate as orthodox Christianity because the "heresy" was simply a competing strain of early Christianity. Yet we find that the Nag Hammadi texts present a Jesus at extreme odds with the one found in the Gospels.

Although the scholarly world has jumped at the opportunity to inspect, critique, and compare the Nag Hammadi texts, controversy has raged over their dating, proper interpretation, and relationship to Christianity. Neither is there scholarly agreement on the origins of Gnosticism, called "the Gnostic problem."[16]

The Gnostic Message: The Secret God Within

Gnosticism in general, and the material from Nag Hammadi in particular, presents a spectrum of beliefs, although a central philosophical core is roughly discernible—a core that scholar Kurt Rudolph calls "the central myth."[17] Gnosticism teaches that something is desperately wrong with the universe, and then delineates the means to explain and rectify the situation.

The universe, as presently constituted, is not good. Nor was it created by an all-good God. Rather, a lesser god, or demiurge (as he is sometimes called), fashioned the world in ignorance. The *Gospel of Philip* says, "The world came about through a mistake. For he who created it wanted to create it imperishable and immortal. He fell short of attaining his desire."[18] The origin of the demiurge, or offending creator, is variously explained. But the upshot is that some precosmic disruption in the chain of beings emanating from the unknowable Father God resulted in the "fallout" of a substandard deity with less than impeccable credentials. The result was a material cosmos soaked with ignorance, pain, decay, and death—a botched job, to be sure. This deity, nevertheless, despotically demands worship and even pretentiously proclaims his supremacy as the one true God.

This creator god is not the ultimate reality but, rather, a degeneration of the unknown and unknowable fullness of Being (or pleroma). Yet human beings (or at least some of them) are in the position potentially to transcend their imposed limitations, even if the cosmic deck is stacked against them. Locked within the material shell of the human race is the spark of this highest spiritual reality, which the creator accidentally infused into humanity at their creation—on the order of a drunken jeweler who accidentally mixes gold dust into junk metal. Simply put, spirit is good and desirable; matter is evil and detestable.

If this spark is fanned into flame, it can liberate humans from the world of matter and the demands of its confused creator. What has devolved from perfection can ultimately evolve back into perfection through a process of self-discovery. This escape of the divine spark from its incarceration in the material can even be understood as the salvation of the deity itself, who wrestles free from ignorance and the domination of dark forces to ascend back to the highest level.[19]

Into this basic structure enters the idea of Jesus as a redeemer of those trapped in materiality. He comes as one descended from the spiritual realm with a message of self-redemption. The body of Gnostic literature, which is wider than the Nag Hammadi texts, represents various views of this redeemer figure.[20] There are, in fact, differing schools of Gnosticism with differing views of Christ. Nevertheless, a basic image emerges.

The Christ comes from the higher levels of intermediary beings (called aeons) not as a sacrifice for sin but as a Revealer, an emissary from error-free environs. He is not the personal agent of the Father-Creator revealed in the Old Testament. (That deluded deity is what got the universe into such a royal mess in the first place.) Rather, Christ has descended from a more exalted level to be a catalyst for igniting the Gnosis latent within the ignorant. He gives a metaphysical assist to underachieving deities (that is, humans), rather than granting ethical restoration to God's erring creatures through the crucifixion and resurrection.

An Ancient Library Unveiled

By inspecting a few of the Nag Hammadi texts, we encounter Gnosticism in Christian guise: Jesus dispenses Gnosis in order to awaken those trapped in ignorance; the body is a prison, the spirit alone is good; and salvation comes by discovering the "kingdom of God" within the Self.

One of the first Nag Hammadi texts to be extricated out of Egypt and translated into Western tongues was the *Gospel According to Thomas,* which is comprised of 114 sayings of Jesus. Although scholars do not believe it was actually written by the apostle Thomas, it has received the lion's share of scholarly attention. The sayings of Jesus are given minimal narrative setting, are largely not thematically arranged, and have a cryptic, epigrammatic bite to them.[21] Although Thomas does not articulate every aspect of a full-blown Gnostic system, some of the teachings attributed to Jesus fit the Gnostic pattern. (Other sayings closely parallel or duplicate material found in the Synoptic Gospels.)

The text begins by saying, "These are the secret sayings which the living Jesus spoke and which Didymus Judas Thomas wrote down. And he said, 'Whoever finds the interpretation of these sayings will not experience death.' "[22] Already we find the emphasis on secret knowledge (gnosis) as redemptive. A comparison with a similar-sounding text in John's Gospel reveals Thomas's Gnostic difference. In John, Jesus says, "I tell you the truth, if a man keeps my word, he will never see death" (John 8:51). F.F. Bruce points out that John's intention is "essentially ethical, whereas that in the *Gospel of Thomas* is mainly intellectual."[23]

Unlike the accounts in the canonical Gospels, Jesus' crucifixion and resurrection are not narrated, and neither do any of the 114 sayings directly refer to these events. Thomas's Jesus is a dispenser of wisdom, not the crucified and resurrected Lord.

Jesus speaks of the kingdom:

> The kingdom is inside of you, and it is outside of you. When you come to know yourselves, then you will become known, and you will realize that it is you who are the sons of the living father. But if you will not know yourselves, you dwell in poverty and it is you who are that poverty.[24]

This emphasis on self-knowledge as redemptive is also seen when, in saying number 70, Jesus says, "That which you have will save you if you bring it forth from yourselves. That which you do not have within you [will] kill you if you do not have it within you."[25] Several other Gnostic documents center on this key same theme.

Pagels states that many of the Gnostics "shared certain affinities with contemporary methods of exploring the self through psychotherapeutic techniques."[26] This includes the premises that, first, many people are unconscious of their true condition; and second, "that the psyche bears within itself the potential for liberation or destruction."[27]

Gilles Quispel notes that for Valentinus, a Gnostic teacher of the second century, Christ is "the Paraclete from the Unknown who reveals . . . the discovery of the Self—the divine spark within you."[28] Stephen Hoeller says that in the Valentinian system "there is no need whatsoever for guilt, for repentance from so-called sin, neither is there a need for a blind belief in vicarious salvation by way of the death of Jesus."[29] Rather Jesus is savior in the sense of being a "spiritual maker of wholeness" who cures us of our sickness of ignorance.[30]

The heart of the human problem for the Gnostics is ignorance, sometimes called "sleep," "intoxication," or "blindness." In the *Gospel of Thomas,* Jesus seems to disparage the physical world but affirms the value of the spirit: "If the flesh came into being because of the spirit, it is a wonder. But if spirit came into being because of the body, it is a wonder of wonders. Indeed I am amazed at how this great wealth has made its home in this poverty."[31]

The *First Apocalypse of James* goes even further. Here Jesus tells James that he will gain wisdom when he throws away the "bonds of flesh which encircle" him. Jesus continues,

"Then you will reach Him-who-is. And you will no longer be James; you are the One-who-is."[32] Likewise, the *Gospel of Philip* speaks of an enlightened one who "is no longer a Christian but a Christ."[33]

And who is Jesus? He says, "It is I who am the light which is above them all. It is I who am the all. From me did the all come forth, and unto me did the all extend. Split a piece of wood and I am there. Lift up stone and you will find me there."[34]

Gnosticism on Crucifixion and Resurrection

Those Gnostic texts that discuss Jesus' crucifixion and resurrection display a variety of views that, nevertheless, reveal some common themes.

In the *Apocalypse of Peter*, Peter has a vision of two Jesuses on the cross, one being impaled and one laughing. The text then reads,

> He whom you saw on the tree, glad and laughing, this is the living Jesus. But this one into whose hands and feet they drive the nails is the fleshly part which is the substitute being put to shame, the one who came into being in his likeness.

Later Jesus derides those who only see the crucified figure, and he "laughs at their lack of perception, knowing that they are born blind."[35] In the *First Apocalypse of James*, James is consoled by a Jesus who says, "Never have I suffered in any way, nor have I been distressed. And this people has done me no harm."[36]

John Dart has discerned that the Gnostic stories of Jesus mocking his executors reverse the accounts in Matthew, Mark, and Luke where the soldiers (Mark 15:20) and chief priests (Mark 15:31) mock Jesus.[37] In the biblical Gospels Jesus does not deride or mock his tormentors; on the contrary, *while suffering from the cross,* he asks the Father to forgive those who nailed him there.

In commenting on the "Treatise on the Resurrection," Bentley Layton notes that in the Valentinian Gnostic theology, "Jesus' suffering, traditionally understood to mean his real death on the cross, would not refer to biological death but simply the suffering sojourn of his spirit or soul on earth within the illusory realm of matter."[38]

Similarly, Gnostic accounts of Jesus' resurrection differ significantly from the New Testament record. A resurrection is enthusiastically affirmed,[39] yet the nature of the postresurrection appearances differs from those in the biblical accounts. Jesus is disclosed through spiritual visions rather than physical circumstances. According to Pagels, the Gnostics insisted that the resurrection "was not a unique event in the past: instead, it symbolized how Christ's presence could be experienced in the present."[40]

The resurrected Jesus for the Gnostics is the spiritual Revealer who imparts secret wisdom to the selected few, usually through visionary appearances. The biblical Jesus has little in common with the Gnostic Jesus. He is viewed as a redeemer in both cases, yet his nature as a redeemer and the way of redemption diverge at crucial points. Yet we need to delve further into this disagreement before we come to our conclusion.

Did Christ Really Suffer and Die?

As in much modern New Age teaching, the Gnostics tended to divide Jesus from the Christ. For Valentinus, Christ descended on Jesus at his baptism and left before his death on the cross. Much of the burden of the treatise *Against Heresies,* written by the early Christian theologian Irenaeus, was to affirm that Jesus was, is, and always will be the Christ. He says:

> The Gospel . . . knew no other son of man but Him who was of Mary, who also suffered; and no Christ who flew away from Jesus before the passion; but Him who was born it knew as Jesus Christ the Son of God, and that this same suffered and rose again.[41]

In dealing with the idea that Christ did not suffer on the cross for sin, Irenaeus argues that Christ would have never exhorted his disciples to take up the cross if he in fact was not to suffer on it himself, but instead fly away from it.[42]

For Irenaeus (who was the disciple of Polycarp, who himself was the disciple of the apostle John), the suffering of Jesus, the Christ, was paramount. While the various Gnostic schools saw Jesus as an Illuminator, Irenaeus, claiming to follow the apostles, knew him as crucified Savior. Because "it was not possible that the man . . . who had been destroyed through disobedience, could reform himself," the Son brought salvation by "descending from the Father, becoming incarnate, stooping low, even to death, and consummating the arranged plan of our salvation."[43]

This harmonizes with the words of Polycarp, who was Irenaeus's teacher and "was instructed by the apostles and conversed with many who had seen Christ"[44]:

Let us then continually persevere in our hope and the earnest of our righteousness, which is Jesus Christ, "who bore our sins in His own body on the tree" [1 Peter 2:24], "who did no sin, neither was guile found in his mouth" [1 Peter 2:22], but endured all things for us, that we might live in Him.[45]

Polycarp's mentor, the apostle John, said, "This is how we know what love is: Jesus Christ laid down his life for us" (1 John 3:16), and "This is love: not that we loved God, but that he loved us and sent his Son as an atoning sacrifice for our sins" (4:10).

The Gnostic Jesus is predominantly a dispenser of cosmic wisdom who discourses on abstruse themes like the spirit's fall into matter. Jesus of Nazareth certainly taught theology, but he dealt with the problem of pain and suffering in a far different way. E. Stanley Jones highlights this:

He did not prove how pain and sorrow in the universe could be compatible with the love of God—he took on himself at the cross everything that spoke against the love of God, and through that pain and tragedy and sin showed the very love of God.[46]

The Matter of the Resurrection

For Gnosticism, the inherent problem of humanity derives from the misuse of power by the ignorant creator and the resulting entrapment of souls in evil matter. The Gnostic Jesus alerts us to this and helps rekindle the divine spark within. In the biblical teaching the problem is ethical;

humans have sinned against a good Creator and are guilty before the throne of the universe.

In light of these differences, the significance of Jesus' literal and physical resurrection should be clear. For the Gnostic who abhors matter and seeks release from its grim grip, the physical resurrection of Jesus would be anticlimactic, if not absurd. Liberation does not come in corporeal packages; a material resurrection would be counterproductive and would only recapitulate the original problem.

If Jesus is the Christ who comes to restore God's creation, he must come as one of its own, a *real-life* human. Although Gnostic teachings show some diversity on this subject, they tend toward Docetism—the doctrine that the descent of the Christ was spiritual, not material, despite any appearance of materiality. From a biblical viewpoint, materiality is not the problem. Disharmony with the Maker is the problem. Adam and Eve were both material and in harmony with their good Maker before they succumbed to the serpent's temptation. Yet in biblical reasoning, if Jesus is to conquer sin and death for humanity, he must rise from the dead in a physical body, albeit a transformed one. A mere spiritual apparition would not provide redemption for a broken creation.[47]

For this reason, the apostle Peter preached Jesus of Nazareth as "a man accredited by God to you by miracles, wonders and signs" (Acts 2:22). Though put to death, "God raised him from the dead, freeing him from the agony of death, because it was impossible for death to keep its hold on him" (verse 24). Peter then quotes Psalm 16:10, which speaks of God not letting his "Holy One see decay" (verse 27). Peter says of David, the psalm's author, "Seeing what was ahead, he spoke of the resurrection of the Christ, that he was not abandoned to the grave, nor did his body see decay. God has raised this Jesus to life, and we are all witnesses of the fact" (verses 31,32)[48]

The Gospels tell us that Jesus' resurrected body was seen (Matthew 28:17), heard (John 20:15,16), and even touched (Matthew 28:9). The resurrected Jesus is also recorded as eating food on at least four occasions (Luke 24:30,42,43; John 21:12,13; Acts 1:4). The apostle Paul confesses that if the resurrection of Jesus is not a historical fact, Christianity is a vanity of vanities (1 Corinthians 15:14-19). And while he speaks of Jesus' (and the believers') resurrected condition as a "spiritual body," this does not mean nonphysical or ethereal; rather, it refers to a body totally free from the results of sin and the fall.[49]

Jesus, Judaism, and Gnosis

The Gnostic Jesus disapproves of Judaism, while the Jesus of the Gospels fulfills its promises. For Gnostics, the God of the Old Testament is something of a cosmic clown, neither ultimate nor good. Many Gnostic documents reverse the meaning of Old Testament stories in order to ridicule him. The serpent and Eve are heroic figures who oppose the dull deity in the *Hypostasis of the Archons* (the *Reality of the Rulers*) and in *On the Origin of the World*.[50] In the *Apocryphon of John*, Jesus says he encouraged Adam and Eve to eat of the tree of the knowledge of good and evil,[51] thus putting Jesus diametrically at odds with the meaning of the Genesis account, where this action is seen as the essence of sin (Genesis 3).

The Jesus found in the New Testament quotes the prophets, claims to fulfill their prophecies, and consistently argues according to the Old Testament revelation, despite the fact that he exudes an authority equal to it. Jesus says, "Do not think that I have come to abolish the Law or the Prophets; I have not come to abolish them but to fulfill them" (Matthew 5:17). When Jesus appeared after his death and burial to two of his disciples on the road to Emmaus, he commented on their slowness of heart "to believe all that the prophets have spoken." He asked, "Did not the Christ have to suffer these things and then enter his glory?" Luke then records, "And beginning with Moses and all the prophets, he explained to them what was said in all the Scriptures concerning himself" (Luke 24:25-27).

For both Jesus and the Old Testament, the supreme Creator is the Father of all the living. They are one and the same. In Gnosticism, there is a chasm between an unknowable "Father God" and a metaphysically impoverished Creator. There is also a separation of the Creator from the Redeemer.

God: Unknowable or Knowable?

Many Gnostic treatises speak of the ultimate reality or godhead as beyond intellectual comprehension. Any hope of contacting this reality, a spark of which is lodged within the Gnostic, must be filtered through numerous intermediary beings of a lesser stature than the godhead itself.

In the *Gospel of the Egyptians* the ultimate reality is said to be the "unrevealable, unmarked, ageless, unproclaimable Father." Three powers are said to emanate from Him: "They are the Father, the Mother, (and) the Son, from the living silence."[52] The text speaks of giving praise to "the great invisible Spirit" who is "the silence of silent silence."[53] In the *Sophia of Jesus Christ,* Jesus is asked by Matthew, "Lord . . . teach us the truth," to which Jesus says, "He Who is is ineffable." Although Jesus seems to indicate that he reveals the ineffable, he says concerning the ultimate, "He is unnamable . . . he is ever incomprehensible. He is imperishable and has no likeness (to anything)."[54]

At this point the divide between the New Testament and the Gnostic documents could not be deeper or wider. The entire contour of Jesus' ministry points to him as God in the flesh. He says, "Anyone who has seen me has seen the Father" (John 14:9). The introduction to John's Gospel says that "In the beginning was the Word [Logos]" and that "Word was with God, and the Word was God" (John 1:1). John did not say, "In the beginning was the silence of the silent silence" or "the unspeakable."

The Incarnation means that God communicated himself in person through life and language. The Creator's truth and life are announced spiritually through the medium of matter. "The Word became flesh and lived for a while among us. We have seen his glory, the glory of the one and only son, who came from the Father, full of grace and truth" (John 1:14). In John's first epistle, he speaks of "that which was from the beginning," and says, "The life appeared; we have seen it and testify to it, and we proclaim to you the eternal life, which was with the Father and has appeared to us" (1 John 1:1,2).

A messianic prophecy in the book of Jeremiah foretells a day when God himself—

> will raise up to David a righteous Branch,
> a King who will reign wisely and do what is just and right in
>   the land.
> In his days Judah will be saved and Israel will live in safety.
> This is the name by which he will be called:
> The LORD Our Righteousness (Jeremiah 23:5,6).

Many Jewish rabbis considered this verse messianic, as they did several other passages speaking of the Branch (Jeremiah 33:15; Isaiah 4:2; Zechariah 3:8; 6:12,13).[55] As we have seen, Jesus claimed to be uniquely God on earth, as the Messiah.[56] Jesus himself, by citing Psalm 110:1, teaches that "Christ" (that is, the Messiah) is King David's Lord (Mark 12:35-37). A classic messianic text affirms that God himself will arrive on the human scene:

> For to us a child is born,
> to us a son is given,
> and the government will be on his shoulders.
> And he will be called
> Wonderful Counselor, Mighty God,
> Everlasting Father, Prince of Peace (Isaiah 9:6).

The apostle John writes of these realities made flesh in Jesus and declares that he "has made him [the Father] *known*" (John 1:18; emphasis added).[57]

Although Jesus revered God the Father as holy and as transcendent, He did not view God as unknown or unknowable. This counters the teaching of Joseph Campbell, who, in many ways, taught a Gnostic view of God. In his popular book and television series *The Power of Myth*, he affirmed a "transtheological" notion of an "undefinable, inconceivable mystery, thought of as a power, that is the source and supporting ground of all life and being."[58] He also said, "God is beyond names and forms. . . . God, the ultimate, is beyond pairs of opposites, that is all there is to it."[59] So strong is Campbell's emphasis on transcendence that he affirms that God "transcends thingness."[60]

Yet Campbell's Gnostic view is confused and contradictory. If God is utterly beyond any names, forms, words, or descriptions, we could then say absolutely nothing about "God." To have a theology of any kind—Gnostic or orthodox—we must use words to describe God. However, Gnostics—ancient and modern—reject some descriptions of God as faulty. They deny that the human problem is sin and that Christ died to atone for our sins. Therefore, the Gnostic mind must forever be tied in suffocating knots. By definition, it can say nothing meaningful of "the silence of the silent silence," but it speaks, nevertheless. The lesson is clear: Let no one vainly attempt to utter the unutterable.[61]

Gnosticism and Modern Thought

Modern Gnostics should also be aware of some Gnostic elements which decidedly clash with modern tastes. Although Elaine Pagels ingratiated the Gnostics to millions with her book *The Gnostic Gospels,* several tenets of Gnosticism are hard to swallow.

First, although Pagels, like Jung, has shown the Gnostics in a positive psychological light, the Gnostic outlook is just as much theological and cosmological as it is psychological. Most modern Gnostics reinterpret Gnostic literature in a psychological fashion in order to remove any objectionable prescientific claims, which are taken to be mythical and not literal.[62] Nevertheless, the Gnostic message is all of a piece; the psychology should not be artificially divorced from the total worldview. Gnosticism should not be reduced to psychology, as if we know better what a Basilides or a Valentinus *really* meant than they did.

The historical Gnostic worldview was exceedingly ripe with personified spiritual forces arranged in descending order from the unknowable godhead. The Gnostic documents do not present their system as a coded psychology (with various cosmic forces representing psychic functions), but as a religious and theological explanation of the origin and operation of the universe. Those who want to adopt consistently Gnostic views should keep in mind what their revered Gnostic texts actually affirm.

Second, the Gnostic rejection of matter as illusory, evil, or at most second-best is at odds with many New Age sentiments regarding the value of nature and the need for an ecological awareness and ethic. Trying to find an ecological concern in the Gnostic corpus is on the order of harvesting wheat in Antarctica. For the Gnostics, as scholar Pheme Perkins puts it, "Most of the cosmos that we know is a carefully constructed plot to keep humanity from returning to its true divine home."[63] There was no love for "Mother Earth."

Third, Pagels to the contrary, the Gnostics were not feminists, nor did they view women as equals in any sense. Gnostic groups did sometimes allow for women's participation in religious activities, and several of the emanational beings were seen as feminine. Nevertheless, even though *Ms.* magazine gave the Gnostic Gospels a glowing review,[64] women fare far worse in Gnosticism than many think. Although Gnosticism uses feminine religious symbolism, this does not guarantee the exaltation of the feminine. Kathleen McVey's critique of Pagels is telling:

> Pagels's citation of excerpts from gnostic writings without their requisite contexts obscures the overall relation of male and female divine powers. For example, when Ialdabaoth boasts (in clear parody of Yahweh) that he is the only God, his Mother reprimands him, "Do not lie, Ialdabaoth." Since nothing of the context is revealed by Pagels, one might imagine that the female divine principle is superior to the male. But the Mother here is herself the "abortion" of Sophia, who is, in turn the youngest of thirty aeons descended from the ineffable Father. Sophia's fall . . . is ultimately the cause of the existence of the material world, from which the gnostic must escape.[65]

The concluding saying from the *Gospel of Thomas* has less than a feminist ring:

> Simon Peter said to them, "Let Mary leave us, for women are not worthy of life." Jesus said, "I myself shall lead her in order to make her male, so that she too may become a living spirit resembling you males. For every woman who will make herself male will enter the kingdom of heaven."[66]

The Jesus of the Gospels never spoke of making the female into the male—no doubt because Jesus did not perceive the female to be inferior to the male. Going against the social customs, he gathered women followers and revealed to an outcast Samaritan woman that he was the

Messiah, which scandalized his own disciples (John 4:1-39).
Jesus was no Gnostic.

Writing in *Parabola*, a journal of mythology, Ann Belford
Ulanov perceptively says:

> Nowhere in the texts of Scripture do we find Jesus treating
> women in degrading ways. Not once. Indeed, we find the
> opposite. To the Samaritan woman he announces that he
> is life giving water. To Martha, he is the coming resurrec-
> tion. To the Magdalene, he is risen. He speaks theology
> with women. . . . He really knew women's lives, really
> spoke to them, called them to follow him.[67]

Fourth, despite an emphasis on reincarnation in some
Gnostic writings, several Gnostic documents speak of the
damnation of those who refuse to become enlightened,[68]
particularly apostates from Gnostic groups.[69] If one chafes
at the biblical Jesus' warning of "eternal destruction," of-
fenses are likewise readily available from Gnostic writers as
well. However, modern Gnostics never refer to these references positively. This is logically inconsistent.

Gnostic Scriptures and the Bible

If the preceding discussion has thrown the contrast between the Gnostic Jesus and the biblical Jesus into clear re-
lief, we still have not completely settled the issue of the
historical reliability of the Gnostic documents. Should
these documents cause us to expand or revise our view of
Jesus? What are their credentials?

Concerning the Gnostic-orthodox controversy, biblical scholar F.F. Bruce is so bold as to say that "there is no reason why the student of the conflict should shrink from making a value judgment: the gnostic schools lost because they deserved to lose."[70] The Gnostics lost once, but do they deserve to lose again?

6

JESUS AND THE
GNOSTIC GOSPELS

THE LAST CHAPTER outlined the stark contrasts between the
Gnostic Jesus and "the Word made flesh." These respective
views of Jesus are lodged within mutually exclusive worldviews concerning claims about God, the universe, humanity,
and salvation. Our next line of inquiry will be historical.
Should the Gnostic sayings of the *Gospel of Thomas* or the
resurrection sermons of the immaterial Gnostic Jesus capture our attention as reliable reports of the mind of Jesus,
or does the Son of Man of the biblical Gospels speak with
the authentic voice?

It is vital to inspect the historical standing of the Gnostic writings in terms of their historical integrity, authenticity,
and veracity—just as we did in chapter 3 with the Gospels
and Paul's writings. Since Gnosticism was the first direct
challenge to Christianity, it is appropriate to lock historical
horns with it before going on to grapple with other challenges to biblical belief.

Although much excitement has been generated by
the Nag Hammadi discoveries, not a little misunderstanding
has been mixed with the enthusiasm. The overriding

assumption of many is that the treatises unearthed in upper Egypt contained "lost books of the Bible" of historical stature equal to or greater than the New Testament books. Much of this has been fueled by the titles of some of the documents themselves, particularly the so-called Gnostic Gospels: the *Gospel of Thomas, Gospel of Philip, Gospel of Mary, Gospel of the Egyptians,* and the *Gospel of Truth.* The connotation of a "Gospel" is that it presents the life of Jesus as a teacher, preacher, and healer and is similar in style, if not content, to Matthew, Mark, Luke, and John.

Yet a reading of these "Gospels" reveals an entirely different genre of material. For example, the introduction to the *Gospel of Truth* in *The Nag Hammadi Library* reads, "Despite its title, this work is not the sort found in the New Testament, since it does not offer a continuous narration of the deeds, teachings, passion, and resurrection of Jesus."[1] The introduction to the *Gospel of Philip* in the same volume says that although it has some similarities to a New Testament Gospel, "The Gospel of Philip is not a gospel like one of the New Testament gospels. . . . [The] few sayings and stories about Jesus . . . are not set in any kind of narrative framework like one of the New Testament gospels."[2] In introducing the *Gospel According to Philip,* Bentley Layton notes that "the term 'gospel' does not here refer to the Christian literary genre called gospel (e.g., the Gospel of Mark)."[3] Biblical scholar Joseph A. Fitzmyer criticized the title of Pagels's *The Gnostic Gospels* because it insinuates that the heart of the book concerns lost Gospels that have come to light, when in fact the majority of Pagels's references are from early church fathers' sources or other non-Gospel material.[4]

The "superstar" of the Nag Hammadi collection in view of scholarly and popular attention is the *Gospel of Thomas*. Yet this also falls outside of the genre of the New Testament Gospels—despite the fact that many of its 114 sayings are directly or indirectly related to Matthew, Mark, and Luke. *Thomas* is more like various beads almost haphazardly strung on a necklace. This, in itself, makes proper interpretation difficult. F.F. Bruce observes that

> the sayings of Jesus are best to be understood in the light of the historical circumstances in which they were spoken. Only when we have understood them thus can we safely endeavor to recognize the permanent truth which they convey. When they are detached from their original historical setting and arranged in an anthology, their interpretation is more precarious.[5]

Bruce contrasts the obscure genre of the *Gospel of Thomas* with the New Testament, which speaks not only of "what the sayings of Jesus meant in the situation of his ministry but also of how they were understood some decades later in the early church."[6]

The Gnostic material on Jesus has a decidedly different "feel" than the biblical Gospels. There, Jesus' teaching emerges naturally from the overall contour of his life. In the Gnostic materials, Jesus seems, in many cases, more of a lecturer on philosophy than a Jewish prophet. In the *Letter of Peter to Philip*, the apostles tell the resurrected Jesus, "Lord, we would like to know the deficiency of the aeons and of their pleroma."[7] Such obscure philosophical abstractions were never on the lips of the disciples—the fishermen, tax collectors, and Zealots of the biblical accounts. Jesus then discourses on the precosmic fall of "the mother" who acted in opposition to "the Father" to produce our imperfect world of matter.[8]

Whatever is made of the historical feel of these documents, their actual status as historical records should be brought into closer scrutiny to assess their factual reliability.

The Reliability of the Gnostic Documents

If a document is historically reliable, it is trustworthy in what it affirms and is faithful to the facts. We can gauge historical reliability by inquiring into how the text stands up to questioning in three areas: integrity, authenticity, and veracity.[9]

Integrity concerns the preservation of the writing through history. Do we have reason to believe the text as it now reads is essentially the same as when it was first written? Or has substantial corruption taken place through distortion, additions, or subtractions?

As we found in chapter 3, the New Testament has been preserved in thousands of diverse and ancient manuscripts which enable us to reconstruct the original documents with a high degree of certainty. But what of Nag Hammadi?

Before the discovery at Nag Hammadi, Gnostic documents not inferred from references in the church fathers were few and far between. Since 1945, though, there are many primary documents. Scholars date the extant manuscripts from A.D. 350–400, which is quite old as documents relating to the origin of Christianity are concerned. The original writing of the various documents, of course, took place sometime before A.D. 350–400, but not, according to most scholars, before the second century.

The actual condition of the Nag Hammadi manuscripts varies considerably. James Robinson, the editor of *The Nag Hammadi Library*, notes that

> there is the physical deterioration of the books themselves, which began no doubt before they were buried around 400 C.E. [then] advanced steadily while they remained buried, and unfortunately was not completely halted in the period between their discovery in 1945 and their final conservation thirty years later.[10]

Reading through *The Nag Hammadi Library*, one often finds notations such as ellipses, parentheses, and brackets, indicating spotty marks in the texts. Often the translator has to venture tentative reconstructions of the writings because of textual damage. The *Zostrianos* and *Marsanes* writings, for example, are extremely fragmentary and difficult to reconstitute. The situation may be likened to putting together a jigsaw puzzle with numerous pieces missing: One is forced to re-create the pieces by using whatever context is available. Robinson adds, "When only a few letters are missing, they can often be filled in adequately, but larger holes must simply remain a blank."[11]

Concerning translation, Robinson relates that "the texts were translated one by one from Greek to Coptic, and not always by translators capable of grasping the profundity or sublimity of what they sought to translate."[12] He notes, however, that most of the texts are more adequately translated, and that when there is more than one version of a particular text, the better translation is clearly discernible. Nevertheless, he is "led to wonder about the bulk of the texts that exist only in a single version,"[13] because these texts cannot be compared with other translations for accuracy.

Robinson comments further on the integrity of the texts:

> There is the same kind of hazard in the transmission of the texts by a series of scribes who copied them, generation after generation, from increasingly corrupt copies, first in Greek and then in Coptic. The number of unintentional errors is hard to estimate, since such a thing as a clean control copy does not exist; *nor does one have, as in the case of the Bible, a quantity of manuscripts of the same text* that tend to correct each other when compared.[14]

Authenticity concerns the authorship of a given writing. Do we know who the author was? Or must we deal with an anonymous or pseudepigraphic one? A writing is considered authentic if it can be shown to have been written by its stated or implied author.[15] In chapter 3 we argued that the Gospels are written by their namesakes: Matthew, Mark, Luke, and John. Who wrote the Nag Hammadi documents?

The *Letter of Peter to Philip,* for example, is dated at the end of the second century or even into the third.[16] This certainly rules out a literal letter from the apostle to Philip. The genre of this text is known as pseudepigrapha, which refers to writings falsely ascribed to noteworthy individuals to lend credibility to the material. Although interesting in explaining the development of Gnostic thought and its relationship to biblical writings, the *Letter of Peter to Philip* should not be considered to deliver reliable history of the events it purports to record.

There are few (if any) cases of known authorship with the Nag Hammadi and other Gnostic texts. Scholars speculate as to authorship but do not take pseudepigraphic literature as authentically apostolic. Even the *Gospel of Thomas*, probably the document closest to the New Testament events, is virtually never considered to be written by the apostle Thomas himself.[17] The marks of authenticity in this material are spotty at best.

Veracity concerns the truthfulness of the author of the text. Was the author in a position to relate adequately what is reported, in terms of both chronological closeness to the events and observational savvy? Did he or she have sufficient credentials to relay historical truth?

Some, in their enthusiasm over Nag Hammadi, have roped texts into the historical corral that actually date several hundred years after the life of Jesus. For instance, in a review of the movie *The Last Temptation of Christ*, Michael Grosso speaks of Jesus' sexual life "right at the start of the Christian tradition." He then quotes from the *Gospel of Philip* to the effect that Jesus often kissed Mary Magdalene on the mouth.[18] The problem is that the text is quite far from "the start of the Christian tradition," being written, according to one scholar, "perhaps as late as the second half of the third century."[19] As we have already noted in regard to the *Letter of Peter to Philip*, several of the texts referring to Jesus were written quite late and would be better viewed as later commentaries on his life than as primary historical sources.

Craig Blomberg states that "most of the Nag Hammadi documents, predominantly Gnostic in nature, make no pretense of overlapping with the gospel traditions of Jesus' earthly life."[20] He observes that "a number claim to record conversations of the resurrected Jesus with various disciples, but this setting is usually little more than an artificial framework for imparting Gnostic doctrine."[21]

What, then, of the veracity of the documents? We do not know with any high probability who wrote most of them. Whatever the philosophical merits of the Nag Hammadi texts (and we found several defects in the last chapter), their historical veracity concerning Jesus seems slim. Yet some scholars advance a few candidates as providing historically reliable facts concerning Jesus.

In the case of the *Gospel of Truth,* some scholars see Valentinus as the author[22] or at least as authoring an earlier version.[23] Yet Valentinus dates into the second century (d. A.D. 175) and was thus not a contemporary of Jesus. Harold Attridge and George MacRae date the document between A.D. 140 and 180.[24] Layton recognizes that "the work is a sermon and has nothing to do with the Christian genre properly called 'gospel.' "[25]

The text differs from many in Nag Hammadi because of its recurring references to New Testament passages and the Gospel tradition. Layton notes that "it paraphrases, and so interprets, some thirty to sixty scriptural passages almost all from the New Testament books."[26] He goes on to note that Valentinus shaped these allusions to fit his own Gnostic theology.[27] In discussing the use of the Synoptic Gospels (Matthew, Mark, and Luke) in the *Gospel of Truth,* C.M. Tuckett concludes that "there is no evidence for the use of sources other than the canonical gospels for synoptic material."[28] This would mean that the *Gospel of Truth* gives no independent historical insight about Jesus but rather reinterprets previous material.

The *Gospel of Philip* is thick with Gnostic theology and contains several references to Jesus; however, it does not claim to be a revelation from Jesus but more of a Gnostic manual of theology.[29] According to C.M. Tuckett's analysis, all the references to Gospel material seem to stem from Matthew and not from any other canonical Gospel or other source independent of Matthew. Andrew Hembold has also pointed out that both the *Gospel of Truth* and the *Gospel of Philip* show signs of "mimicking" the New Testament; they both "know and recognize the greater part of the New Testament as authoritative."[30] This would make them secondary, not original documents.

Tuckett has also argued that the *Gospel of Mary* and the *Book of Thomas the Contender* (not to be confused with the *Gospel of Thomas*) are dependent on Synoptic materials, and that "there is virtually no evidence for the use of pre-synoptic sources by these writers. These texts are all 'post-synoptic,' not only with regard to their dates, but also with regard to the form of the synoptic tradition they presuppose."[31] In other words, these writings are simply drawing on preexistent Gospel material and rearranging it to conform to their Gnostic worldview. They may embellish, delete, twist, or revise Gospel information, but they do not contribute historically authentic, new material.

The *Apocryphon of James* claims to be a secret revelation of the risen Jesus to James his brother. It is less obviously Gnostic than some Nag Hammadi texts and contains some more orthodox-sounding phrases, such as "Verily I say unto you none will be saved unless they believe in my cross."[32] It also affirms the unorthodox, such as when Jesus says, "Become better than I; make yourselves like the son of the Holy Spirit."[33] While one scholar dates it sometime before A.D. 150,[34] Blomberg believes it gives indications of being "at least in part later than and dependent upon the canonical Gospels."[35] Its theology certainly puts it at odds with the canonical Gospels, which better attested historically.

The Gospel of Thomas on Trial

The Nag Hammadi text that has provoked the most historical scrutiny is the *Gospel of Thomas*. The Jesus Seminar, discussed in chapter 2, deems Thomas to be a very earlier source for material on Jesus, and puts it in the same category as the biblical Gospels. Hence the title of their book: *The Five Gospels*. Because of its reputation as a lost "fifth Gospel" and its often esoteric and mystical cast, it is often quoted in New Age circles. In *The Fifth Gospel: A Verse-by-Verse New Age Commentary on the Gospel of Thomas (1988)*, Robert Winterhalter claims that Thomas knows "the Christ both as the Self, and the foundation of individual life."[36] Some of the sayings in the *Gospel of Thomas* do seem to teach this. But is this what the historical Jesus taught?

Because it is more of an anthology of mostly unrelated sayings rather than an ongoing story about Jesus' words and deeds, *Thomas* is outside the genre of "Gospel" in the New Testament. Yet some of the 114 sayings closely parallel or roughly resemble statements in the Synoptics,[37] either by adding to them, deleting from them, combining several references into one, or by changing the sense of a saying entirely.[38]

The above explanation of *Thomas* uses the Synoptic Gospels as a reference point for comparison. But is it likely that *Thomas* is independent of these sources and gives authentic, although "unorthodox," material about Jesus?

There certainly are sayings that harmonize with biblical material, and direct or indirect relationships can be found to all four canonical Gospels. In this sense, *Thomas* contains both orthodox and unorthodox material, if we use *orthodox* to mean the material in the New Testament. For instance, the Trinity and unforgivable sin are referred to in the context of blasphemy:

> Jesus said, "Whoever blasphemes against the father will be forgiven, and whoever blasphemes against the son will be forgiven, but whoever blasphemes against the holy spirit will not be forgiven either on earth or in heaven" [#44].[39]

In the next saying, Jesus speaks of the "evil man" who "brings forth evil things from his evil storehouse, which is in his heart, and says evil things" [#45][40] (see Luke 6:43-46). This can be read to harmonize with the New Testament Gospels' emphasis on human sin, not just ignorance of the divine spark within.

Although it is not directly related to a canonical Gospel text, the following statement seems to state the biblical theme of the urgency of finding Jesus while one can: "Jesus said, 'Take heed of the living one while you are alive, lest you die and seek to see him and be unable to do so'" [#59][41] (cf. John 7:34; 13:33).

At the same time, we find texts of a clearly Gnostic slant, as noted earlier. How can we account for this?

The original writing of *Thomas* has been dated variously between A.D. 50 and 150 or even later, with many scholars opting for a second-century date.[42] Unlike the Gospels, we have no mention of *Thomas* until Hippolytus and Origen cite it early in the third century. This silence would be unlikely if it was a first-century document.[43] Of course an earlier date would lend more credibility to it, although its lack of narrative framework still makes it more difficult to understand than the canonical Gospels. While some argue that Thomas uses historical sources independent of those used by the New Testament, this is not a uniformly held view, and arguments are easily found which muster evidence for *Thomas*'s dependence (either partial or total) on the canonical Gospels.[44]

Blomberg claims that "where Thomas parallels the four gospels it is unlikely that any of the distinctive elements in Thomas predate the canonical versions."[45] When *Thomas* gives a parable found in the four Gospels and adds details not found there, "they can almost always be explained as conscious, Gnostic redaction [editorial adaptation]."[46]

James Dunn elaborates on this theme by comparing *Thomas* with what is believed to be an earlier and partial version of the document found in Oxyrhynchus, Egypt, near the turn of the century.[47] He notes that the Oxyrhynchus "papyri date from the end of the second or the first half of the third century, while the *Gospel of Thomas* found at Nag Hammadi was probably written no earlier than the fourth century."[48]

Dunn then compares similar statements from Matthew, the Oxyrhynchus papyri, and the Nag Hammadi text version of *Thomas*:

Matthew 7:7-8 and 11:28—". . . Seek, and you will find; . . . he who seeks finds . . ." "Come to me . . . and I will give you rest."

Pap.Ox. 654.5-9—(Jesus says:) Let him who see(ks) not cease (seeking until) he finds; and when he find (he will) be astounded, and having (astoun)ded, he will reign; an(d reigning), he will (re)st. (Clement of Alexandria also knows the saying in this form.)

Gospel of Thomas 2—"Jesus said: He who seeks should not stop seeking until he finds; and when he finds, he will be bewildered (beside himself); and when he is bewildered he will marvel, and will reign over the All."[49]

Dunn notes that the term "the All" (added to the earlier document) is "a regular Gnostic concept" and that, "as the above comparisons suggest, the most obvious explanation is that it was one of the last elements to be added to the saying."[50] Dunn further adds that the Nag Hammadi version of *Thomas* shows a definite "gnostic colouring" and gives no evidence for the thesis that a form of Gnostic Christianity already existed in the first century. He continues:

Rather it confirms the counter thesis that the Gnostic element in Gnostic Christianity is a second century syncretistic outgrowth on the stock of the earlier Christianity. What we can see clearly in the case of this one saying is probably representative of the lengthy process of development and elaboration which resulted in the form of the *Gospel of Thomas* found at Nag Hammadi.[51]

Other authorities substantiate the notion that whatever authentic material *Thomas* may convey concerning Jesus, the text from Nag Hammadi shows signs of Gnostic tampering. Marvin W. Meyer judges that *Thomas* "shows the hand of a gnosticizing editor."[52] Winterhalter, who reveres *Thomas* enough to write a devotional guide on it, nevertheless says of the Nag Hammadi *Thomas* that "some sayings are spurious or greatly altered, but this is the work of a later Egyptian editor."[53] (He thinks, though, that the wheat can be successfully separated from the chaff.[54])

Here we find ourselves agreeing with the writings of the early Christian defenders of the faith who maintained that Gnosticism in the church was a corruption of original truth and not an independently legitimate source of information on Jesus or the rest of reality. Fitzmyer drives this home in criticizing Pagels's view that the Gnostics have an equal claim on Christian authenticity. He says that her way of handling the Nag Hammadi material

> throughout the book gives the unwary reader the impression that the difference between "orthodox Christians" and "gnostic Christians" was one related to the "origins of Christianity." Time and time again she is blind to the fact that she is ignoring a good century of Christian existence in which those "gnostic Christians" were simply not around.[55]

It is also telling that outside of the *Gospel of Thomas,* which does not overtly mention the resurrection of Jesus, other Gnostic documents claiming to impart new information about Jesus do so through spiritual, postresurrection dialogues. These are often visions that are not subject to the same historical verification as claims made about the earthly life of Jesus. This leads Dunn to comment that:

> Christian Gnosticism usually attributed its secret [and unorthodox] teaching of Jesus to discourses delivered by him, so they maintained, in a lengthy ministry after his

resurrection (as in *Thomas the Contender* and *Pistis Sophia*).
The *Gospel of Thomas* is unusual therefore in attempting to
use the Jesus-tradition as the vehicle for its teaching. . . .
Perhaps Gnosticism abandoned the *Gospel of Thomas* format because it was to some extent subject to check and re-
buttal from Jesus-tradition preserved elsewhere.[56]

Dunn thinks that the more thoroughly the Gnostics
challenged the already established orthodox accounts of
Jesus' earthly life, the less credible the Gnostics became; but
with postresurrection accounts, no checks were forthcoming. They were claiming additional information vouchsafed
only to the elite. He concludes that Gnosticism

> was able to present its message in a sustained way as the
> teaching of Jesus only by separating the risen Christ from
> the earthly Jesus and by abandoning the attempts to show
> a continuity between the Jesus of the Jesus-tradition and
> the heavenly Christ of their faith.[57]

What is seen by some as a Gnostic challenge to historic,
orthodox views of the life, teaching, and work of Jesus was
actually in many cases a retreat from historical considerations entirely. Only by doing so could the Gnostics attempt
to establish the credibility of the Gnostic documents.

Gnostic Underdogs?

Although Pagels and others have provoked sympathy, if not
enthusiasm, for the Gnostics as the underdogs who just happened to lose out to orthodoxy, the Gnostics' historical

credentials concerning Jesus are less than compelling. While it is romantic to "root for the underdog," the Gnostic underdogs show every sign of being heretical hangers-on who tried to harness Christian language for conceptions clearly opposed to early Christian teaching.

Many sympathetic with Gnosticism make much of the notion that the Gnostic writings were suppressed by the early Christian church. But this assertion does not, in itself, provide support one way or the other for the truth or falsity of Gnostic doctrine. If truth is not a matter of *majority* vote, neither is it a matter of *minority* dissent. It may be true, as Pagels says, that "the winners write history," but that doesn't necessarily make them bad or dishonest historians. If so, we should hunt down Nazi historians to give us the real picture of Hitler's Germany and relegate all opposing views to that of dogmatic apologists who just happened to be on the winning side.

In *Against Heresies,* Irenaeus went to great lengths to present the theologies of the various Gnostic schools in order to refute them biblically and logically. If suppression had been his concern, the book never would have been written as it was. Further, to argue cogently against the Gnostics, Irenaeus and the other anti-Gnostic apologists would presumably have had to be diligent to correctly represent their foes in order to avoid ridicule for misunderstanding them. Patrick Henry highlights this in reference to Nag Hammadi:

> While the Nag Hammadi materials have made some corrections to the portrayal of Gnosticism in the anti-Gnostic writings of the church fathers, it is increasingly evident that the fathers did not fabricate their opponents' views; what distortion there is comes from selection, not from

invention. It is still legitimate to use materials from the writings of the fathers to characterize Gnosticism.[58]

It is highly improbable that all of the Gnostic materials could have been systematically confiscated or destroyed by the early church. James Dunn finds it unlikely that the reason we have no unambiguous first-century documents from Christian Gnostics is because the early church eradicated them. He believes it more likely that we have none because there were none.[59] But by archaeological virtue of Nag Hammadi, we now do have many primary-source Gnostic documents available for detailed inspection. Yet they do not receive superior marks as historical documents about Jesus. In a review of *The Gnostic Gospels*, noted biblical scholar Raymond Brown affirmed that from the Nag Hammadi works "we learn not a single verifiable new fact about Jesus' ministry, and only a few new sayings that might plausibly have been his."[60]

Another factor foreign to the interests of Gnostic apologists is the proposition that Gnosticism expired largely because it lacked life from the beginning. F.F. Bruce notes that "Gnosticism was too much bound up with a popular but passing phase of thought to have the survival power of apostolic Christianity."[61]

Exactly why did apostolic Christianity survive and thrive? Robert Speer pulls no theological punches when he proclaims, "Christianity lived because it was true to the truth. Through all the centuries it has never been able to live otherwise. It can not live otherwise today."[62]

7

THE LOST YEARS
OF JESUS

WE ALL LOVE secrets, especially when we are the recipients of a particularly juicy one. And the more significant the subject matter, the more precious the secret. Hidden wisdom is a scarce and treasured commodity that elevates the initiated into rarefied realms. What the masses have lost, the knowers have found. Blessed are the knowers who see through convention to reality—those who solve the mystery of "the lost years of Jesus." Many people entranced by the new spirituality embrace a Jesus unknown to traditional Christians: a world traveler.

The conventional Christian understanding of Jesus places him in Jewish sandals worn only in ancient Palestine. The Christ came to the Jewish people, as promised by the prophets, to mend the lame, feed the poor, raise the dead, proclaim the kingdom, obey the Father, die as a ransom for many, and be raised from the dead as the final demonstration of his unique mission and deity. Before his ascension, Jesus charged his disciples to make disciples of all the nations (Matthew 28:18-20; Acts 1:8), yet his own earthly ministry was limited to his homeland, Palestine.

In the biblical understanding, Jesus need not be a world traveler to be the Savior of the world. Matthew records Jesus' trip to Egypt as an infant, but the significance of this flight from Herod's sword is explained as a fulfillment of the prophecy, "Out of Egypt I called my Son" (Matthew 2:15; see Hosea 11:1). God called Jesus "out of Egypt," not toward Egypt or any other Eastern site.

When Jesus taught in the synagogue in his hometown, many were amazed at his teaching and wondered, "What's this wisdom that's been given him, that he even does miracles! Isn't this the carpenter? Isn't this Mary's son and the brother of James, Joseph, Judas and Simon? Aren't his sisters here with us?" (Mark 6:2,3; cf. Matthew 13:53-58). They were shocked that the Jesus they knew—this hometown boy—would teach with power and work miracles.

Jesus' biblical biography sums up his life between the ages of about 12 to 30 with one sentence in Luke: "And Jesus increased in wisdom and in years, and in divine and human favor" (2:52, NRSV). However, there is no hint that he left Palestine. As a carpenter, he would have no reason to do so. As the Son of Man, he said, "I was sent only to the lost sheep of Israel" (Matthew 15:24). Jesus never showed any desire to explore the world in search of greater teaching; in fact, he confidently affirmed to the Samaritan woman that "salvation is from the Jews" (John 4:22). A reading of the Gospels does not reveal a gaping hole in Jesus' life. No years are "lost"; rather, some years are summarized. Given Jesus' later ministry and his interest in theology displayed as a child, we can well imagine him studying the Scriptures while learning the trade of carpentry from his father. Commenting on the supposed "lost years," biblical scholar

Edgar Goodspeed assumes that it was no wonder Jesus could use the Hebrew prophets "with such power in his brief ministry; he had studied and pondered them for many years, as no one has ever done, before or since."[1]

In the Gospels, the key to Jesus' public ministry is not a sojourn to the East, but his baptism. This is the time when God the Father publicly endorsed and commissioned him and when the Holy Spirit came upon him in power. Jesus' subsequent ministry and teaching was not that of a Hindu guru or Buddhist sage. He preached resurrection, not re-incarnation. He instructed his disciples to relate to a personal God, not an impersonal principle. He declared and demonstrated himself uniquely to be God in the flesh, not one of many God-realized masters.[2]

Nevertheless, two passages from the New Testament are sometimes used to justify Jesus as a world traveler. The first is John 21:25: "Jesus did many other things as well. If every one of them were written down, I suppose that even the whole world would not have room for the books that would be written."[3] This is thought to allow for eastward adventures. However, a parallel passage adds more clarity to this verse.

> Jesus did many other miraculous signs in the presence of his disciples, which are not recorded in this book. But these are written that you may believe that Jesus is the Christ, the Son of God, and that by believing you may have life in his name (John 20:30,31).

John is overwhelmed with Jesus' miraculous power, but he has selected certain accounts in order to encourage belief in Jesus. His statement that all the books in the world could not contain a complete record of Jesus' deeds is not a general endorsement of anything that might be said about him. In fact, in John's first letter he warns of Antichrists who distort the doctrine of Christ (1 John 4:1-4). Someone might say that all the biographies the world has to offer on Mother Teresa are not sufficient to record the extent of her loving deeds, but this would in no way open the door to a biography claiming that she spent her teenage years as a glamorous fashion model in France! John is referring to those things Jesus did *when he was with his disciples in Palestine.* Lost years are not in question.

In her book *The Jesus Mystery* (1984), Janet Bock refers to John 1:31, where John the Baptist says he did not know Jesus, as evidence that Jesus had been away from Palestine for quite some time. Otherwise, John—Jesus' cousin— would have recognized him.[4] Bock fails to note the obvious fact that John was a recluse who "lived in the desert until he appeared publicly to Israel" (Luke 1:80); he may not have known Jesus at all because he had not grown up with him. Or this may mean that John would not have known Jesus was *the Messiah* if not for the fact that the Holy Spirit had descended on him (John 1:29-34). In any case, lost years and world travels are not the issue.

Nevertheless, these silent or "lost" years have mystified and preoccupied many who believe that within these summarized years lies the entire meaning of Jesus.

Enter Nicholas Notovitch

In 1894 a Russian journalist named Nicholas Notovitch published a book in France called *The Unknown Life of Jesus*

Christ, which became quite popular and controversial, going through eight editions in one year. Later in that same year, three English translations appeared, along with Italian and German translations, followed a few years later by Swedish (1896) and Spanish (1909) translations.[5] Notovitch's story was as exotic as his claims were bold. If he was right, historic, institutional Christianity was wrong.

The controversy centered on a supposedly lost Tibetan text called "The Life of Saint Issa: Best of the Sons of Men," which claims that Jesus left Palestine from ages 13 to 29 to travel east. Notovitch made this rather short text the heart of his book. He also added essays explaining how he happened to find the lost text and what he made of its significance.

In 1907, Levi Downing offered a channeled book, *The Aquarian Gospel of Jesus the Christ,* which echoed many of Notovitch's claims. (We will deal with Downing in chapters 11 and 12.) Several books—such as *The Lost Years of Jesus* by Elizabeth Clare Prophet (1984), *The Jesus Mystery* by Janet Bock, and *Jesus Lived in India* (1986) by Holger Kersten— present the claims of Notovitch, Downing, and others as serious challenges to historic Christianity. With certain variations, they all believe that Jesus was no stranger to the mystic East. He lived there, imbibed the ancient teachings, and returned to Palestine an enlightened master. But it all began with the obscure Russian journalist, Notovitch. Just what did he claim and what was his evidence?

In the preface of *The Unknown Life of Jesus Christ,* Notovitch reports that after the Turkish War (1877–78) he journeyed to India to study "the peoples who inhabit India and their customs, the grand and mysterious archaeology, and the colossal and majestic nature of their country."[6] After various travels he arrived at Ladakh, Tibet, from where he intended to return to Russia. But while there, he heard from a chief lama of "very ancient memoirs relating to the life of Jesus Christ,"[7] contained in certain great monasteries. With renewed vigor, Notovitch decided to hunt down this material instead of returning to Russia. While at Leh, the capital of Ladakh, he visited the Himis monastery, where the chief lama informed him that copies of the manuscripts were housed. Notovitch says that in order not to arouse suspicion, he decided to depart for India.[8]

After his departure, Notovitch says he fortuitously broke his leg, which brought him back to Himis for treatment and, ultimately, for the recovery of the "lost" years of Jesus. He claims that upon his request, the chief lama brought to him "the manuscripts relating to Jesus Christ and, assisted by my interpreter, who translated for me the Thibetan [sic] language, transferred carefully to my note book what the lama read to me."[9] He says that since he did not doubt the authenticity of the chronicle, which was "edited with great exactitude by the Brahminic, and more especially the Buddhistic historians of India and Nepaul [sic],"[10] he sought to publish a translation.

Notovitch claimed to be so sure of the document's authenticity that he essentially threw down the gauntlet to those who favored the New Testament Gospels, saying his discovery was "compiled three or four years after the death of Jesus, from the accounts of eyewitnesses and contemporaries, [and] has much more probability of being in conformity with truth than the accounts of the Gospels," which he held to be written much later.[11]

So runs a streamlined account of the alleged uncovering of the text (we will return to other key details in the next chapter). But what does the text say?

The Life of Saint Issa (Jesus)

Notovitch published the text under the title "The Life of Saint Issa: Best of the Sons of Men," within his book *The Unknown Life of Jesus Christ.* It is divided into 14 chapters with verses within the chapter. It begins with a prologue lamenting "the great crime committed in the land of Israel" (1:1) of murdering "the great and just Issa, in whom was manifest the soul of the universe" (1:2). Issa (Jesus) was incarnated to lead people back to "the one and indivisible Creator whose mercy is infinite" (1:4).

The next verse speaks of "the merchants coming from Israel" who gave the account reported in the text (1:5). A discussion of Israel's bondage in Egypt follows, speaking of Prince Mossa's (Moses') role in securing the liberation of God's people from Pharaoh. Mossa leads Israel back to God, but they soon return to idolatry.[12]

We then hear of Israel's unfaithfulness being punished by God through the Roman oppression. Yet God heard his people's prayers and decided to "re-incarnate in a human form" (4:1). "The eternal Spirit" came in human form so "He might teach man to identify himself with the Divinity and attain to eternal felicity" (4:3).

God spoke through this child, and even as a youth Issa gathered a following by talking of "the only indivisible God" and "exhorting the strayed souls to repent and purify themselves from [their] sins" (4:8). Yet at age 13, just when he expected to marry, Issa left Jerusalem with a train of merchants and "journeyed toward the Sinda [India]" (4:13) in order to perfect "himself in the knowledge of the word of God and the study of the laws of the great Buddhas" (4:13).

At age 14, Issa "came this side of the Sindh and settled among the Aryas, in the country beloved by God" (5:1). After his fame spread in the northern Sindh, "the devotees of the god Djaine" (5:2) sought him, but he "left the deluded worshippers" (5:3) and went to "Djagguernat, in the country of Orsis" (5:3), where Brahma priests taught him to comprehend the Vedas, to cure physical ills by prayer, to teach the sacred scriptures, to drive out evil desires from man and remake him in the likeness of God (5:4).

During six years here and in "other holy cities" (5:5), Issa lived and loved the lower Hindu classes and sided with them against the oppressing higher classes. He even "denied the divine inspiration of the Vedas and the Puranas" in favor of the universal law of worshiping God alone (5:12-13). Issa denounced all idolatry, and called down the anger of God on those who worship inanimate objects (5:15-26). God is the "cause of the mysterious life of man, into whom He has breathed part of His divine Being" (5:18).

Although the higher classes of priests and warriors took offense at Issa's rejection of their teaching and sought to kill him, he escaped to "the country of the Gautamides, where the great Buddha Sakya-Muni came to the world, among a people who worshiped the only and sublime Brahma" (6:2). In other words, Issa moved from Hinduism to Buddhism, although a Buddhist worshiping Brahma is anomalous to say the least.[13] He then mastered the Pali language and studied the sacred Sutras (Buddhist scriptures) for six years, after which he could "perfectly expound the sacred scrolls" (6:4).

He then left Nepal and the Himalayan mountains and descended to the valley of Radjipoutan. He later moved to the west and everywhere preached "the supreme perfection attainable by man" (6:5). Issa continued to condemn idolatry among "the Pagans" (6:7-16), warning that those who create idols "will be the prey of an eternal fire" (7:10). Many forsook their idols (7:1).

Issa's next stop was Persia, where he excoriated the Zoroastrians for viewing God as both good and evil and for worshiping the sun (chapter 8). This was less than warmly received by the "Magi," who abandoned Issa on a highway outside the city in the middle of the night, hoping he would become breakfast for wild beasts. Yet he escaped.

Issa, then age 29, returned to Israel for three years. There he preached high ethical standards of reverence for God, altruism, and nonresistance in relation to Roman oppression. He was unopposed by the Jewish religious leadership but was feared by Pilate, who worried that he would incite insurrection. Pilate gave Issa over to the Jewish judges, who found no fault in him and washed their hands in a sacred vessel saying, "We are innocent of the blood of this righteous man" (13:25).

Nevertheless, Pilate prevailed, and Issa was crucified. After a full day on the cross, Issa "lost consciousness and his soul disengaged itself from the body, to reunite with God" (14:4). "Thus ended the terrestrial existence of the reflection of the eternal Spirit under the form of a man who had saved hardened sinners and comforted the afflicted" (14:4).

Pilate then ordered that the body be given to relatives, who placed it in a tomb where many came to wail and lament. Three days later, Pilate had Issa's body put in another place, fearing a rebellion among the people (14:6). When some of Issa's followers visited the now-empty tomb, a rumor spread that "the Supreme Judge had sent his angels from heaven, to remove the mortal remains of the saint in whom part of the divine Spirit had lived on earth" (14:7).

This caused Pilate to become angry and to impose the death penalty for proselytizing in Issa's name (14:8). Nevertheless, despite persecution, Issa's disciples left Israel and preached to the heathen to "abandon their gross errors, think of the salvation of their souls and earn the perfect bliss" for the immaterial world of the great Creator (14:10). And they met with success (14:11). So ends "The Life of Saint Issa."

Reality According to Issa

The theology of the text is a curious mixture of Judaism, Christianity, Hinduism, and Buddhism. The God of Issa seems to be a personal and moral being who demands worship and hates idolatry (hence Judaism), even threatening unrepentant idolaters with hell! The Christian element is present in that some of Issa's teachings are close to those found in the Gospels, particularly when he says he did not come to disown the laws of Moses but to "reestablish them in the hearts of men" (10:21; cf. Matthew 5:17-20). Yet the appearance of Issa is closer to the pantheistic Hindu idea of an avatar (periodic manifestation of God) than the Christian view of God uniquely incarnate as a man, because Issa is said to "manifest the soul of the universe." Issa seems most favorably disposed toward Buddhism which, unlike the other religions he is exposed to, he does not criticize. He leaves Israel with the express purpose of studying "the laws of the great Buddhas" (4:13). Zoroastrianism and Jainism fare far less well.

Notovitch's narrative and the Issa the text presents are drastically detached from the biblical record at many points, but we will only mention a few decisive dissimilarities.

We read of Issa learning from the Hindus how "to cure physical ills by means of prayers" (5:4), but the text gives us no record of him doing so or of any supernatural touch upon his ministry. Issa, unlike Jesus, is a stranger to the miraculous.

In the story of Issa, the Jewish religious leaders side with Issa against Pilate, begging him to not execute him. This contradicts all four Gospels, which present both the Jewish leadership and Roman rule as equally responsible for his death. The growing tension between Jesus and the Jewish religious establishment, so keenly felt in the Gospels, is absent from the account of Issa.

Although Issa is somehow a revelation of God, he is not an incarnation in the biblical sense. He is said to be a manifestation of "the soul of the universe" (1:2) and "a saint in whom part of the divine Spirit had lived on earth" (14:7). These descriptions are absolutely alien to biblical theology, which declares Jesus to be "the Word made flesh," who Himself created the universe (John 1:1-18).

Issa and the narration repeatedly speak of sin and the need to repent from sin, especially idolatry, yet Issa is silent about any atoning sacrifice being offered for sin. Rather, "the good he must do to his fellow man [is] the sure means of speedy union with the eternal Spirit" (6:6). "He who has recovered his primitive purity shall die with his transgressions forgiven" (6:6). Issa teaches that part of God dwells in each person (5:18; 9:15), and it is intimated that salvation involves identifying oneself with this indwelling part (4:3). Issa is more an ethical teacher and preacher than a Redeemer who atones for our sin through his crucifixion.

The account of Issa's crucifixion occupies only a small fraction of the text, whereas the Gospels emphasize it more than any other aspect of Jesus' life. This betrays the theology: Issa dies a martyr's death, not a Savior's death. His life is more important than his death. His death is the end, not the beginning.

What the Gospels present as the climax of Jesus' ministry and his ultimate vindication—the resurrection, "The Life of Saint Issa" flatly denies. Issa's body was secretly moved by Pilate, after which his followers *mistakenly* assume his body was supernaturally transported to heaven, when in reality it was rotting in an unmarked grave of Pilate's choosing.

The text provides no reason why Pilate would think that moving the body to another grave would discourage an insurrection, nor is any reason evident. But if Pilate feared a mass Christian movement and knew where Jesus' body was located, it would have only made sense to produce the corpse in order to squash all preaching of the resurrection. History knows nothing of this.

But before looking at the evidence for and against Notovitch's claims, we should note that the theology of Issa itself is at odds with much of the new spirituality. This is especially ironic considering that many often invoke Issa to support their view of Jesus as a mystical guru.

The text seems to speak of God as a personal and moral being, not the impersonal force, principle, or vibration of much of the new spirituality. Issa's God is often angry at humans for their disobedience, particularly concerning idolatry. Hinduism, which provides much of the spiritual muscle for the new spirituality, takes it on the theological chin several times.

Although Issa speaks of humans as having at least part of the divine spirit in them, he calls people to repent of sin (sin being understood as actions and attitudes that displease a personal God). This is at odds with the human potential aspect of the new spirituality, which stresses our sinlessness and infinite potential. At one point Issa says that miracles cannot be performed by man (11:7), thus putting him at some distance from the paranormal propensity of much New Age thinking.

Further, Issa comes out against divination, saying that "he who has recourse to diviners soils the temple of his heart and shows his lack of faith in his Creator" (11:10). This puts the brakes on any number of divining practices, such as Tarot card reading, casting the I Ching, using crystal divination, and psychic readings, which are accepted by many spiritual seekers.

The story of Issa seems unclear on reincarnation. It says that God was in some sense "reincarnated" in Issa, but it also speaks of the Judgment Day as if it were a final judgment. Issa does deny transmigration, saying that God "will never humiliate his child by casting his soul for chastisement into the body of a beast" (6:11). So we can say the text is at least ambiguous on the doctrine of reincarnation.

"The Life of Saint Issa: Best of the Sons of Men" is really a theological hodgepodge. It does not clearly support many core New Age doctrines, despite the fact that books like *The Jesus Mystery* by Janet Bock claim that Jesus' supposed travels reveal him to be more of an Eastern mystic than the church wants to believe.

Janet Bock and other writers tend to supplement the Notovitch book with various spiritual revelations received by people like Edgar Cayce and Levi Downing during trance states. What *historical* evidence do we have for the objective truth of Jesus as Saint Issa? We turn to this in the next chapter.

8

DID JESUS TRAVEL
TO INDIA?

IF JESUS JOURNEYED east to India and elsewhere, traditional Christianity has neglected a vital aspect of his life and ministry. Are the Gospels partial biographies that need to be supplemented by outside sources that speak of Jesus' Oriental adventures? Has the church locked itself into a flawed view of Jesus? To assess these concerns, we need to test the claims of the documents discussed in the last chapter. As in previous chapters, we will apply the historical tests of *integrity, authenticity,* and *veracity* to Notovitch's text. We will commence with the criterion of veracity. What is the nature of the text itself? Does it appear to be true to fact?

Edgar J. Goodspeed, an expert on ancient manuscripts, observes that "the whole cast of the book is vague and elusive."[1] He also notes, "It presents no difficulties, no problems—whereas any really ancient work newly discovered bristles with novelties and obscurities."[2] We saw this especially in the ferment of scholarly disagreement that ensued after the discovery of both the Dead Sea Scrolls and the Nag Hammadi texts. Speaking of the text, Goodspeed continues: "Here the message of Issa is a pallid and colorless morality, amiable and unobjectionable enough, but devoid of the flashes of insight and touches of genius that mark the early gospels."[3]

Goodspeed also recognizes that the text "identifies itself with no recognizable type of primitive thought," although it "shows a superficial acquaintance with the leading New Testament" accounts.[4] As we argued in the last chapter, it is more of a hodgepodge, or theological patch-quilt, than a well-integrated belief system.

The veracity of the document is also called into question when we consider some historical inaccuracies concerning world religions. Per Beskow, a Swedish New Testament scholar, points out that the reference to "the god Djaine" (5:2) discloses "a considerable lack of knowledge about Indian religions." He continues:

> The Jains, or Jainas, do not believe in any god at all, but in certain jinas ("Conquerors"), who are enlightened spiritual leaders. The a in Jain comes from the same phonetic law that makes the [Hindu] worshippers of Shiva into Shavias and the [Hindu] worshippers of Vishnu into Vaishnavas.[5]

There is no "god Djaine."

The fact that "The Life of Saint Issa" would err so terribly concerning the Jain religion does not bode well for its overall veracity.[6] Nor does another error concerning religious belief.

The text was purportedly reconstructed from manuscripts in a Buddhist monastery and speaks more highly of Buddhism than any other religion. It even speaks of Issa as having been "elected" by Buddha "to spread his holy word"

(6:4). Buddha seems to be interchangeable with God in this case. It also speaks of Buddhists worshiping Brahma, which is an odd combination of Hinduism and Buddhism. It also speaks of a jealous Creator God who can punish and forgive sin and who hates idols. This has little to do with most of historic Buddhism, which is either atheistic, agnostic, or pantheistic and abounds in images of the Buddha as proper objects of religious veneration and contemplation.[7] The "Buddhism" of the text looks more like a syncretistic creation of an attempt to graft elements of Buddhism onto Judaism than it does to any identifiable Buddhism of that time in history.[8]

It is instructive to know that theories relating Christianity to Buddhism were very much in vogue when Notovitch published his *Unknown Life of Jesus Christ*. Many Westerners sought to synthesize the two religions in novel ways. Historian Carl Jackson, in reviewing this phenomenon, says that Notovitch "may be said to have carried the controversy to its ultimate *reductio ad absurdum*" by his claim that the supposed resemblances between Christianity and Buddhism are accounted for by Jesus studying Buddhism with Buddhists.[9] The attempt to link Buddhism and Christianity was appealing to many, but not based on fact.[10]

It is also rather odd that while certain commonly known English names take on exotic spellings (supposedly following the language of the text) in the text, such as Issa for Jesus (which *is* faithful to the Tibetan), [11] Mossa for Moses, and Romeles for Romans, Pontius Pilate remains unchanged.[12] This inconsistency is another strike against the text being historically believable.

So we find several reasons to question the veracity of "The Life of Saint Issa," in light of historical facts, whether from the New Testament or from other sources.

Concerning its *authenticity*, we have only one verse in the text claiming that the account was written by "the merchants" who presumably accompanied Jesus on his trek from Israel to the East. These merchants are not named, and their identity is never mentioned in the entire text. Neither is there any strong external tradition as to the text's authorship, as we find for the New Testament Gospels (see chapter 3). We are left in the dark as to where the merchants were from (India or Palestine?),[13] how they gained their facts, or their abilities to record the facts—assuming they wrote the text at all!

So far, we have found substantial reasons to doubt the veracity and authenticity of this controversial text. However, the greatest difficulties are in regard to the matter of its *integrity*. Do we have reason to believe this text has been accurately transmitted over the centuries? Or is it a modern invention, a mere forgery?

F. Max Muller (1823-1900), the great Orientalist of the nineteenth century and translator and editor of the multivolumed *Sacred Books of the East*, subjected the Issa thesis to critical scrutiny soon after its publication. Lest anyone accuse him of ill intentions,[14] in 1882, 12 years before Notovitch's publication, he had written that he "would be extremely grateful if anybody would point out to me the historical channels through which Buddhism influenced early Christianity," because he had been searching in vain for this his entire life.[15] Muller thought that if the Issa text were legitimate, it would help establish the historicity of Jesus, despite the text's difference from the New Testament accounts.[16]

Writing in 1894, Muller found it exceedingly difficult to believe that a text of this importance was not listed in the Kandjur and Tandjur collections, the "excellent catalogues of manuscripts and books of the Buddhists in Tibet and China." He found it "impossible or next to impossible . . . that this Sutra of Issa, composed in the first century of our era, should not have found a place either in the Kandjur or in the Tandjur."[17] Notovitch responded by saying that those catalogs didn't exhaust the manuscript resources at his disposal at the Himis monastery.[18] Yet how plausible is it that Issa would not be well-known in India if, in fact, Jesus had actually been there? We would expect this text to be listed in the major catalogs if Issa had the impact in India that "The Life of Saint Issa" claims that he did. We should also remember Notovitch's lack of scholarly standing and Muller's world renown.[19] Muller is the authority.

This brings us to Notovitch's account itself. Even if we take him at face value, we are quite distant from the supposed original writing of the Issa text. Notovitch's own words make this clear:

> The two manuscripts, from which the lama of the convent Himis read to me all that had a bearing upon Jesus, are compilations from divers [sic] copies written in the Thibetan language, translations of scrolls belonging to the library of Lhassa and brought, about two hundred years after Christ, from India, Nepaul and Maghada, to a convent on Mount Marbour, near the city of Lhassa.[20]

In light of this, Goodspeed notes that Notovitch's claims are extremely unscholarly and improbable:

> It is evident that the scholar's desire to see the manuscript
> of the work, or failing that to see a photograph of it or a
> part of it, or at least to have precise directions about how
> and where to find it (its place and number in the Himis
> library) is not in this case to be satisfied.[21]

We are at least three times removed from the manuscript. Notovitch tells us that first, the lama read aloud from
the manuscripts; second, the interpreter interpreted; and
third, Notovitch recorded it. But Notovitch also admits that
he "arranged all the fragments concerning the life of Issa in
chronological order and [took] pains to impress upon
them the character of unity, in which they were absolutely
lacking."[22] Goodspeed complains that "this is just what a
scholar would not have done; he would wish to present the
fragments just as the manuscripts had them, unaffected by
his own views and tastes."[23]

While it is not impossible for a nonscholar to stumble
across a valuable manuscript, Notovitch's testimony loses
credibility given the many inaccuracies already noted and
considering the fact that Notovitch was "a man of no known
attainments in any direction, certainly not in the direction
of biblical history and criticism."[24] Notovitch's lack of scholarship, or even basic biblical knowledge, is especially evident when he describes the Gospel of Luke as saying that
Jesus "was in the deserts until the day of his showing in Israel" (1:80). This, he believes, proves that no one knew
where he had gone until he reappeared 16 years later.[25]
However, this biblical reference has nothing to do with
Jesus, but with *John the Baptist!* (Whether anyone claims
John went to India, I do not know.)

Even more problems are evident in Notovitch's tale. He describes the manuscripts about Issa as scrolls or books, when, as Per Beskow points out, "Tibetan books are neither scrolls nor bound in our way. They consist of oblong leaves, imitating palm leaves; they are kept loose between wooden plates, and the whole is kept wrapped in a piece of cloth."[26] Notovitch was wrong again.

Let us bring together the facts on Issa and Notovitch. The Issa of the manuscript bears little resemblance to the Jesus Christ of the Gospels. The doctrine of Notovitch's text is a sloppy syncretism that cannot fully support a New Age platform. Concerning the tests of historicity: The text contains several obvious falsehoods regarding Jainism and Buddhism. We have no idea who supposedly wrote the text outside of a vague reference to unidentified "merchants." Even if the text is what Notovitch claims, it is *textually* uncertain with regard to integrity because of 1) its being transcribed through a translator, 2) its unavailability for scholarly inspection, and 3) Notovitch's admittedly substantial reworking of the original material.

Another Gospel Forgery

Beyond these considerable problems, several witnesses came forth shortly after the publication of *The Unknown Life of Christ*, who claim that Notovitch never discovered the manuscript. In a finely detailed article published in a scholarly journal called *The Nineteenth Century*, in April 1896, Professor J. Archibald Douglas recounts his trip to the Himis monastery to check up on Notovitch's claims.

Douglas says he was open-minded and initially expected to confirm Notovitch's discovery. He seems to have had no personal or monetary motive to discredit Notovitch.

Douglas begins by agreeing that Notovitch visited the monastery, noting that the chief lama remembered several European gentlemen visiting in 1887 and 1888, which could very well have included Notovitch, a Russian.[27] But Douglas notes that Notovitch's name does not appear on the list of travelers kept at the bungalow in the city of Leh, where Notovitch said he stayed. Douglas did find that a Notovitch was treated there—not for a broken leg, but for a toothache.[28]

A translator was enlisted by Douglas to read extracts from Notovitch's book to the chief lama, in order to gain his response. The lama's comments were recorded in a statement signed by the lama, Douglas, and the translator, Shahmwell Joldan, late postmaster of Ladakh.

In the document, reprinted in the journal, the lama contradicts all of Notovitch's major assertions. When asked about the Issa document, the Chief Superior Lama replied:

> I have been for forty-two years a Lama, and am well ac-
> quainted with all the well-known Buddhist books and man-
> uscripts, and I have never heard of one which mentions
> the name of Issa, and it is my firm and honest belief that
> none exists. I have inquired of our principal Lamas in
> other monasteries of Tibet, and they are not acquainted
> with any books or manuscripts which mention the name of
> Issa.[29]

When asked if the name Issa was held in high respect by Buddhists, the lama replied, "They know nothing even of his name; none of the Lamas has ever heard it, save through missionaries and European sources."[30] The lama further denied that any Westerner had stayed there to nurse a broken leg (contra Notovitch)[31]; he denied having spoken with Notovitch about the religions of the ancient Egyptians, Assyrians, and people of Israel (contra Notovitch) and even denied knowing anything about these religions[32]; he likewise denied that the monastery contained any Buddhist writings in the Pali language (contra Notovitch).[33] Beskow confirms this, saying (contra Notovitch) that "Pali, which is the sacred language of Theravada Buddhism, has never been used in Tibet, and the Tibetan translations have usually been done from Sanskrit or from Chinese."[34]

Douglas reports that when parts of Notovitch's book were read to the lama, he burst out with, "Lies, lies, nothing but lies,"[35] and on another occasion asked Douglas if Notovitch could be punished by law for his untruths.[36]

Douglas also questions Notovitch's reference to using a resident (*shikari*) from a nearby village as an interpreter, because such a person is always a simple peasant, unable to handle the theological and philosophical concepts found in Notovitch's book.[37]

In response to these charges, Notovitch later claimed that the lama lied to Douglas because he was afraid the precious manuscripts would be stolen by Westerners; only Notovitch's "Eastern diplomacy" put him on the good side of the lama.[38] This is very unlikely. Even if the lama had confessed to the existence of such a manuscript, he would not have needed to reveal its location in the large collection. He could certainly have refused to show it, sell it, or donate it to foreigners. I also assume that the monasteries had adequate means to keep their precious documents secure. Further, if the monks were so reticent, how did Notovitch, visiting there for the very first time, gain access to the manuscripts, despite his "Eastern diplomacy"? We should remember that Douglas was accompanied by the postmaster of Ladakh—someone surely on better terms with its citizens than Notovitch, a total stranger.

Elizabeth Clare Prophet tries to strengthen the case that the monks feared the manuscripts would be stolen. She quotes from a passage in *The Cultural Heritage of Ladakh* to the effect that because the Himis monastery attracted so many visitors, the monks had a condescending, if not contemptuous attitude toward them and seemed convinced that all the foreigners would steal from them if possible. The book goes on to say that the monastery experienced some quite serious losses of property "in recent years," which were being investigated when the authors were there. (It was found, though, that foreigners were not responsible.[39]) This information, Prophet avers, lends credence to Notovitch's idea that his own "Eastern diplomacy," not possessed by Douglas, won him a precious peek at the manuscripts.

This argument reveals at least three serious weaknesses. First, the reference to supposedly stolen property is only in "recent years." The Notovitch incident dates to 1887, which is presumably not "recent." Second, the original quote from *The Cultural Heritage of Ladakh* goes on to mention something crucial omitted by Prophet: that "Hemis [sic] suffers greatly from the absence of its head lama."[40] It is just such a head lama who plays a prominent role in both Notovitch's and Douglas's accounts. Surely, the Himis of today is different enough from that of 1887 to render Prophet's selective quotation moot with regard to defending Notovitch! Third, the very book she cites concerning Himis and the region of Ladakh has absolutely no reference to Notovitch, Jesus, Christ, or Issa in its index. If the Notovitch story had any credibility, wouldn't it be mentioned in this source? This is a telling omission, indeed.

We must consider one more item before giving a verdict on Notovitch: Could the Issa story have been created out of his imagination if he named the specific site at which he claimed to have found the manuscript? Prophet[41] and Notovitch himself[42] say it is unlikely that a liar would make such particular claims. Is it really?

Notovitch could have easily realized that very few people have access to an obscure Tibetan monastery. He could have expected that his book would be in print for many months, while he pocketed considerable royalties, before someone checked him out. (This, in fact, is exactly what happened.) He may have even made contingency plans to use if he were challenged, such as the "Eastern diplomacy" response. Furthermore, he himself backtracked after Douglas's and Muller's criticism. In the preface to the edition of his book reprinted by Prophet, he confessed that there was probably no one manuscript about Issa but that the story had been gathered from various books in the monastery[43]—a revision of his earlier comments.[44]

So what is the verdict on Notovitch and his *Unknown Life of Jesus Christ*? Beskow calls his "discovery" the "best known Gospel forgery of modern times."[45] Goodspeed, Douglas, and Muller agree. Albert Schweitzer calls it a "fictitious" life of Christ and "a bare-faced swindle and an impudent invention."[46] This verdict is, I believe, accurate.

Nevertheless, Elizabeth Clare Prophet's book *The Lost Years of Jesus* adds three other witnesses who claim to have seen the documents and, in the case of one Swami Abhedananda, made a translation of them. The reader can consult her arguments for the details, but at least four salient and stubborn facts remain. [47]

First, the Issa manuscripts remain unavailable for scholarly inspection. Prophet has not shown otherwise. In addition to Prophet's arguments, Fida Hassnain, an Islamic professor and author of *A Search for the Historical Jesus* (1994), also claims to have visited the Himis monastery several times in search of the Issa manuscript. Although he never saw the manuscript, he claims that he found in a local church a journal entry dated 1890 by a Moravian missionary named Dr. Marx which mentioned Notovitch's visit to the monastery and his discovery of the manuscript.

Hassnain says he photographed two pages from Marx's diary and translated them from German. He claims that the diary mentions Notovitch as "a Russian traveler who broke his leg at Hemis in Ladakh, and who was nursed by the Moravian Mission doctors. Mention is made of the claim of Notovitch that he had seen Tibetan scrolls about Jesus in the Hemis monastery."[48]

Although Hassnain includes several photographs of the monastery in his book, strangely, he does not provide a photograph of this journal entry. The entry mentioned only Notovitch's *claim* to have seen the Tibetan manuscripts. Dr. Marx says nothing of having himself seen the manuscript. If this diary is authentic (which is very hard to establish given the lack of evidence), it could be that Notovitch simply lied to Marx. Given what we have found in this chapter, this is very likely. Furthermore, the supposed diary entry contradicts the testimony of the Chief Superior Lama interviewed by Archibald Douglas.

Hassnain's claim adds another small piece to the Notovitch puzzle. However, it fails to establish either the actual existence of the supposedly lost Tibetan manuscript or its historical reliability as a source about Jesus Christ.

Second, no one has come up with an adequate picture of the text that reveals its distinctive features and unique identity.[49] Prophet includes a photo of a monk holding some kind of scroll with the caption, "These books say our Jesus was here,"[50] but this hardly qualifies as sound evidence, especially since *books* is the wrong word to use (as noted above).

Third, Prophet's and Hassnain's anecdotal claims do nothing to rehabilitate the text's dubious historicity and Notovitch's inaccuracies. The arguments given above stand fast.

Fourth, and most importantly, the reliability of "The Life of Saint Issa" must be compared with the biblical record of Jesus. As discussed in chapter 3, the New Testament marshals impressive credentials. It has historical *integrity*, which Issa lacks. It has historical *authenticity*, which Issa lacks. It has historical *veracity*, which Issa lacks. In the bright light of this threefold argument for the New Testament, it is safe to say that the burden of proof is on "The Life of Saint Issa"—a burden that is very difficult to bear. To put it another way, 5366 ancient Greek New Testament manuscripts in the hand are worth more than (at most) one inaccessible and idiosyncratic manuscript in the Tibetan bush.

Given the above considerations, *even if* it could be established that a genuine manuscript of "The Life of Saint Issa" exists, this, in itself, would not prove it to be true to fact. Such a manuscript could easily be a legendary fabrication which makes use of biblical materials about Christ but also interweaves them with non-Christian and nonhistorical teachings. Ron Rhodes, who also doubts that the Issa manuscript exists, makes this case strongly:

> Christians acknowledge that news of Jesus eventually reached India and Tibet as a result of the missionary efforts of the early church. It is conceivable that when devotees of other religions heard about Jesus, they tried to modify what they heard to make it appear that Jesus and his teachings were compatible with their own belief systems. It is possible that sometime between the first and nineteenth centuries these unreliable legends were recorded on scrolls and circulated among the converts in India. This would not be unlike the distorted versions of the life of Jesus that emerged among the early Gnostics and were recorded in the Gnostic gospels.[51]

Did Jesus Die in India?

While Notovitch's "discovery" leaves the body of Issa decomposing in Palestine, other New Age revisionists have him surviving the crucifixion and retiring in India. After dying there, he was supposedly interred in a tomb in Kashmir. Ironically, one article defending this view begins by citing Notovitch as a source, even though his account of Issa does not permit Jesus returning to India.[52]

Before dealing with these claims, we should again keep in mind the case for the historical reliability of the New

Testament. Any historical claim that contradicts this record in any important way needs to assume the burden of proof. The New Testament, of course, records that Jesus died on the cross, was buried, rose again, and ascended to heaven. We will deal specifically with the historicity and significance of the resurrection of Jesus in chapter 15, but we should remember from chapter 3 that Jesus' death *on the cross* was integral to his life and mission. He was a man born to die and emphasized his destiny throughout his ministry in different ways. Therefore, to claim that he did not die on the cross is to question the entire biblical portrait of Jesus. But how is this done?

One notion is that Jesus was crucified but did not die on the cross. He only appeared to die. He was brought to a tomb where he revived, only to leave Palestine and head eastward. This is a new twist on an old idea called the "swoon theory."

First, it is maintained by some that Jesus was not on the cross long enough to have died from crucifixion. Richard Walters says, "Writings on crucifixion state that, when the person crucified was in normal health, in no case did death occur within 12 hours." He concludes that "it is improbable that Jesus died after just three hours on the cross."[53] Second, some claim that Jesus was drugged when someone put a sponge up to his mouth to drink. This caused the appearance of death that deceived those present.[54] Third, the fact that blood spurted out from Jesus' side when it was pierced by the Roman's sword is thought to be another indication he was still alive.[55] Kersten and Gruber further argue that the nature of the shroud of Turin provides evidence that Jesus did not die on the cross.[56]

Before moving to the claims of Jesus' tomb being in India, we should briefly address these arguments.

As a general point, one has to wonder why those who trust the Gospel accounts enough to affirm that Jesus was crucified depart from the narratives when they clearly report that Jesus was dead as dead could ever be. Why believe at one point and doubt at another? If critics do not establish sufficient criteria for their doubts, their rejection of Jesus' death is simply arbitrary.

More specifically, first, there was sufficient time for Jesus to die on the cross. We must not view the crucifixion in isolation from what preceded it. As Michael Green notes:

> It is incredible that Jesus, who had not eaten or slept before his execution, who was weakened by a loss of blood through the most brutal flogging [see 1 Peter 2:24], who was pierced in both hands and feet, could have survived unaided had he been alive when taken down from the cross.[57]

Jesus was so weakened from his beatings that he was unable to carry his cross all the way to Golgotha, the execution site (Matthew 27:32). The authors of a technical article called "On the Physical Death of Jesus Christ," in the *Journal of the American Medical Association,* remarked that the time of survival for Roman crucifixions "ranged from three or four hours to three or four days and appears to have been inversely related to the severity of the scourging."[58]

Pilate showed surprise that Jesus died so rapidly (Mark 15:44), but he did not question that Jesus was really dead. The Romans were no beginners when it came to crucifixion. The squad of four soldiers broke the legs of the two men crucified with Jesus (a practice that would hasten death), but did not bother to break Jesus' legs because they saw he had already expired.

Second, the theory that Jesus arranged to be given some potion to feign death is problematic in several ways. The Gospel of John reports that Jesus was given a drink *in full view of the Roman guards* before he died (John 19:28,29). It was their job to be executioners, not accessories to a hoax. They had a vested interest in being accurate coroners because "had the centurion, had the governor made a mistake over the execution of a messianic pretender, their jobs and probably their lives would have been on the line."[59] Surely, they would have been wise to such a ploy. Moreover, if we assume that Jesus somehow arranged for his last-minute rescue, he is no less than a grand impostor and not worthy of any respect, because he preached the necessity of his own death. We might then say that Jesus rivaled Houdini, but we could never view him with religious veneration, let alone worship.

Third, the fact that blood and water came from Jesus' side is positive evidence for his death. The Roman soldiers pierced his side because they wanted to make doubly sure he was dead. This was a standard practice to ensure death.[60] What followed confirmed Jesus' death, as explained in the just-mentioned article in the *Journal of the American Medical Association*. Here is the conclusion of the authors:

> Clearly, the weight of historical and medical evidence indicates that Jesus was dead before the wound to his side was inflicted and supports the traditional view that the spear, thrust between his right ribs, probably perforated not only

the right lung but also the pericardium and heart and thereby ensured his death. Accordingly, interpretations based on the assumption that Jesus did not die on the cross appear to be at odds with modern medical knowledge.[61]

The view that the shroud of Turin somehow gives evidence that Jesus did not die on the cross must clear two huge hurdles. First, the authenticity of the shroud is far more in doubt than the reliability of the New Testament, which clearly indicates that Jesus died on the cross. The crucifixion is also corroborated by secular historians (as noted in chapter 3). Second, even if the shroud is the death wrapping of Jesus, it is highly unlikely that this artifact could, 2000 years later, establish that Jesus did not die on the cross. If the scroud is authentic, the evidence points in the other direction: Jesus died and was raised from the dead.[62]

Various authors have spoken of legends in Eastern lands claiming Jesus as their own. A tomb thought by some to contain Jesus' remains is in Kashmir, India, supposedly occupied by a mysterious Yuz Asaf.[63] But here again, a heavy burden of proof rests on such a revisionist view, given the historical reliability of the New Testament and considering the fact that Jesus could not have lived through the crucifixion. The resurrected and ascended Christ proclaims in the book of Revelation, "I was dead, and behold I am alive for ever and ever!" (Revelation 1:18). Paul is confident that "since Christ was raised from the dead, he cannot die again; death no longer has mastery over him" (Romans 6:9).

Those who claim that Jesus ended up in India must also explain the existence of the primitive church's faith in the resurrected and ascended Lord. And what sort of a teacher would Jesus be if he escaped to India while permitting an entire religion to be hinged on a threefold falsehood— namely, his death, resurrection, and ascension?[64]

But the real evidence against Jesus' death in India is a developed argument for his bodily resurrection and ascension. Jesus cannot be both rotting in Kashmir and ruling in heaven. We must save this for the chapter "Jesus and the Cosmic Christ."

One more revisionist historical view casts doubt on the biblical Jesus. Many claim Jesus was a member of the mystical Essene community and that his life and teachings can be explained by this connection. Was Jesus an Essene? Is this the great secret of the New Testament?

9

JESUS AND THE
DEAD SEA SCROLLS

ANOTHER STRATEGY TO revise the Jesus of traditional Christian understanding is to place him in a spiritual environment closer to his home than the mystic East. This portrait finds Jesus not in eastern lands but influenced by, or even a member of, the Essene community located on the shores of the Dead Sea in Palestine. Although it existed during the time of Jesus, this ancient Jewish religious group is not mentioned by the New Testament. Yet it has a strong spiritual allure for many modern seekers of the spiritual.

Some people view the Essenes as a kind of halfway house between orthodox Judaism and Eastern mysticism. They are revered as having captured the hidden essence of Jewish religion, while the other Jewish parties of the day were lost in external legalities. The Essenes, for many, represent a "third way" of Jewish spirituality closely akin to modern New Age thinking. Various esoteric or mystery organizations such as Theosophy, Anthroposophy, and Rosicrucianism see the Essenes as members of the Great White

Brotherhood or Lodge—a mystical brotherhood tracing its origins back to earlier mystery religions.[1]

Manly P. Hall, a prolific esoteric author, asserts that the Essenes "were a link between pagan and Christian mysticism, and were absorbed into the new faith or into orthodox Jewish communities as the result of the conflict between Christians and orthodox Jews."[2] One writer calls them "a new age religious sect in matters of belief and philosophy."[3] Shirley MacLaine views Essenes as prototypical New Agers, finds Essenism in the best of all world religions, and confidently identifies Jesus as an Essene.[4] The early Theosophist Annie Besant in *Esoteric Christianity* affirms that Jesus was groomed for ministry by studying in Essene environs.[5] The medium Edgar Cayce affirmed much of the same in his trance readings.[6]

Before 1947, what was known of the Essene community was gleaned from the Jewish philosopher Philo (c. 20 B.C.–A.D. 50), Jewish historian Josephus (A.D. 37–c. 100), Pliny the Elder, writing in the period A.D. 73–79, and Hippolytus, the Christian writer of Rome at the early part of the third century. We no longer need to rely on secondary documents. The discovery of the Dead Sea Scrolls in 1947 dwarfs even the Nag Hammadi discoveries and has been the center of much more critical attention and acclaim. Primary documents have been unearthed dating from about the first century B.C. to roughly A.D. 70. The Essenes can now speak for themselves. By comparing the classical sources on the Essenes with the documents found beginning in 1947 at the Dead Sea, most scholars have concluded that the community at Qumran was an Essene group.[7] But who exactly were the Essenes?

What Did the Essenes Believe?

Although the word *Essene* covers a sect that spanned many decades, and not all Essenes had the same status or exact beliefs, a general picture does emerge from our sources.[8]

The Essenes at Qumran were largely a group of ascetics who separated themselves from the orthodox Judaism of the temple because of its perceived religious laxity. They viewed themselves as a remnant voice, crying "in the desert" (Isaiah 40:3), preparing for a new era of righteousness. They lived communally with strict standards of religious and ceremonial discipline, especially regarding ritual purity. They were deeply rooted in the Old Testament Scriptures, which they transcribed and wrote commentaries on. Among other writings, the Dead Sea Scrolls contain fragments from all the books of the Hebrew Bible except Esther, giving us manuscripts 1000 years older than those previously known.[9]

Can the material on the Essenes culled from the Dead Sea Scrolls and the secondary sources support the notion that these people were substantially New Age in their orientation and that Jesus was either an Essene or had strong affinities with the sect?

The Dead Sea Scrolls themselves are comprised of biblical commentaries, apocryphal writings, pseudepigrapha, and writings relating to the Essene community's rules of order.[10] Interestingly, although the community possessed scriptures other than Old Testament texts, it seems that only books presently in our Old Testament were deemed worthy of interpretive commentary.[11] Pfeiffer notes that "scholars who have examined the manuscripts assert that the Biblical scrolls are written in a style of writing that is distinctive, as if to mark them off for special consideration."[12] This is instructive because, despite various non-Jewish elements discernible in the Dead Sea Scrolls, the predominating worldview is that of *Jewish monotheism, not pantheistic monism.*[13] Confessional poetry from the Community Rule (the rule of order for the Qumran Essenes) displays a deep sense of remorse over sin in the face of a personal and holy God:

> As for me,
> I belong to wicked mankind,
> to the company of ungodly flesh.
> My iniquities, rebellions, and sins,
> together with the perversity of my heart,
> belong to the company of worms
> and to those who walk in darkness.
> For mankind has no way,
> and man is unable to establish his steps
> since justification is with God
> and perfection is out of His hand.[14]

The hymn writer finds himself to be a sinful person in the company of sinful humanity, whose only hope of justification lies in a personal God who is in no sense identified with the self. This directly contradicts the New Age teaching that God is a principle, not a person.[15] Many other similar passages are found in this book, as well as in the Thanksgiving Hymn, that emphasize human sinfulness, God's holiness, and the necessity of God's action for humans to be justified in God's sight. In the Thanksgiving Hymn, the writer says that "a creature of clay" is "in iniquity from the womb" (compare Psalm 51:5) and "in guilty unfaithfulness until old age."[16] This is hardly New Age theology.

Much of the new spirituality professes that we, as divine beings at various levels of manifestation, create our own reality and control our own destiny. Such affirmations of autonomy are absolutely alien to the theology of the scrolls. For the Essenes, God is the sovereign Lord and moral Governor of the universe who knows the beginning from the end and who is bullied by no one. The Community Rule declares:

> There is none beside Thee to dispute Thy counsel
> or to understand Thy holy design,
> or to contemplate the depth of Thy mysteries
> and the power of Thy might.[17]

Such declarations certainly chafe at ambitions to human sovereignty.[18]

Although many claim that the Essenes believed in reincarnation, the Dead Sea documents do not support or confirm this. It is questionable whether they held to a pharisaical view of the physical resurrection or to a more Greek-inspired view of the immortality of the soul, but, in any case, they did not teach reincarnation.[19]

The evidence points to the Essenes' belief in heaven and hell as final destinations. The Community Rule speaks of the "eternal joy in life without end, a crown of glory and a garment of majesty in unending light"[20] for the just and "eternal torment and endless disgrace together with shameful extinction in the fire of the dark regions"[21] for sinners. This is far less mellow and much more black-and-white than most New Age scenarios.

The historical evidence recovered at the Dead Sea, along with secondary sources, shows that the Essenes deviated from mainstream Judaism at some points but not in their basic worldview. The Essenes were fiercely mono-theistic. Despite being more interested in angelic beings than other Jewish sects, the Essenes worshiped the Creator alone. Despite their emphasis on receiving special knowledge and status in relation to other Jews, they attributed this to God's grace, not to mystical achievement. Despite the fact that they were probably influenced by Greek and possibly Persian thinking to some degree, any foreign influence on the Essenes was secondary to the teachings of their sacred Jewish Scriptures. Moses was God's lawgiver, not Plato. Despite some tendencies to exalt the spiritual over the material, the Essenes were still essentially Jewish mono-theists, not Gnostics.

These factors alone damage the program to paint Jews in New Age colors by dipping into the Essenes' theological palette. *Even if* we could connect Jesus with the Essenes (which we will dispute below), this would not in itself make Jesus into a pantheistic monist who believed in human per-fectibility and reincarnation.

Can a connection be made between the Essenes and Jesus? If so, what kind of a connection would it be?

Was John the Baptist an Essene?

We need to start with John the Baptist, Jesus' forerunner and, according to Jesus, a prophet worthy of high honor. Some allege that John was an Essene or that he had strong connections with the group. This is because of the location of his stay in the wilderness, his ascetic life, and his practice of baptism. Did Jesus, then, endorse an Essene?

The Gospels record John as coming from the wilderness (Luke 1:80; 3:2). This likely was near the Qumran community. John may have been somewhat influenced by the Essenes, but he stands apart from them in distinctive ways. His clothing was not the white linen of Essenes but was made of camel's hair. His diet of locusts and wild honey was also more austere than that of the Essenes.[22] A life of ascetic renunciation was known among the Jews apart from the Essenes through the Nazarite vow (1 Samuel 1:11,28). Moreover, Luke even seems to pattern his recounting of John's early life after the Hannah and Samuel story of the Old Testament.[23] Since John's parents, Zechariah and Elizabeth, were of the priestly line, it is highly unlikely that they would commit their young son to an order so hostile to the established priesthood in Jerusalem.[24]

John's baptismal practice and theology were also at odds with the Essenes. Although the Qumran community thought Isaiah 40:3 ("A voice of one calling: 'In the desert prepare the way for the LORD; make straight in the wilderness a highway for our God' "), referred to them, their interpretation differed greatly from John's. The Essenes retreated into the wilderness to prepare the way of the Lord by searching the law of Moses and purifying themselves to be united with the godly and separated from the ungodly. John, on the other hand, preached from the wilderness, delivering a message of repentance to prepare the public at large for the coming of the Messiah.[25] F.F. Bruce notes that:

> John chose for the inauguration of his ministry the most public part of the wilderness of Judea, the crossing of the Jordan north of the Dead Sea, where traffic between Judea

and Peraea passed this way and that; and he addressed his message to all who would hear, including the "men of the pit" from whom the pious sectaries of Qumran swore to keep aloof.[26]

Luke presents John not as a monk, but as a prophet (Luke 3:2) who directly receives and proclaims the word of the Lord. This puts him some distance from the Essenes' understanding.

John's baptizing also differs from the Essenes' baptism because it signified an immediate repentance as a kind of one-time initiation. The Essenes, to the contrary, engaged in ritual bathing that was administered only after a probationary period, and afterward on a daily basis. John's baptism was messianic; he was preparing people for Jesus. The Essenes' washings were unrelated to any messianic or religious figure per se.[27]

If John the Baptist had ever been an Essene, he certainly must have left the ranks of the remnant before his public ministry—or he must have been an incredibly poor student![28]

Was Jesus an Essene?

Our question now becomes, Can we establish a positive connection between Jesus himself and the Essenes? Is it true that Christianity is the Essene movement that succeeded?

The Dead Sea Scrolls never mention Jesus of Nazareth by name, nor does the New Testament mention the Essenes,[29] even though the events of the Gospels, Acts, and much of the rest of the New Testament overlap with the Qumran community's existence, which probably came to a violent end sometime around A.D. 70 with the fall of Jerusalem. Therefore, we find no direct evidence for Jesus in the material.

Some have tried to identify Jesus with an important leader (or founder) of the sect, who is referred to in the Dead Sea Scrolls as the Teacher of Righteousness. Yet this is more imaginative than historical, as many scholars have noticed. Besides the fact that the Teacher of Righteousness is usually dated as having lived a century or more before Jesus, the defining aspects of the biblical Jesus are absent from the Teacher of Righteousness. These include Jesus' divine preexistence, virgin birth, miracles, sinless life, crucifixion, and resurrection.[30] We can, however, look to the teachings of the scrolls, and information derived from secondary sources, to find similarities and dissimilarities between the Nazarene and the Essenes.

If John differed from the Essenes because of his stricter asceticism, Jesus differed from both in that he was accused of being a glutton and drunkard (Matthew 11:19). Although Jesus encouraged his disciples to fast when needful, he issued no rule regarding fasting, nor did he encourage it during his public ministry. He refused the devil's offer of turning stones into bread, but he refused few dinner invitations afterward. He even turned water into wine at a wedding feast (John 2:1-11). Jesus frequently dined with tax collectors and Pharisees alike, using his conviviality as a means for teaching about the kingdom of God. Such activities would have scandalized even the most liberal of the Essenes.

Josephus related that the Essenes, unlike the other religious sects of the day, thought "that oil is a defilement; and if any of them be anointed without his own approbation, it is wiped off his body."[31] Jesus allowed himself to be anointed with costly oil before his crucifixion (Mark 14:3-9), commissioned his disciples to anoint with oil (Mark 6:13), and advised putting oil on one's head when fasting (Matthew 6:17).

Jesus also differed from his austere Jewish brothers in that he brought his message to all the people face-to-face. He was no monk who retreats, but a prophet who confronts. "For the Son of Man came *to seek and to save* what was lost" (Luke 19:10, emphasis added). This assignment required walking mile after dusty mile on the streets and roads of Palestine for about a three-year period. Jesus was a door-to-door preacher, not a behind-closed-doors recluse. He urged his followers to forsake all to follow him, yet they found themselves in the middle of everyday life as evangelists of the kingdom.

Jesus, the leader, did not divide his followers into strict hierarchical order, as was the order of Qumran. Nor did he require any probationary period for kingdom service. He drew disciples to himself by the sheer force of his messianic magnetism, and repelled those who would not comply. He cultivated disciples on a personal, noninstitutionalized basis. When the 12 disciples began to jockey for power, he said the greatest was he who was the servant of all (Matthew 23:11). Although it seems Jesus developed deeper relationships with some disciples than with others, there was no official ranking within his group. The Essenes, however, divided members into four classes: priests, Levites, lay members, and applicants.[32]

Unlike the Essenes, Jesus did not identify himself and his band of followers with the kingdom of light and give up on all others as children of darkness. Although Jesus did demand a decision concerning his identity and his kingdom—a decision that would put a person on one side of the eternal fence or the other—he did not write off all those not yet his disciples. He pursued people in the hope of their becoming his disciples, and he trained his disciples to do the same. Jesus moved toward the lost, not away from them, even lamenting over Jerusalem's rejection of his mission (Matthew 23:37). This is different in spirit from the approach of the Dead Sea documents, which taught that only the Essenes were saved, and that they were to remain separate from the unsaved. (The Essenes did seek some converts, but their identity was wrapped up in exclusivism.)

The Essenes were avid law-keepers and viewed the Pharisees as too lax on the law. They retreated into the wilderness to become immune from such lawlessness. Jesus never flouted the law of Moses, and affirmed its principles, yet he criticized a legalism that exalted the law over the Lawgiver and that replaced a heartfelt obedience to God with a mechanical legalism. Although we saw earlier that the Qumran community could emphasize the grace of God in salvation, their views on the law differed from Jesus' views in several ways.

The Dead Sea document called the Damascus Rule says, "No man shall assist a beast to give birth on the Sabbath day. And if it should fall into a cistern or a pit, he shall not lift it out on the Sabbath."[33] After declaring himself the Lord of the Sabbath, Jesus argued against the Pharisees' view of the Sabbath by asking, "Suppose one of you has only one sheep and it falls into a pit on the Sabbath; will you not lay hold of it and lift it out? How much more valuable is a human being than a sheep!" (Matthew 12:11,12, NRSV). We do not know if Jesus was speaking against the Essenes, but his argument does not square with their teaching. Neither would his revolutionary statement: "The Sabbath was made for humankind, and not humankind for the Sabbath" (Mark 2:27, NRSV), have won him favor with Essene audiences.

Jesus' views on ritual purity and impurity also put him in a different category than the Essenes. James Charlesworth speaks of the "Essenes' virtual paranoia about becoming unclean."[34] Especially ostracized were the lepers. The Temple Scroll says, "In every city you shall set aside areas for those stricken with leprosy, with plague and with scab, who shall not enter your cities and profane them."[35] Jesus *touched* lepers and made them whole (Matthew 8:2,3). He also deliberately stayed at the home of Simon the leper (Mark 14:3).

The Essenes looked forward to messianic redemption from God. Jesus claimed to be that redemption in the flesh (John 4:25,26). He fulfilled the law as the Son of God and announced the kingdom of God as coming in his own person. Christianity was built on this premise.

These fundamental differences between Jesus and the Essenes cannot be diluted by the similarities that can be found. The similarities should be seen as stemming not from the direct influence of the Essenes, but because of the common Jewish theological influence on both Jesus and the Essenes. F.F. Bruce explains the commonalities of Jesus and various Jewish groups without demoting Jesus' uniqueness:

> It is easy to go through the recorded teachings of Jesus and list parallels—some of them quite impressive—with what we find in the Qumran texts. . . . It is idle to feel alarm at

this, as though the originality of Jesus and the divine authority of Christianity were imperiled by such a recognition. For he accepted the same Biblical revelation as did the Qumran conventers and the rabbis in the mainstream of Jewish tradition, and it would be surprising if no affinity at all were found between their respective interpretations of that revelation, on which their respective teachings were based.[36]

It is not impossible that Jesus as a Jew of his day knew of, and in some cases may have been influenced by, the Essenes' teachings to the degree that he used some of their phrases or recognized good aspects of their lives.[37] However, this is conjecture because Jesus never mentioned the Essenes by name. Even if some influence is granted, this does not mean that Jesus was an Essene or that his theology was indebted to the Essenes. Speaking of the uniqueness of Jesus, Charlesworth says, "It is startling to discern how true it is that the genesis and genius of earliest Christianity, and the one reason it was distinguishable from Judaism, is found essentially in one life and one person."[38]

According to the classical secondary sources and the Dead Sea Scrolls, the Essenes were not the ancient New Agers as some think they were. Even if it could be established that they were forerunners of the New Age, the reliability of the New Testament picture of Jesus (see chapter 3) is such that Jesus cannot be fit into the mold of an Essene. Nevertheless, some writers continue to make this controversial case in interesting ways. To them we turn in the next chapter.

10

MORE DEAD SEA SCROLL INTRIGUE

IN THE LAST chapter we discovered that the historic Essenes were not New Agers and that Jesus was not an Essene. We built this case on the Dead Sea Scrolls themselves in relation to the New Testament. Nevertheless, other versions of the Essene Jesus theory are still heard in the marketplace of ideas. Should they cause us to question the reality of the Jesus we find in the New Testament?

Jesus Without Miracle

One Australian writer has recently caused something of a media sensation with her theories on Jesus and the Dead Sea Scrolls. Barbara Thiering offers a new and unorthodox view of Jesus' relationship to the Dead Sea Scrolls, which she claims should revolutionize our understanding of Christianity entirely. Rather than seeing Jesus as Essene-New Ager, Thiering argues that Jesus' life can be explained without appealing to the spiritual dimension at all. In this approach, she joins the ranks of the debunkers who explain away all the supernatural elements of Christianity such as the virgin birth, Jesus' miracles, and his resurrection. "Christianity does not stand or fall by these as literal events; they never were literal events,"[1] Thiering states. She adds spice to her story by claiming that Jesus married Mary Magdalene, fathered three children by her, was divorced, and married again.

Her bestselling book *Jesus and the Riddle of the Dead Sea Scrolls* (1992) is a popular work built mostly on material from two more scholarly books, both of which failed to win any approval in the scholarly community.[2] The book was produced in the wake of a sensational television documentary shown on Palm Sunday, 1990, on the Australian Broadcasting Network.[3] Going against the whole grain of scholarship on the Dead Sea Scrolls, Thiering claims that the scrolls' cryptic comments on the Teacher of Righteousness refer neither to a pre-Christian figure (as virtually all scholars believe) nor to Jesus (as some misguided speculators believe), but to John the Baptist. She further alleges that Jesus is to be identified with the scrolls' comments about "the wicked priest" who opposed the Teacher of Righteousness. The Essene community, she claims, split into two factions: one led by Jesus, the other by John the Baptist. On what basis can Thiering advance such audacious claims?

Thiering rightly recognizes that the community that produced the Dead Sea Scrolls interpreted the Old Testament in such a way as to view itself as the fulfillment of ancient prophecy. The Essenes claimed to have uncovered the secret meaning of the scriptures by deciphering their code. This method of interpretation, called *pesher* (Hebrew for "interpretation"), becomes Thiering's tool for dismantling the traditional understanding of the New Testament. She introduces the idea that the Qumran community recorded its history in code, and that this coded history is found in the Gospels. This permits Thiering to say that the miracle stories in the Gospels do not refer to miracles at all, but are coded statements about events in the Qumran community. The healing miracles of Jesus are really veiled accounts of Jesus promoting his followers to higher ranks. For instance:

> The two "miracles" of the feeding of five thousand and the feeding of the four thousand are not intended, *for the critical reader,* to show Jesus as an extravagant wonderworker who would rather perform miracles than go and buy bread. They are records of the first ordinations to the Christian ministry, in a highly memorable form.[4]

Most controversially, Thiering claims that Jesus was not crucified in Jerusalem but at Qumran, along with Simon Magus (see Acts 8) and Judas Iscariot. All three somehow failed to die on their crosses and were revived in their tombs, with Jesus receiving lifesaving medicinal assistance from Simon Magus. Thus, Jesus never rose from the dead as the divine Savior and Lord. He simply survived the crucifixion, and "it is probable that he died of old age in seclusion in Rome" after A.D. 64.[5] She dismisses the traditional New Testament evidence and quotes a third-century Gnostic source (*The Gospel of Philip*) that claims that Jesus did not die on the cross.[6] Christianity must give up its supernatural claims and adjust itself to Thiering's nonsupernatural explanations. The idea of the supernatural is for "babes in Christ" who cannot handle the hard facts.[7]

Does Thiering's daring reconstruction of Christian history give us any reason to abandon historic Christianity? New Testament scholar N.T. Wright notes that "the only scholar who takes Thiering's theory with any seriousness is Thiering herself."[8] There are many reasons for scholars to reject her.

First, Thiering's entire argument depends on an idiosyncratic dating of the scrolls themselves. We have argued that there is no good reason to date the scrolls as late as she does in order to allow them to refer to Jesus.[9] If this is true, then the scrolls could not be speaking of Jesus and John the Baptist at all, since they were not yet born. Wright comments that "this of itself would be enough, in fact, to bring the whole structure toppling down."[10]

Second, although Thiering correctly observes that the Qumran community used the *pesher* method to find itself referred to in certain Hebrew scriptures, this method was never used in writing the history of the community itself. As Wright notes, the *pesher* method "was a way of hooking in to the past, not of writing quite new works for the future."[11] This style of interpretation was "a way of saying 'we are the people spoken of by the prophets,' not 'we are the people who can set new crossword puzzles for others to solve.'"[12] If this code was employed to interpret the Gospels and Acts, we would expect to discover some ancient writings to back up this point. Thiering provides no such evidence. She simply asserts her *pesher* interpretations. Neither does she attempt to explain why this *pesher* understanding of the Gospels and Acts was supposedly lost.[13] Therefore, there is no reason to believe that the Gospels and Acts are written in some secret code language.

Third, Thiering's claim that Jesus had children rests on material from late and unreliable Gnostic documents and tortuous misinterpretations of New Testament passages. For instance, she interprets Acts 6:7, which says "The Word of God increased," to mean that Jesus' family grew larger.[14] Of course, the book of Acts is the history of the early church after the resurrection and ascension of Christ into heaven (Acts 1:1-11). Jesus' "family" increases as people accept him as Lord, not as he physically fathers children. When Luke writes that "the Word of God increased," he means that God's truth was received by more and more people, as is clear from the rest of the verse: "The number of disciples in Jerusalem increased rapidly, and a large number of priests became obedient to the faith." The idea of Jesus divorcing and remarrying is similarly unhistorical and illogical.[15]

Fourth, Thiering is not even consistent in applying her far-flung innovations. She abandons the *pesher* method in her account of Jesus' crucifixion and subsequent appearances. As Wright notes, "Granted her own method, this ought to have been 'code' for Jesus' demotion within the community and then his promotion to high office once more. Instead, she resorts to a laughably incredible retelling of the story."[16]

In chapter 8, I argued against the notion that Jesus survived the crucifixion and staged a resurrection. Thiering's theory does nothing to strengthen this farfetched notion.[17] Her quotation of Gnostic sources to verify Jesus' surviving the cross falls flat when we remember that they were written long after the Gospels themselves as reinterpretations of the original events (see chapter 6). As we will see in chapter 15, there are many solid reasons to believe that

Jesus physically rose from the dead and founded the Christian movement. Thiering's imaginative revision of Christian history may make for enchanting fiction, but its historical credibility is entirely lacking.

Although Thiering tries to render the Christian story more believable for skeptical moderns by dispensing with the miraculous, in so doing she cuts out the very heart of Christianity: the resurrected Christ (1 Corinthians 15:1-34). Moreover, her conjectures are far less believable than the Gospel accounts themselves (see chapter 3). Biblical scholar Luke Timothy Johnson does not exaggerate when he declares that "Thiering's 'history' is the purest poppycock, the product of fevered imagination rather than careful analysis. The way she works with the data defies every canon of sober historical research, and operates outside all the rules of textual analysis."[18]

Several books claim to reveal other information on the Essenes not normally recognized. While the basic historical reliability of the Dead Sea Scrolls and other material on the Essenes is generally not questioned, these exotic documents need closer inspections.

Szekely and *The Essene Gospel of Peace*

In her popular book *Going Within* (1989), Shirley MacLaine speaks of "Edmond Bordeaux Szekaly's [sic] translations from the original Hebrew and Aramaic texts" concerning the Essenes, and later says that "of course, Jesus was an Essene teacher and healer."[19] Although she does not mention it outright, MacLaine was probably influenced by

Szekely's edition of *The Essene Gospel of Peace,* purportedly a record of the life of Jesus as an Essene master,[20] which he claims has sold hundreds of thousands of copies over its long publication history. Fida Hassnain's revisionist book *A Search for the Historical Jesus* (1994) invokes Szekely as an authority in a chapter on Jesus and the Essenes.[21]

Szekely claims to have discovered an Aramaic manuscript buried in the secret archives of the Vatican library while doing research there in 1923–24. Two other manuscripts are said to duplicate this manuscript: one in Old Slavonic, said to be in the National Library of Vienna, and Hebrew fragments that had resided in the now-destroyed Benedictine Monastery in Cassino, Italy. Before scrutinizing the historical reliability of these documents, we need to understand the Jesus that Szekely finds in them.

The Essene Gospel of Peace, Szekely's supposed translation of this Aramaic manuscript, was first published in 1937, with second and third installments published in the 1970s. Jesus is portrayed as giving many long discourses having to do mainly with health concerns and the sacredness of the earth. He says:

> Your Mother is in you, and you in her. She bore you; she gives you life. It was she who gave you your body, and to her shall you one day give it back again. Happy are you when you come to know her and her kingdom; if you receive your Mother's angel and if you do her laws, I tell you truly, he who does these things shall never see disease. For the power of the Mother is above all. And it destroys Satan and his kingdom, and has rule over all your bodies and all living things.[22]

The "Earthly Mother" plays just as important, if not more vital a role in the Essene Jesus' theology as the "Heavenly Father." Jesus advises the needy to purify their bodies and receive the natural gifts of the Mother. Instead of healing miraculously with a word of command, as in the Gospels, Jesus leads the sick into natural cures:

> And many unclean and sick followed Jesus' words and sought the banks of the murmuring streams. They put off their clothing, they fasted, and they gave up their bodies to the angels of the air, of water, and sunshine. And the Earthly Mother's angels embraced them, possessing their bodies both inwards and outwards. And all of them saw all evils, sins and uncleanness depart in haste from them.[23]

The Essene Jesus teaches that God's law is not to be found in the Scriptures—which are only humanity's product—but in nature. The "living word" is found "in the grass, in the tree, in the river, in the mountain, in the birds of heaven, in the fishes of the sea; but seek it chiefly in yourselves."[24] Meat-eating is not an option for the Essene Jesus who preaches that everything beyond "the fruits of the trees, the grain and grasses of the field, the milk of the beasts and the honey of the bees" is "of Satan."[25]

The Essene Gospel of Peace: Book Two, published four decades after the first book, contains three pages called "Fragments from the *Essene Gospel of John*" that give a new gloss on Jesus' view of being born again (compare John 3). The Essene Jesus says that unless "a man be born of the Earthly Mother and the Heavenly Father, and walk with the Angels of the Day and the Night he cannot enter into the Eternal Kingdom."[26]

The theology of the texts is pantheistic, monistic, and earth-centered. The Essene Jesus is a cosmic naturopath, who waxes lyrical about the healing power of various angels of water, air, sun, and so on sent by the Earthly Mother. His idea of sin is not that of moral transgression, but physical mistreatment. Sin is flushed out by natural processes, not atoned for by the death of Jesus himself.

Szekely synthesizes the supposedly Essenian material in another book called *The Essene Jesus: A Revelation from the Dead Sea Scrolls*.[27] According to Szekely, all religions teach the same truths at the esoteric level, and the Essene Jesus is the esoteric master missed by the masses.[28] He claims that Jesus said he was "no longer a man but had become as God,"[29] and that Jesus saved mankind not by his death but by his life and teachings on cosmic and natural law,[30] or to put it better, "He did not save mankind, but showed mankind the path to salvation" because "each must save himself; no one else can save him."[31] This is not the Jesus of the New Testament.

Szekely's Lack of Evidence

The above should be sufficient to give the mystical flavor of Szekely's "Essene Jesus." Before examining the case for the documents, we should realize that both Szekely's version of the Essenes and his picture of Jesus are highly unorthodox. His mystical, nature-loving Essenes bear almost no resemblance to the Essenes of the Dead Sea Scrolls and the classical secondary sources. Szekely's Essenes have no awareness of sin and are more concerned with the Earthly Mother than with the Heavenly Father. ("Earthly Mother" is a designation never found in the writings of the historical Essenes.) Although the Essene Jesus uses biblical terminology and phraseology such as "Verily" and "Happy are they," and biblical passages are interspersed in the material, the theology is at odds with the New Testament. Jesus is presented as a nature-healer, not the Savior. Instead of eating the Passover lamb, he requires vegetarianism. He reveres the Earthly Mother more than his Heavenly Father (making him more of a bi-theist, instead of a monotheist). He never speaks of sin as an offense against a holy God, but as a physical imbalance. He is evolved highly enough to have become as God, but this is not his unique status. [32]

Clearly, the burden of proof is on Szekely to disprove not only the scholarly world's view of the Essenes, but also the historic Christian understanding of Jesus as the Christ. Can he rise to this challenge?

We run into trouble concerning the *integrity* of Szekely's texts. We know nothing of how they were supposedly transmitted over time. In fact, we have only his word on their existence. There is no external corroboration. He claims that one complete Aramaic manuscript of *The Essene Gospel of Peace* is lodged in the secret archives of the Vatican, and that he translated it during a stay there. [33] Translating a large ancient manuscript in a dead language is not as simple as Szekely makes it sound. Yet he says he "read" it and left shortly thereafter. He makes no mention of taking photographs. But as Beskow notes, "Not even today with sophisticated phototechnology, would it be possible to produce copies useful for a scholarly edition in such haste." [34] Neither does Szekely give any scholarly details concerning the nature of the manuscript, whether it was a scroll or a codex. Beskow notes that an official at the secret archives informed him that no such manuscript is housed there and that there is no record of Szekely's visit there.[35] He even documents a letter from the prefect of the secret archives to this effect.[36] Szekely claims he presented his finds at the University of Paris in 1925, but he says his thesis has been lost, and he does not mention the name of his advising professor.[37]

We are given precious little information on the supposed Old Slavonic manuscript, which Szekely says belongs to the National Library of Vienna. It is not even mentioned in his book dealing with the discovery of *The Essene Gospel of Peace*. Beskow notes that manuscripts in official libraries invariably have code numbers, and if Szekely had been working with this manuscript for 50 years, it would be a moral obligation to let others know where it can be found.[38] But he never did. Beskow also observes that it is not uncommon for the National Library of Vienna to receive inquiries about Szekely's material; but it is not to be found there.[39]

Szekely further claims that Hebrew fragments of the document were found in Mount Cassino, which has since been destroyed in World War II. Although Szekely published a Hebrew edition of *The Essene Gospel of Peace,* he did not translate it, annotate it, or explain how it was reconstructed from the original fragments—procedures required in scholarly circles to establish credibility.[40]

There is little evidence for the *veracity* of Szekely's supposed find. It fails to correspond to other known facts. It is contradicted repeatedly by other much better attested sources both from the Dead Sea Scrolls and the New Testament. Stylistically, *The Essene Gospel of Peace* does not read like ancient Jewish literature. It resembles Romantic impressions more than biblical narrative or poetry.[41]

Concerning *authenticity,* recent editions do not say who wrote *The Essene Gospel of Peace* (except that the author was an Essene). Szekely claims to have a fragment from "the *Essene Gospel of John,*"[42] which is little more than a rewriting of part of John with the addition of "the Earthly Mother" and other Szekelian trademarks. As for the *integrity* of the document, Szekely asserts his best texts supposedly date to the third century; but we have no way of verifying their *existence,* let alone their integrity. If these manuscripts actually existed as Szekely claimed, it seems unlikely that he would not have revealed them to the scholarly world, because their import would rival the Dead Sea Scrolls and the Nag Hammadi manuscripts. Yet he never did so.[43]

Many more criticisms could be leveled regarding inconsistencies in Szekely's writings, logical gaps, the general unreliability of his claims, and his predilection to inflate his achievements,[44] but we will conclude with Beskow:

> *The Gospel of Peace* is a sheer forgery, written entirely by Szekely himself. It is one of the strangest frauds we know of in the biblical field, as it has been carried through by stages during a whole lifetime and has been built into an entire body of research based on imagination only.[45]

Szekely's Essene Jesus is attractive to many, Shirley MacLaine among them, because the sting of the biblical Jesus is entirely lacking. The Essene Jesus provokes no controversy, makes no enemies, issues no ethical demands, and never divides the world into those who are for him and those who are against him. He is a mellow metaphysician and an organic physician who bears no cross, sheds no blood, and startles no disciples as the resurrected Lord. Instead he, fictitious though he may be, validates the message of the New Age.

An Essene Eyewitness to the Crucifixion?

Another obscure source claims that Jesus was an Essene who survived the crucifixion after being revived in the tomb. *The Crucifixion by an Eyewitness,* first published in English in 1907, is purportedly written by an Essene who witnessed the crucifixion of Christ and wrote of it seven years later. The document expresses some views similar to Barbara Thiering's: It claims that Christ was an Essene, and it extracts any supernatural element from the life of Christ. This work has been used extensively by the heretical Ahmadiyya sect of Islam to help substantiate their claim that Jesus did not die on the cross.[46] It is also cited uncritically in a chapter on the crucifixion in Fida Hassnain's *A Search for the Historical Jesus.*[47]

Despite its exotic appeal, *The Crucifixion by an Eyewitness* lacks any historical credibility. It claims to have been written originally in Latin six years after the crucifixion, when the Essenes of that time wrote in Hebrew or Aramaic. Not a single document from the Dead Sea Scrolls is written in Latin.[48] The book also speaks of the four Gospels as already written, when they did not yet exist only seven years after the crucifixion.[49] Unlike the New Testament documents, there are no ancient manuscripts of this text to verify its antiquity. Upon close analysis, biblical scholars Per Beskow and Edgar J. Goodspeed dismiss the work as a piece of fiction that expresses both the antisupernaturalism of the Enlightenment and the romantic tendency to recast Jesus as an initiate into a secret order. It was, in fact, largely plagiarized from a work of fiction called *Natural History of the Great Prophet of Nazareth*, published by K.H. Venturini (1800–02).[50] Again, wishful thinking about Jesus does not make for historical factuality.

A Buddhist Jesus Misrepresented by Qumran?

We find another slant on Jesus and the Essenes in *The Original Jesus: The Buddhist Sources of Christianity* (1995), which alleges that Jesus was a Buddhist whose teachings were eventually suppressed and distorted. The book is based on many of the unfounded assumptions criticized in chapters 7 and 8 concerning Jesus' purported trips to the East. The Essenes and the Dead Sea Scrolls, however, play a crucial role in these extravagant speculations.

Authors Gruber and Kersten claim that Jesus associated with the Qumran community after spending time with the Egyptian Buddhists.[51] The Qumran people, they claim, were not Essenes, but a secessionist group that corrupted the Essenes' Buddhist-like ideas. Jesus influenced the Qumran people with his Buddhist ideas, but failed to win them over completely to Buddhism. Instead they largely kept their non-Buddhist beliefs. Gruber and Kersten's conclusion is that "leading ideas that had been developed in Qumran circles thus ultimately gained entrance into the Gospels," with the result being that "the original Jesus's purely Buddhist views" were "increasingly pushed into the background."[52] They conclude that "the story of Jesus's mission must be regarded as one of the most splendid failures in the whole of history. As the transmitter of his message the original Jesus stands before us today as a loser."[53]

This reconstruction is couched in scholarly terms, but the theory is erroneous for many reasons. First, the idea that the Qumran community was separate from the Essenes is a questionable position and a minority view among scholars. Even if the Qumranists were not Essenes, Gruber and Kersten's conclusions about the Qumran influence on the New Testament are still very questionable, as chapter 9 has argued.

Second, what we know of the Essenes's doctrines (even if we exclude the scrolls and refer only to the classical secondary sources such as Josephus) does not square with Buddhist teachings at all. They believed in a personal God, the soul, sin, and a literal heaven and hell—beliefs all denied by the Buddhists. Any similarities between the groups are found in basic ethical teachings (such as the importance of love), which are shared by most religions. There is no evidence of Buddhist influence.

Third, there is no evidence that Jesus visited Buddhist communities in Egypt or anywhere else, as I argued in chapter 8. This is wishful thinking at best.

Fourth, as chapter 9 argued, the teachings and actions of John the Baptist and Jesus were significantly different from the practices of the Qumran people. Similarities between the two groups can be explained by their shared reverence for the Hebrew Scriptures, not by any direct influence—either positive or negative—from the Qumran community on the New Testament.

Fifth, the assertion that the Qumran group imposed its ideas on the Gospels does not harmonize with the nature of the Gospels themselves, which were written a short time after the life of Jesus by four separate authors who were eye-witnesses or who consulted eyewitnesses (John 21:24; Luke 1:1-4). It is extremely unlikely that Qumran's influence could have dominated the earliest Christian documents available to us. If the Qumran people did control the writing of the Gospels, why would they retain so many teachings that contradict their way of life, such as Jesus' more tolerant view of the Sabbath and other matters mentioned above? The idea fails to make any sense.

Sixth, the Qumran-Buddhist theory cannot explain the rapid expansion of Christianity in a hostile climate. How could an illegitimate synthesis of Buddhism and Qumran teachings concocted by misguided followers of Jesus have resulted in a successful movement based on the resurrection of Jesus himself—something Gruber and Kersten believe never happened to their wandering Buddhist sage?[54]

The authors of *The Original Jesus* paint the "original" Essenes and the "original" Jesus in a Buddhist light and vilify both the Dead Sea Scrolls and the New Testament as distortions of these foundational truths. Yet their revisionist theory whitewashes the facts more than it paints a historically accurate picture.

The upshot of this chapter and the previous one is that Jesus was not an Essene, and Essenes were not Buddhists or New Agers. Any hope of redefining the orthodox view of Jesus must come from other circles. The next two chapters explore the contribution that channeling makes to the new view of Jesus.

11

CHANNELS OF DECEPTION

"This is a course in miracles. It is a required course. Only the time you take it is voluntary." So begins the increasingly popular three-volume, 1200-page *A Course in Miracles*. The short introduction concludes with, "Nothing real can be threatened. Nothing unreal exists. Herein lies the peace of God."[1] Over 160,000 sets of the expensive *A Course in Miracles* have been sold since its publication in 1975.[2] The books list no author, but they claim to be transcribed from the voice of Jesus himself.[3]

This Jesus says, "There is nothing about me that you cannot attain."[4] And also: "*There is no death because the Son of God is like his Father. Nothing you can do can change Eternal Love. Forget your dreams of sin and guilt and come with me instead to share the resurrection of God's Son.*"[5] The *Course* further teaches that "it is impossible to kill God's Son; nor can his life in any way be changed by sin and evil, malice, fear, or death."[6] Therefore, "all your sins have been forgiven because they carried no effect at all."[7]

The leading evangelist for *A Course in Miracles* is Marianne Williamson, a charismatic minister to Hollywood stars who officiated at the wedding ceremony for Elizabeth Taylor and Larry Fortensky. Williamson's book *Return to Love* (1992) is a popular explanation of *A Course in Miracles* and has been promoted widely by Oprah Winfrey. Williamson speaks often of Christ, but not in biblical terms: "The concept of a divine, or 'Christ' mind, is the idea that, at our core, we are not just identical, but actually the same being. 'There is only one begotten Son' doesn't mean that someone else was it, and we're not. It means we're all it."[8] She understands Christ not as the central figure of the Gospels but as "the common thread of divine love that is the core and essence of every human mind."[9]

A Course in Miracles has had close to miraculous success in its short career, in no small measure because of its asserted authorship and its heavy use of biblical terminology. The book claims to cut through the illusions that enslave us and to reveal our true spiritual condition. Speaking of Jesus, it asks, "Is he the Christ? O yes, along with you."[10] Jesus became the Christ by seeing "the face of Christ in all his brothers" so that "he became identified with Christ, a man no longer, but one with God."[11]

Truth Beyond History?

In earlier chapters we have seen Jesus presented as the Gnostic revealer, the world traveler, and the Essene mystic. Many lay claim to these revisions of the orthodox picture of Jesus of Nazareth by appealing to certain historical documents. The Nag Hammadi library was unearthed, inspected, and consulted to derive the Gnostic Jesus. We found that this unbiblical Jesus did not exist. "The Life of Saint Issa: Best of the Sons of Men" was hailed by Notovitch in his *Unknown Life of Jesus Christ* as establishing Jesus' trips eastward. We found this life to be unknown because it was nonexistent. The Dead Sea Scrolls and other documents are said to reveal Jesus as a mystical Essene. This case also fails to survive thoughtful scrutiny. In analyzing each of these claims, we have applied various historical tests for the reliability of the documents in question.

Yet the New Age movement is pregnant with revelations about, and even from, Jesus or the Christ that are untethered any earthly record. *A Course in Miracles* cites no footnotes and speaks of no historical corroboration. These revelations allegedly issue from either disincarnate entities or from impersonal cosmic records. The messages may include historical events but are not derived from historical sources such as archaeology, manuscripts, or oral traditions. They are believed to have been intuited, received, transcribed, or channeled from higher levels of reality not normally accessible.

Channeling has recently become a centerpiece for spiritual interests, with hundreds of channelers (or channels) claiming secret contact with a host of paranormal teachers. These range from Ramtha, a 35,000-year-old warrior spirit hosted by J.Z. Knight; to Lazaris, a more mellow entity hosted by Jach Pursel; to Jesus or the Christ, hosted by assorted channelers. Although the interest in some individual channelers may come and go, channeling itself is a primary source for unorthodox views of Jesus. Channeling, otherwise known as mediumship or spiritism, is an ancient phenomenon that seems to come in waves of interest over the centuries. Channeling proponent Jon Klimo's concise definition of channeling is helpful:

> The process of receiving information from some level of reality other than the ordinary physical one and from beyond the self as we currently understand it. This includes messages from any mental source that falls outside one's own ordinary conscious or unconscious and is not anyone else incarnate on the physical plane of reality.[12]

Both the method of channeling and the kinds of entities channeled vary considerably. Some people claim that channeling is a kind of "voluntary possession" in which the entity takes complete control of the human. After the channeled message the channeler has no recollection of what his or her vocal cords were doing during this time. Others claim a more cooperative endeavor such as hearing a voice, seeing a vision, or being strongly impressed in some manner that does not swallow up the channeler's personality completely in the communication process.[13]

Many of the thousands of modern channelers make mention of Jesus at least in passing, hailing him as a great spiritual master of one sort or another. Yet the myriad messages converge on Jesus as an example of Christ consciousness, rather than as the unique Lord and Savior. Consequently, notions of human limitation, sin, death as the result of sin, and hell are rejected in favor of the self as intrinsically divine and unlimited.[14] For example, Ramtha says that "for two thousand years, we have been called *sinful creatures*. That stigma automatically takes away our ability to remind ourselves that we are great, or that we are equal with God or Christ or Buddha, or whomever."[15]

Rather than chronicle a welter of words about Jesus from the channelers, we will explain and assess in this chapter three channeled sources that center on Jesus and the Christ, namely, *A Course in Miracles, The Aquarian Gospel of Jesus the Christ,* and the Edgar Cayce readings. All of these sources highly esteem Jesus as the Christ and present themselves as essentially Christian. The claims of supposedly extraterrestrial messages will be investigated in the following chapter.

Jesus According to *A Course in Miracles*

We have already sampled a portion of *A Course in Miracles,* but we need a larger serving to understand its appealing elements. The human transcriber of the revelations was Helen Schucman who, after several visionary experiences, began to hear an inner voice in 1965 say, "This is a course in miracles. Please take notes." After many protests, Schucman, a Jewish atheist, began a seven-year process of recording what eventually became the three-volume set and the basis of a worldwide organization known as the Foundation for Inner Peace.[16] Although Schucman died in 1981, the teachings she received have skyrocketed in popularity since then.[17]

The *Course* teaches that we are all potentially Christs, that Jesus is not touched by evil, that he never died, that sin and guilt are unreal, and that there is no death. Despite these unbiblical assertions, the teaching repeatedly uses biblical terminology. Atonement, according to the *Course,* has nothing to do with any blood sacrifice for sin. It says, "The crucifixion did not establish the Atonement; the resurrection did."[18] The Jesus of the *Course* says that the idea of "taking away the sins of the world" means to show people their true, original innocence, and "innocence is wisdom because it is unaware of evil, and evil does not exist."[19] True perception sees that "sin does not exist."[20]

The perspective of the *Course* is that humans are imprisoned by the illusion of a separate ego that is distinct from God. We are not separate from God either by being created by God or because of sin against God. Sin, evil, guilt, and any separation from God are ultimately unreal, as is death itself: "There is no death, but there is belief in death."[21] Therefore, Jesus is not viewed as the Savior from sin's penalty or as one who defeated death by his own death on the cross. *Sacrificial* atonement is unnecessary for innocent beings. Humans suffer from ignorance of their true reality, not from any inherent moral problem. Christ is not to be worshiped; rather, "Christ waits for your acceptance of Him *as yourself.*"[22] This Jesus also says, "I have stressed that awe is not an appropriate reaction to me because of our inherent equality."[23]

It is not surprising, then, that the *Course* recommends that every person say to himself or herself, "My salvation comes from me. It cannot come from anywhere else."[24] Salvation has nothing to do with entering a literal heaven and escaping a literal hell. According to Marianne Williamson: "Love in your mind produces love in your life. This is the meaning of Heaven. Fear in your mind produces fear in your life. This is the meaning of hell."[25]

The "miracle" of *A Course in Miracles* is a shift in perception that sees all things as one and divine without sin, guilt, and death. It has nothing to do with a supernatural intervention in human affairs. Judith Skutch, cofounder and president of the Foundation for Inner Peace, sums this up: "By not seeing anyone else as guilty, and by extending love instead of fear, we can begin to recognize the truth about our real identity as a sinless Son of God."[26] Williamson puts it this way: "there is no guilt in anyone, because only love is real. . . . Actually, then, there is nothing to forgive."[27]

According to proponent Robert Perry, the *Course* is "intended not as a restatement, but as a purification, of traditional Christianity." This is "most easily seen in its use of Christian terminology . . . [which is] changed to reflect a purified and more universal perspective."[28] Skutch admits that the *Course* "combines a lot of Eastern themes and approaches them within a more familiar Western framework—the strongest of which is the nondualistic."[29] This means that "our only reality lies in spirit, with God as our source,"[30] and the physical world is not ultimately real.

Many of those associated with the *Course* seem to accept its teaching because they believe it to be compatible with biblical doctrine. However, a strong promoter of the *Course*, Kenneth Wapnick, commented that if the Bible were the literal truth, the *Course* would have to be viewed as inspired by demons.[31] He correctly saw an incompatibility.[32]

Others seem to embrace the *Course* because they view it as superior to a dead Christianity unable to meet people's needs. The benefit they derive from the *Course* is all the proof they require. Yet while the message of sinlessness, Christhood, and unconditional love seems appetizing, the experience of these realities demands hard work. "Salvation is nothing more than 'right-mindedness,'. . . which must be *achieved* before One-mindedness is restored."[33] "Salvation is your happiest *accomplishment*."[34]

One must unflinchingly deny all guilt in order to earn salvation from the illusion of guilt. Dean Halverson's analysis of the *Course* brings this into perspective:

> While it may be true that guiltlessness is unconditional, *manifesting guiltlessness* is the condition for overcoming the illusion of guilt. Thus living a guiltless life is the condition that must be met for that illusion to be banished and for salvation to be achieved.[35]

The experiential price for exchanging the biblical view of Jesus Christ's atoning death on behalf of sinful humanity for the *Course*'s "atonement" of remembering one's true innocence is the hard psychological labor of convincing oneself that sin, guilt, and death do not exist. The only thing left to feel guilty about is guilt itself. But one should not fret too much over an illusion, no matter how incorrigible that illusion may seem. It will give way . . . someday, they hope.

The *Course* has been viewed as a "purification" of Christianity, but it more resembles a reversal of every important aspect of Jesus' teaching found in the New Testament. Atonement is inverted to mean there is no need for reconciliation with a holy God through Jesus' death and resurrection. Sin is rejected as unreal. Harboring the illusion of guilt, sin, and death is the real problem. Any supposed separation from God is merely an illusion, a dream. Nevertheless, the illusion is universally compelling and demands the solution offered by the *Course*.

Dean Halverson contrasts the cleavage between the biblical view and the perspective of the *Course*:

> In the *Course*, salvation is earned through the perfect demonstration of our awareness of sinlessness and unity

with God. In the Bible, salvation is a gift that cannot be earned; it can only be received by trusting in the completed work of Jesus Christ.[36]

The ultimate reality for the *Course* is a God who is an impersonal oneness; final salvation means being absorbed into this abstraction in a realm beyond distinctions, words, and events.[37]

The worldview of the *Course* cannot provide a meaningful foundation for the love of which it speaks so often. This problem is glaring in Williamson's book *A Return to Love*, which speaks of God as an infinite continuum of love energy. "We are part of a vast sea of love, one indivisible divine mind," she claims.[38] This means that all is one; there is no difference between us and the universal energy. However, she also affirms that God cares for us,[39] that he has a will for our lives,[40] and that he guides us.[41] These qualities, however, are personal and relational; they presuppose that God is a person who is distinct from us and who chooses us as objects of his love. It makes no sense to speak of God's care, will, and direction if we are all part of the "one indivisible divine mind." Williamson cannot logically apply these personal attributes to a sea of divine energy from which we cannot separate ourselves. There is no divine love without the separation between the Lover and the loved one.[42]

Williamson attempts to mask this impersonal worldview with words stolen from the Christian view of God as a personal and loving Being distinct from his creation. Nevertheless, Williamson's ploy is what Christian apologist Francis Schaeffer called "semantic mysticism"—a deception whereby a faulty worldview is safeguarded from criticism by using appealing words that have no meaning within that worldview itself.[43] Calling the stench of a skunk "sweet aroma" does not make it so. Calling an impersonal force "loving" does not make it so.

Comparing the teaching of the *Course* with Jesus' words to the criminal on the cross beside him shows the vast gulf between it and Christianity. After the man confessed to Jesus that he was being punished justly, he cried out and said, "Jesus, remember me when you come into your kingdom" (Luke 23:42). Jesus replied, "I tell you the truth, today you will be with me in paradise" (Luke 23:43). Repentance and faith were required of the thief. His sin was real. His pain was real. His literal death would soon be real. Jesus' pain was more real than any ever experienced before or since. He, too, would truly die, only to rise again. But this thief, because he was redeemed by Jesus' sacrifice, would be with Jesus himself in a real paradise—not beyond distinctions, words, or events, but full of undiluted Life himself. *A Course in Miracles* cannot offer this kind of hope.

An Aquarian Gospel

"Then hear, you men of Israel, hear! Look not upon the flesh; it is not king. Look to the Christ within, who shall be formed in every one of you, as he is formed in me."[44] So speaks the Jesus of another channeled source that has become a New Age classic. First published in 1907, *The Aquarian Gospel of Jesus the Christ* has interested a score of seekers wanting a greater knowledge of Jesus than given in the Bible. The book has the appearance of a "fifth Gospel" in that it is divided into chapters and verses much like modern translations of the Bible.[45] The subject matter overlaps with the biblical accounts at certain places, but the document makes no claim on historical tradition. Although *The Aquarian Gospel* finds Jesus in India (as well as Greece and Egypt), it is unlike Notovitch's effort in that it does not appeal to any lost physical manuscript. Rather, it is purported to be a receipt of a heavenly revelation to one Levi H. Downing, who went by his first name only.

Although Levi is listed as the author, he is better understood as the receiver because the book is, according to the title page, "transcribed from the Akashic Records." Levi (1841-1911) had a Christian background, but as a boy he is said to have become sensitive to the "finer ethers and believed that in some manner they were sensitized plates on which sounds, even thoughts, were recorded."[46] He "entered into the deeper studies of etheric vibration" and after 40 years spent in meditation and study "found himself in that stage of spiritual consciousness that permitted him to enter the domain of superfine ethers and become familiar with their mysteries."[47]

These "ethers" are also known as the Akashic Records, which Levi says refers to "the Primary Substance" or "Universal Mind" in which everything that has ever happened is recorded. This spiritual substance is not relegated to any one part of the universe. It is everywhere present, but only accessible to those trained to pick up the higher frequencies.[48] Levi wrote *The Aquarian Gospel* "between the early morning hours of two and six—the absolutely quiet hours,"[49] thus becoming the channeler of the Akashic accounts.

Other sensitives, particularly those connected with Theosophy, have appealed to the Akashic Records for hidden wisdom about Jesus and the universe. Klimo describes it as a "nonphysical 'cosmic memory bank' of all that has occurred, which can be tapped by certain individuals, physical and nonphysical."[50]

The Aquarian Gospel differs from the *Course* in that it was supposedly received not from a personal spirit, but from an impersonal record. It also makes factual claims about the historical Jesus—something the *Course* finds no need to do, since it views matter as illusory anyway.

Who Is the Aquarian Jesus?

In the introduction to the book, Levi clearly spells out the relationship between Jesus of Nazareth and the Christ:

> Orthodox Christian ecclesiastics tell us that Jesus of Nazareth and the Christ were one; that the true name of this remarkable person was Jesus Christ. They tell us that this man of Galilee was the very eternal God clothed in flesh of man that men might see his glory. Of course this doctrine is wholly at variance with the teaching of Jesus himself and of his apostles.[51]

In order to anchor this rather bold assertion, Levi must place his purported revelation above the New Testament, which clearly teaches that "Jesus and the Christ were one." The Aquarian Jesus is less a Savior than a magus—a world traveler in search of religious wisdom and initiation into deeper mysteries.[52] His journeys take him to India, Tibet, Persia, Assyria, Greece, and Egypt. Levi's account of Jesus in India echoes Notovitch's in places, as when Jesus visits Leh, the capital of Ladahk. There Notovitch claims to have found "The Life of Saint Issa" at the Himis monastery. Yet the account differs from Notovitch's in several ways.

First, the Aquarian Jesus is much more Eastern than the Jewish-Christian-Buddhist mix of Notovitch. We find him clearly teaching reincarnation as the explanation for musical prodigies. He says, "In one short life they surely could not gain such a grace of voice, such knowledge of harmony and tone." Instead, he says, "These people are not young" because "ten thousand years ago these people mastered harmony" and "they have come again to learn still other lessons from the varied notes of manifests."[53]

Second, the Aquarian Jesus is not like Notovitch's teacher of wisdom, who became a martyr, but is instead an initiate into the esoteric mysteries. In Egypt, Jesus visits the temple in Heliopolis to be received as a pupil of Egyptian wisdom. He passes through six degrees of initiation—sincerity, justice, faith, philanthropy, heroism, and love divine—before entering the Chamber of the Dead. Here, clothed in purple, Jesus receives the seventh and highest degree from the hierophant who says:

> Brother, man, most excellent of men, in all the temple tests you have won out. Six times before the bar of right you have been judged; six times you have received the highest honours man can give; and now you stand prepared to take the last degree. Upon your brow I place this diadem, and in the Great Lodge of the heavens and earth you are THE CHRIST. This is your great Passover rite. You are a neophyte no more; but now a master mind.[54]

Third, the Aquarian Jesus, unlike Issa, performs miracles and is resurrected from the dead. He even appears to various people in India, Persia, Greece, Rome, and Egypt after the resurrection. Yet the resurrection appearances are much closer to spiritistic "materializations" than the New Testament accounts of Jesus' resurrected body.

The essential message of the Aquarian Jesus is the Christhood of all people. He says near the end of the book:

> You know that all my life was one great drama for the sons of men; a pattern for the sons of men. *I lived to show the possibilities of man.* What I have done all men can do, and what I am all men shall be.[55]

The possibilities of human beings are great, according to the Aquarian Jesus, because "all things are God; all things are one."[56] Although the Aquarian Gospel sometimes speaks of Jesus giving his life for humanity, the real message is that Jesus is a model of Christ consciousness, not the unique Lord and Savior. This Jesus says he will resurrect "just to prove the possibilities of man."[57] The resurrected Jesus addresses a royal feast in India and says, "You shall go to all the world and preach the gospel of the omnipotence of man."[58]

Because *The Aquarian Gospel* makes historical claims, despite its supposedly spiritual and nonhistorical origin, it can be checked for accuracy through outside sources. Much of the text repeats material found in the Gospels, either word for word or in altered form. Other material has no Gospel parallels, but some can be compared with general historical knowledge.

The account opens by affirming that "Herod Antipas was the ruler of Jerusalem" during the birth of Jesus.[59] This is close, since the ruler at that time was a Herod, but not close enough, because it was Herod *the Great.* Nonbiblical historical sources say Herod *Antipas,* Herod the Great's son, ruled after and not during the time of Jesus' birth. The Gospels tell us Herod Antipas put John the Baptist to death (Matthew 14:1-12) and tried Jesus (Luke 23:6-15).

The Aquarian Jesus is found studying in a temple in Lassa, Tibet, with one Meng-ste, "greatest sage of all the farther East."[60] This is reminiscent of Meng-tse (notice Levi's reversal of the fifth and sixth letters), sometimes known as Mencius, the Chinese sage. If this is Levi's reference, he is only off by 300 years, because Mencius died in 289 B.C.[61]

Jesus is said to have traveled from Tibet to Lahore.[62] This is interesting since the city is "not known in history until the seventh century A.D."[63] Another anachronism pops up when Jesus appears "fully materialized" to Magian priests in Persepolis.[64] This city was destroyed by Alexander the Great in 330 B.C. and never rebuilt.[65]

Although *The Aquarian Gospel* mixes in much biblical material (as well as material from the apocryphal *Gospel of James*),[66] it contradicts the New Testament record many times, especially concerning Jesus' supposed sojourns in the East. The theology from the Akashic Records is also at odds with the biblical records, which we have argued are reliable historical documents (see chapter 3). To give credence to this *Aquarian Gospel,* one must jettison the New Testament as untrue and overlook several blatant historical inaccuracies. However, there is no reason to do so.

The Sleeping Prophet's Jesus

Edgar Cayce (1877-1945), known as the "sleeping prophet," was one of the foremost mediums of the century. For over four decades he gave "readings" on medicine, lost civilizations, the future, and Jesus himself. These readings have gone public through many popular books. The Association for Research and Enlightenment (A.R.E.) continues to disseminate his materials widely.

As a child, Cayce experienced various visions and would enter a trance state to memorize his school lessons. In 1900, after an untreatable paralysis of the throat, a friend named Al Layne helped him reenter the trance state during which he said, "Yes, we can see the body." This indicated that other beings saw Cayce's body. The voice diagnosed the problem as bad circulation, and Cayce recovered after Layne suggested his body heal itself.[67] So began Cayce's psychic career.

Cayce's readings were given during this deep trance state and originally only concerned matters of personal health. He would amaze those who came to him with the effectiveness of the often-unorthodox prescriptions and recommendations given while he was unconscious. After 13 years of medical readings, someone asked Cayce questions of a more spiritual and philosophical nature. Cayce was initially shocked upon awaking to find that his readings were deviating considerably from what he himself had taught in Sunday school as biblical truth. Concerning his readings that taught reincarnation, he said:

> What the readings have been saying, is foreign to all I've believed and taught, and all I have taught others, all my life. If ever the Devil was going to play a trick on me, this would be it.[68]

Cayce, nevertheless, continued to entertain metaphysical questions in his trance readings, many of which concerned

Jesus. The answers reveal a Jesus unknown to the New Testament.

Reincarnation is the heart of Cayce's worldview. His readings repeatedly assert that Jesus had been incarnated many times before "becoming the Christ." When asked to list "the important incarnations of Jesus in the world's history," Cayce replied, "In the beginning as Amilus, as Adam, as Melchiezek [sic], as Zen, as Ur, as Asaph, as Jeshua—Joseph—(Joshua)—Jesus."[69] On another occasion, Cayce said 30 incarnations were required for Jesus to become the Christ.[70] Cayce also affirmed that Jesus first knew that he would be the Savior "when he fell, in Eden."[71]

Like *The Aquarian Gospel,* the Cayce readings also find Jesus heading eastward to India, Persia, and Egypt. In India, Jesus learned of "those cleansings of the body related to preparation for strength in the physical as well as the mental man."[72] In Persia, he learned of "the unison of forces as related to those teachings of that given by Zu and Ra."[73] Cayce agrees with *The Aquarian Gospel* in saying that Jesus visited the temple in "Hilleopolis [sic] for the period of attaining to the priesthood; in the taking of the examinations there."[74] Cayce differs from Levi in saying that Jesus did not study with Greek philosophers because he "never appealed to the worldly wise."[75] But the key point is that Jesus was an initiate who gradually attained a realization of inner Christhood.

When asked the significance and meaning of the words *Jesus* and *Christ,* Cayce replied:

Jesus is the man—the activity, the mind, the relationships that he bore with others. . . . He grew faint, He grew weak, and yet gained in strength which He had promised in becoming the Christ. . . . Ye are made strong in body, in mind, in soul and purpose, by that power in Christ. The power, then, is in the Christ. The pattern is in Jesus.[76]

Although some of the readings sound biblical, the overall context is that of souls gradually reaching perfection through a long series of reincarnations. According to Cayce, "Jesus who became the Christ" may serve as a spiritual boost for those on this journey, but Jesus is not the Savior who ensures eternal salvation for those who come to him by faith. Cayce says that the "whole gospel of Jesus Christ" is the great commandment to completely love the Lord and our neighbor as ourselves.[77] This is not the *gospel* at all but the demand of the *law*. According to the New Testament, no one can merit eternal life through the works of the law (Romans 3:10-18; Galatians 3:10-12),

Cayce saw all knowledge as residing within. Understanding the creation of souls to be emanations of God or "portions of [God] himself,"[78] he could agree with the statement, made by one of his questioners during a reading, that the Christ consciousness is "described as the awareness within each soul, imprinted in pattern on the mind and waiting to be awakened by the will, of the soul's oneness with God."[79] He also said, "All ye may know of God is within your own self."[80]

The Cayce material, although filled with biblical language, offers a Jesus foreign to the New Testament. Instead of Jesus being the Christ from birth, he became the Christ through successive incarnations and occultic initiation. Instead of being the first and last incarnation of the eternal Word (John 1:1,2,18), Cayce's Jesus evolves upward through 30 earthly advents. Cayce's Jesus omits or misinterprets the many biblical references to an eternal judgment immediately after death (Matthew 25:31-46; Hebrews 9:27).

Cayce was thought to have filled in the gaps of the biblical record by consulting the Akashic Records with his subconscious mind.[81] Hugh Lynn Cayce believed that such records "may be the source of a much truer and more complete understanding of the life of Jesus than the Bible alone."[82] But how should we assess portraits of Jesus withdrawn from the Akashic Records or bestowed from personal channeled entities? To this we now turn.

12

CHANNELING
ON TRIAL

As WE FOUND in the last chapter, assorted channelers and mediums regale us with reports about Jesus—or even from him. These accounts agree in denying the biblical picture of Jesus, but they do not harmonize with each other in all particulars. Even other sources claim to have acquired new information about Jesus from extraterrestrial experts. Can any of these sources be trusted?

Even in New Age circles, the credibility of channeled reports is an issue. A book satirizing much of the New Age movement (but written by a someone sympathetic to New Age interests) presents an advertisement for TCT Ultima II, "a cosmic aptitude test" for evaluating channeled entities:

> Just because they're dead doesn't mean they're smart. Channeling, like anything else, requires that the consumer be discriminating and careful. THERE ARE IDIOT ENTITIES, spooks from the other side who are tired of talking to each other. They're desperate to gab, and will do so whether or not their information is valuable or even true.[1]

A reported spiritual source does not ensure truth. It is interesting to note that while both Levi Downing and Edgar Cayce supposedly consulted the same cosmic memory bank, they withdrew contradictory facts about Jesus. Levi says Jesus went to Greece. Cayce says he did not. They cannot both be right. If we compare the material on Christ received through channeling, many discrepancies are evident. Of course, this in itself doesn't necessarily discredit all channeling, but it makes one wonder how to choose between competing claims, especially if one is unable to consult the cosmic Source oneself. The deeper question involves the reliability of these channeled messages—whether from Ramtha, Jesus, the Akashic Records, the Collective Unconscious, the Universal Mind, or whatever.

A clue to evaluating this material is given by a follower of Rudolf Steiner (1861–1925), the German occultist and philosopher, who also tapped into the Akashic Records for an unorthodox view of Jesus. In describing Steiner's rather complex views of Jesus, Stewart Easton explains the ultimate basis of Steiner's school of thought, which is called Anthroposophy:

> We must emphasize once again that Anthroposophy must rest its case on the truth of Steiner's revelations from the Akasha Chronicle and that his teachings represent in no sense an interpretation of the Bible.[2]

Easton is more honest about Steiner's orientation than many others who consult channeled material. The acceptance of Steiner's basically Gnostic views must rest on the reliability of the supposed supernatural source, not on historical considerations.[3]

By staking this claim, Steiner and his followers must deny all contrary historical evidence with a wave of the Akashic wand. We found *The Aquarian Gospel* wanting in historical aptitude at several embarrassing points, which should lead us to question its general veracity. The Cayce readings prophesied many events which failed to materialize, such as a shifting of the earth's axis in 1936 and the rise of Atlantis in 1968 or 1969.[4] (The very existence of Atlantis as a lost continent is highly suspect historically as well.[5])

This puts channeled materials in a precarious position logically. If channelers make claims regarding recorded history, the channeled assertions can be verified or falsified. But if the claims are independent of historical authorization or disqualification, we are left with a brute trust that the spiritual realm is dispensing truth. For instance, *A Course in Miracles* redefines the person and work of Jesus completely without giving any historical detail about Jesus of Nazareth. Why should we believe this claim—supposedly from Jesus himself—and reject the abundant historical evidence for the reliability of the New Testament?

If one casts off any normal historical testing of channeled pronouncements, there is the further difficulty of accurately identifying the channeled source and testing its veracity. How can the accuracy of the channeled messages be gauged, especially when they contradict each other? We are left without any anchor.

Extraterrestrial Messages About Jeses?

Other people claim to supplement or challenge the biblical understanding of Christ on the basis of messages channeled from extraterrestrial entities. According to some thinkers, extraterrestrials are highly evolved beings who communicate with selected earthlings in order to help us avoid destroying ourselves and lead us to a higher state of spiritual development. Many of these messages warn of an impending apocalypse should their advice not be heeded. There are many variations on this theme, but it is common for these transmissions to speak of Jesus in highly unorthodox terms.

Brag Steiger, who has written extensively on the occult and extraterrestrials, reinterprets the second coming of Christ according to teachings supposedly received from extraterrestrials. He offers that the second coming "refers to the entire race as it experiences its second opportunity to express Christ or cosmic consciousness on the Earth, as before the fall of man into physical matter."[6] Ken Carey writes in *The Starseed Transmissions* (1983) that extraterrestial intelligences informed him that "Christ is the single unified being whose consciousness all share."[7] Many other writers reinforce the basic notion that the Christian view of Christ is wrong and that we must adjust our understanding according to extraterrestrial theology.

These alleged revelations from extraterrestials (or the "space brothers," as they are sometimes called), echo much of the ancient Gnostic message: Humans are enmeshed in matter, but they can liberate the Christ energy within them. The reports render the second coming democratic since they take it to be a raising of the collective consciousness to the divine level. These communiqués claim that an awakened humanity is the second coming, thus denying the literal second coming of Jesus Christ at the end of the age (Acts 1:9-11). They invert the biblical message by claiming that humans will ascend to the divine consciousness rather than Jesus descending to earth at the second coming to eternally separate the saved from the lost (Matthew 25:46).

The Urantia Book: Another Extraterrestrial Angle

I recently received a call from a young radio announcer for a Christian station, who wanted information on a Christian view of UFOs and life on other planets. After a few minutes the man reluctantly confessed that his interest was based on *The Urantia Book* (1955), a revelation that supposedly supplements, corrects, and updates the Bible. Despite his Christian background, this man had doubts that Jesus had to die in order to atone for our sin and turn away the wrath of God. I spoke with him for almost an hour, earnestly arguing for the biblical teachings on Christ's sacrificial death. Near the end of the conversation, his troubled soul seemed to come back to the Bible. What is this *Urantia Book,* and how could it lead someone away from the teachings of Scripture?

The Urantia Book is a mammoth tome that credits no human author. Rather, it claims to have been assembled by extraterrestrial entities or "Revelators"—with ostentatious names such as Perfector of Wisdom, Number, Divine Counselor, and One Without Name—and channeled by one unidentified human. This 2097-page volume gives a fantastically convoluted and obscure account of cosmology, anthropology, theology, and history. One of its more objectionable anthropological claims is that the black (or "indigo") race was the most inferior, although it claims that these people "have exactly the same standing before the celestial power as any other earthly race."[8] Martin Gardner observes that this "is exactly what southerners in the United States, including their minister, used to say about the African American slaves."[9]

One of Urantia's devotees, Peter Bergman of the comedy group "The Firesign Theatre," said of it: "It's been this major influence on my life since 1972. . . . I find it to be the most complete expression and explanation of our relationship to God and where we're going and where we come from."[10] Under the leadership of the Urantia Foundation in Chicago, the book has gone through 11 printings in the United States, with translations in Spanish and Finnish appearing in 1993. Work is being done on Russian and Dutch editions, and there are plans for other languages as well.[11] My search of the Internet yielded several home pages dedicated to spreading the gospel according to *The Urantia Book.* Some of the materials offered were aimed specifically at reaching Christians.

The Urantia Book supplies us with over 774 pages on the life of Christ—much of it concerning his supposed world travels during the "lost years of Jesus" not addressed in the New Testament (see chapters 7 and 8). It tips the extraterrestrial hat to the biblical Gospels, deeming them influential but inadequate, partial, and imperfect records.[12] From the alien angle, the New Testament was corrupted by the influence of Paul, Peter, and others, and only dimly reflects the real teachings of Jesus.[13]

To attempt to fathom *The Urantia Book,* one must descend into a dark and foreboding labyrinth of quirky terminology, pseudoscientific pronouncements, and revisionist ideas about Jesus. In barest outline, the book informs us that God is a "Trinity of Trinities," that humans are unfallen beings who have a divine spark within them (called a "Thought Adjuster"), that they can become fused with God through evolutionary development, and that Jesus' death on the cross did not atone for our sin against God.

In its attack on the idea that Jesus sacrificed his life for ours, *The Urantia Book* states that "the Father in Paradise did not decree, demand, or require the death of his Son as it was carried out on earth."[14] And: "Jesus did not die . . . to atone for the racial guilt of man nor to provide some sort of effective approach to an otherwise offended and forgiving God."[15] Furthermore, the resurrection of Jesus was, it claims, spiritual and not physical, since his body instantáneously decomposed in the tomb.[16] It says: "This material or physical body was not a part of the resurrected personality."[17] These notions contradict the preaching of the apostle Peter, who proclaimed shortly after Pentecost:

> Jesus of Nazareth, a man attested to you by God with deeds of power, wonders, and signs that God did through him among you, as you yourselves know—this man, handed over to you according to the definite plan and foreknowledge of God, you crucified and killed by the hands of those outside the law. But God raised him up, having freed him from death, because it was impossible for him to be held in its power (Acts 2:22-24, NRSV).

Peter was only echoing his Master, who solemnly asserted that "the Son of Man did not come to be served, but to serve, and to give his life as a ransom for many" (Matthew 20:28). The most ancient and reliable records available clearly teach that Jesus offered his life on a bloody cross in obedience to the will of his Father for the redemption of humanity. The first Christians, such as Peter, witnessed and declared that Christ rose from the dead in a perfected physical body, not as a disembodied spirit (Luke 24:36-43; 1 Corinthians 15:1-34; see also chapter 15). However, *The Urantia Book*, with its Gnostic devaluation of the body, would have us abandon the biblical record and embrace its own unhistorical and idiosyncratic perspective, which it claims is a revelation superior to the Bible or any other source.

The Urantia Book declares that "the gospel of the kingdom is: the fact of the fatherhood of God, coupled with the resulting truth of the sonship-brotherhood of man."[18] The true gospel as taught by Paul is that: "Christ died for our sins according to the Scriptures, that he was buried, that he was raised on the third day according to the Scriptures" and that he appeared to many witnesses (1 Corinthians 15:3-4). These apostolic words bear the marks of historical facticity and personal integrity. For these truths Paul lived and died. On these truths Christianity was born, survived through bloody adversity, and makes its unique appeal today. For all its physical bulk and metaphysical murk, *The Urantia Book* is devoid of this transformative authority and power.

Christianity, the Supernatural, and History

Some have called the Bible a channeled document, but it is significant to realize that, unlike channeled documents, it claims to be both supernaturally inspired by a personal God and rooted in space-time factuality. The apostle Paul was initially converted through a supernatural vision of the risen Christ. Yet Paul also speaks of historical details of Jesus' life that completely agree with those given in the Gospels, and he cites Christian hymns and creeds which predate his own letters. And although historic Christianity views Paul's writings and the rest of the Bible as inspired by God, this does not make the authors wholly passive, nor does it mean that they received their material through divine dictation. The sovereign Spirit so directed their lives as to guide them into the truth—truth that was rooted in history.[19] The God-inspired visions recorded in Scripture always relate in some way to historical events and do not contradict previously revealed truth, even if the manner in which God relates to his people develops over time from the Old Testament to the New Testament.

The apostle John gives an important warning for weeding out false spirits:

> Dear friends, do not believe every spirit, but test the spirits to see whether they are from God, because many false prophets have gone out into the world. This is how you can recognize the Spirit of God: Every spirit that acknowledges that Jesus Christ has come in the flesh is from God, but every spirit that does not acknowledge Jesus is not from God. This is the spirit of the antichrist, which you have heard is coming and even now is already in the world (1 John 4:1-3).

John targets any spiritual manifestation that denies the historical Incarnation. Earlier in his letter he says:

> Who is the liar? It is the man who denies that Jesus is the Christ. Such a man is the antichrist—he denies the Father and the Son. No one who denies the Son has the

Father; whoever acknowledges the Son has the Father also (1 John 2:22-23).

John teaches that lying spirits populate the supernatural world and that discernment is demanded. The touchstone for discernment is the doctrine of the Incarnation. Jesus is, and forever remains, *the* Christ; one cannot be rightly related to God without confessing this fundamental fact. In his Gospel, John records Jesus as saying, "I am the way and the truth and the life. No one comes to the Father except through me" (John 14:6). For John, no one can lay hold of God without recognizing Jesus as the unique and final revelation of God.

Jesus himself repeatedly warned that false teachers, false prophets, and false Christs would lead many astray (Matthew 7:15-23; 24:23-25). He said to judge them by their fruit. Any spiritual communication that denies the essential message of the gospel, according to the biblical Jesus, bears bad fruit. It is both false and dangerous.

Jesus also clearly believed in the reality of the devil and the demonic realm as a source of confusion, deception, and spiritual derangement. He says more about the devil than does anyone else in the entire Bible. He called the devil a liar and the father of lies (John 8:44), and taught his disciples to pray, "deliver us from the evil one" (Matthew 6:13). One cannot read the Gospels without feeling the conflict between Jesus and the devil. The demonic cannot be edited from the Gospels without doing historical, theological, and literary violence to the texts. Michael Green notes that:

> We have to give full weight to the tremendous moral earnestness of his teaching and living in this whole area of the satanic. His teaching is bound up with it. His exorcisms

are bound up with it. His death is bound up with it. At all
the major points in his life and ministry the conflict with
Satan is of cardinal importance.[20]

We see in the Gospels that demons can exert tremendous control over individuals, causing illnesses and insanity,
as well as giving supernatural strength and causing other
manifestations. We also find in the book of Acts that a slave
girl had a spirit that was used profitably in fortune-telling
for her masters. The apostle Paul recognized this and cast
out the spirit "in the name of Jesus Christ" (Acts 16:16-18).

These verses and other biblical texts recognize that the
devil and demons can impart certain information to those
they influence. They can deceive and counterfeit the truth.
Yet even a supernatural demonstration, such as a prediction
of the future, is no guarantee of the veracity of the message
(Deuteronomy 13:1-4). Paul, who was converted through a
heavenly vision, warned his readers to test the spirits, irrespective of their apparent grandeur. In defending the
gospel message to the Galatian church, he said:

> I am astonished that you are so quickly deserting the one
> who called you by the grace of Christ and are turning to a
> different gospel—which is really no gospel at all. Evidently
> some people are throwing you into confusion and are try-
> ing to pervert the gospel of Christ. But even if we or an
> angel from heaven should preach a gospel other than the
> one we preached to you, let him be eternally condemned!
> (Galatians 1:6-8)

Not only do the channeled messages invariably and in-
sistently deny the biblical Jesus, they also repeat a message

first offered in the Garden of Eden when the serpent seductively and successfully offered a temptation to the unfallen couple, saying that disobedience to God was not harmful because they would not die but would be as God themselves (Genesis 3:1-5). The serpentine seduction succeeded, resulting in spiritual death. The entities and impersonal cosmic sources that are influencing the New Age are simply replaying the same old serpentine message from Genesis chapter 3, which is the essence of sin and rebellion against God. The apostle John identifies the serpent as the devil himself (Revelation 12:9).

Supposed revelations from supposed extraterrestrials may have nothing to do with physical beings from other planets. Whether or not there is intelligent life on other planets, the nature of many "close encounters" with UFOs and the messages received from extraterrestrials may indicate a demonic origin. David Spangler, a leading New Age thinker and channeler, received a message from an entity named John who said that "some of the space Beings . . . are actually very high heirarchial Beings and Masters [spirit guides] who adopt planetary garb simply because there are some people who will accept their teachings only in this way. . . . There has been a good deal of beneficent masquerading going on."[21] If Satan can masquerade as an angel of light, and his ministers appear as servants of righteousness (2 Corinthians 11:14,15), extraterrestrial posing by demons cannot be ruled out.[22]

What or who, then, is behind this "Jesus of the spirits"? The evidence points to an overarching spiritual liar armed with ingenuity and craftiness, commanding a number of subordinates, and able to recycle one basic message in an appealing number of versions—but unable to speak the saving truth. John Ankerberg and John Weldon ask, "Isn't it interesting that [Satan's] spirits have not deviated from their master's first lies? If channeled beings are not demons, the consistency and persistence of these themes throughout the history of spiritistic revelations is nothing short of amazing."[23]

Every channeled word may not be breathed by Satan or other seductive spirits, but as with the fortune-telling slave girl in Acts, we should note that spirits can directly intervene with their messages. Sometimes other, less supernatural explanations can account for the phenomenon of channeling.

Conscious fraud should not be ruled out in many cases, especially when histrionics and recycled spiritual verbiage seem to exhaust the "mystery" of the channeling event. One ex-follower of Ramtha reported in *Newsweek* that J.Z. Knight could impersonate Ramtha without going into her characteristic, traumatically induced trance. She said; "We thought she did a better job of doing Ramtha than Ramtha. In fact, we couldn't tell the difference."[24] One linguist also subjected the accents of several channeled entities (who claimed previous embodiment on earth) to linguistic analysis and found them to be pseudo-accents, better understood as the channeler's invention than an entity's intervention.[25] Martin Gardner has argued at length that the existence of *The Urantia Book* is best explained by covert human authorship.[26]

Other manifestations of channeling may be explained by some kind of dissociative mental disorder resulting in a secondary personality.[27] Some instances of channeling may be explained in terms of conscious or unconscious self-hypnotism. In these kinds of cases, it is more likely that the channelers are expressing a nonsupernatural message spun out of their own subjective disorders rather than delivering a direct demonic message.[28]

One option not open to those who believe the biblical Jesus is that the channeled interpretations of Jesus are trustworthy. The channeled material may agree with the biblical record on generalities or inessentials, but on essentials such as the unique and unrepeatable Incarnation, the sacrificial death of Jesus, his bodily resurrection, and his cosmic rule, they take the predictable esoteric detours. A clear case is a statement channeled from "the Christ" who says of his embodiment as Jesus: "It was not my intention to be deified and to be called a savior of mankind. My role was that of way-shower."[29] In light of this kind of misrepresentation, Brooks Alexander's comments are not too harsh:

> The practice of spiritism is terminal because it represents the ultimate confusion of values. It trades humanity's privilege of intimacy with God for sheer fascination with a liar who secretly hates all that is human and all that humans hold dear.[30]

Yet some will still protest that material derived from channeled and other New Age sources "works" where traditional Christianity does not. We have suggested that the "good news" of the channeled sources may not be as good as it initially sounds because of the effort involved in attaining the ever-elusive Christ consciousness. But more needs to be said about this. So we will next consider the fundamental message of the biblical Jesus in relation to challenges made by those who reject the biblical understanding of him. What did Jesus really do? What did he say? What does it matter?

13

JESUS: WHAT HE DID, WHAT HE SAID

CARICATURE IS AN awful enemy of truth, and not a few misunderstandings of the Jesus of the New Testament stem from partial pictures, selective perceptions, out-of-focus impressions, casual hearsay and, in some cases, outright distortions. The same can be said of the founders of other religions. Proponents of the world's religions may even unintentionally slander their own avowed prophets, holy men and women, and revelators when intellectual sloppiness and religious ignorance replace the desire for accuracy and clarity.

In light of this propensity for confusion, a careful look at the central character of the New Testament is in order for those both within and without Christian circles. We should be bloodhounds after the fundamental facts and follow the scent until the prize is found.

Each Gospel offers a distinctive portrait of Jesus, rich with hard historicity. We hear of rulers, cities, provinces, rivers, mountains, festivals, and the like. Although not a detail is uttered about, let's say, Jesus' specific taste in food or his choice of sandals, all the Gospels enter into great detail regarding the last few days of his earthly life leading to his crucifixion. This is no biographical accident, because the cross is central to the story. Remove it or minimize it, and all else crumbles. The Gospels could thus be called focused biographies or distilled reports. Their purpose is not to relate exhaustive detail but to offer essential events. Historical facts are never secondary to or removed from the theological message; rather, they fit as smoothly as a soft hand into a silk glove.

This chapter will present the Jesus of the Gospels and of the rest of the New Testament, with a concern for the interpretations offered by those who are open to new approaches. Our focus is on the circumstances of Jesus' early life and something of his teaching on God, humanity, and ethics. In the next chapter we will highlight Jesus' claims and credentials as the Christ.

The Virgin Birth of Jesus

Historians tell us that Jesus entered a world of religious confusion and social unrest. The "promised land" of Palestine had become occupied territory, a satellite of the vast Roman Empire. Although the centralized power of Rome provided the *Pax Romana* (the Peace of Rome) over much of the known world, the Jews of the first century were subjugated to Caesar. How could God allow it? they questioned. And how could he provide deliverance? God's deliverance would begin in a virgin's womb.

Matthew tells us that "Jesus was born in Bethlehem in Judea, during the time of King Herod" (Matthew 2:1), setting him squarely in history. In appearance he looked no different than any other Jewish newborn boy, yet his origin was unique. Matthew (1:18-25) and Luke (1:26-38) write that Jesus was conceived without the intervention of a human father when the Holy Spirit overshadowed his mother, Mary. So it is proper to speak of both a virginal conception as well as a virgin birth.

Jesus' unique origin brackets him off from all other humans.[1] Although fully human, Jesus did not inherit a sinful human nature. His human genesis is not primarily natural but supernatural; not initiated by humanity, but by God. From conception, Jesus is a one-of-a-kind gift from God. Mary becomes the vessel for divine service and cries out in praise, "My soul praises the Lord and my spirit rejoices in God my Savior, for he has been mindful of the humble state of his servant" (Luke 1:46-48).

Yet this supernatural conception is not an artificial invasion by an alien intruder bent on violating everything natural. While unique, it is not "out of place," for earth is the ordained theater of redemption. The Incarnation is "in character" for God. C.S. Lewis observed, "If God creates a miraculous spermatozoan in the body of a virgin, it does not proceed to break any laws. The laws at once take over. Nature is ready. Pregnancy follows, according to all the normal laws, and nine months later a child is born."[2]

The virginal conception signifies and contributes to the uniqueness of Jesus; it should not be confused with stories of divine-human propagation as found in other religions. One Rosicrucian writer, H. Spencer Lewis, accepts the virgin birth not only of Jesus but of all avatars (special periodic manifestations of God), of which Jesus is only one.[3] This is both totally foreign to the biblical account, which views the event as singly significant, and at odds with accounts in other religious contexts.[4] John Frame notes that:

> There is no clear parallel to the notion of a virgin *birth* in pagan literature, only of births resulting from intercourse between God and a woman (of which there is no suggestion in Matthew and Luke), resulting in a being half-divine, half-human (which is far different from biblical Christology).[5]

Frame further notes that none of the pagan stories fix the event in specific history as do Matthew and Luke.[6]

In a recent book called *The Original Jesus* (1995), Elmar Gruber and Holger Kersten argue that the virgin birth story was borrowed from a Buddhist source, which claims the same kind of origin for Buddha.[7] This view overlooks the significant differences between the Buddhist story and the Gospel accounts. The preincarnate Buddha comes in the form of a white elephant who enters the side of his mother. Parrinder notes that it "was not a virgin birth, since she was married, and in this story . . . it is celestial influence rather than a divine seed that enters her."[8]

Most importantly, Gruber and Kersten ignore the fact that the Buddhist sources are dated long after the writing of Luke and Matthew. The story comes from a fifth-century text and is absent from the most ancient Pali canon of Buddhism.[9] If any borrowing is going on, it is more likely that Buddhists selectively borrowed from the Gospels than vice versa.[10] Furthermore, the oldest accounts of the life of Buddha do not depict him as a supernatural figure, but as an illuminated sage. As discussed in chapter 3, the New

Testament documents were all written in the mid-to-later portions of first century. According to J. Gresham Machen, the virgin-birth material "can easily be shown to have been in existence only a few decades from the time when Jesus lived."[11] This is a far cry from the late emergence of the Buddhist stories.

Christhood in a Manger

The events surrounding Jesus' infancy also point toward his distinctiveness, even in his very name.

Joseph is told in a dream by an angel not to be afraid to take Mary as his wife because "what is conceived in her is from the Holy Spirit. She will give birth to a son, and you are to give him the name Jesus, because he will save his people from their sins" (Matthew 1:20,21). *Jesus* is a transliteration of the Hebrew *Joshua*, which means "Jehovah is salvation" or "Jehovah is Savior." The name recognized the saving power of God alone to rescue his people and was common for a Jewish man at the time.[12] His name does not commemorate a work done by another but explains his unrivaled identity.

Another angelic messenger met shepherds tending their flocks near the birthplace of Jesus. As the glory of the Lord shone around the angel, they were terrified, but the angel replied, "Do not be afraid. I bring you good news of great joy that will be for all the people. *Today* in the town of David a Savior has been born to you; he is Christ the Lord" (Luke 2:10,11, emphasis added; cf. Matthew 1:18).

The word *Christ* here is not a proper name, as is *Jesus*, but a title (although "Jesus Christ" later became a shortened way to say "Jesus, the Christ"). The title *Christ* refers to being "anointed" by God, and is used in the ancient Greek translation of the Old Testament (the Septuagint) to refer to God's favor on those especially equipped by God, such as the priest anointed with holy oil (particularly the high priest), the Old Testament prophets and, on occasion, a king of Israel.[13] But Jesus does not become the Christ at a given point in his life. He is the Christ from birth—and even from conception. Not only that, "he is Christ *the Lord*." None of the priests, prophets, or kings of the Old Testament are called "the Lord." Thus did the wise men (Magi) come from the East, not to instruct the Christ but to worship him "who has been *born king* of the Jews" (Matthew 2:2, emphasis added).

This understanding sets the Christ of the New Testament against various views that see Jesus as a man who realized his Christhood later in life through initiation (baptism, meditative techniques, or other methods), just as we, too, can attain our Christhood. As the *Metaphysical Bible Dictionary* (used in Unity) puts it, "Each of us has within him the Christ, just as Jesus had, and we must look within to recognize and realize our sonship, our divine origin and birth, even as he did."[14] According to the New Testament, he alone is virgin-born; he alone saves people from sin; he alone is *the* Christ.

It is not enough simply to explain the significance of the words *Jesus* and *Christ*. We need to examine his short but stunning life, because it is here most dramatically that we discover his character and power.

Besides the infancy narratives and few other items, the Gospels do not give us detailed descriptions of Jesus' childhood and early manhood, but from the context there is every reason to assume that he matured, as any Jewish boy would, by receiving religious instruction in the family, attending services and festivals, and learning the trade of his father—namely, carpentry (see Mark 6:3). Luke summarizes the time between Jesus' circumcision (at eight days) and age 12 by saying, "And the child grew and became strong; he was filled with wisdom, and the grace of God was upon him" (Luke 2:40).

Jesus showed a precocious interest in theology. During the feast of Passover, the 12-year-old Jesus spent a good deal of time in the temple courts talking with the religious leaders. When Jesus was confronted by his parents concerning his behavior, he responded, "Why were you searching for me? . . . Didn't you know I had to be in my Father's house?" (Luke 2:49). What the Gospel writers see as Jesus' special and unique relationship with the Father was conspicuous even in his childhood.

The Gospel of Luke then sums up the rest of Jesus' youth and early manhood with one sentence: "And Jesus grew in wisdom and in stature, and in favor with God and man" (Luke 2:52).

Jesus in the Public Eye

The lion's share of the Gospel accounts track Jesus' public ministry, crucifixion, and resurrection. Despite the fact that any summary of the ministry of Jesus will be inadequate, we will accent several aspects of his character and teaching.

Before Jesus preached his first sermon or healed his first disabled person, his cousin John the Baptist was electrifying the country around the Jordan, preaching a baptism of repentance for the forgiveness of sins (Matthew 3:2). His call to repentance was not an abstract appeal to moral uplift; he was the forerunner of Jesus, of whom he said, "He is the one who comes after me, the thongs of whose sandals I am not worthy to untie" (John 1:27). Some thought John the Baptist might be the Christ, but when they asked him who he was, John replied plainly, "I am not the Christ" (John 1:20). John did not assert his own Christhood (either actual or potential), but deferred to Jesus as the Christ.

Jesus came to be baptized by John, not to repent of sins but to identify with John and the people (Matthew 3:14,15). After Jesus was baptized, as he was praying, "Heaven was opened and the Holy Spirit descended on him in bodily form like a dove. And a voice came from heaven: 'You are my Son, whom I love; with you I am well pleased'" (Luke 3:21,22). Although his baptism identified Jesus with the people, it also isolated him from the rest because the Holy Spirit and God the Father ratified him as "the Son" with a special mission.

There is no indication that Jesus received, attained, or discovered Christhood at this point, as Gnostics and others have suggested. His baptism, rather, specially equipped him to begin his divine mission. Luke tells us that "Jesus himself was about thirty years old when he began his ministry" (Luke 3:23).

Just as Herod schemed to destroy the infant Jesus, so did the devil want a shot at the mature Jesus face-to-face. Being filled with the Holy Spirit, Jesus was led into the wilderness to be tempted by the devil. After Jesus fasted, the devil presented four temptations, each of which was intended to destroy Jesus' trust in the Father and to derail his divine mission. Each time Jesus countered the devil's distortion of Scripture and logic with the true revelation of God in the Old Testament by quoting from the book of Deuteronomy. After the devil's fourth unsuccessful attempt, Jesus dispatched him and returned from the wilderness to begin gathering disciples (see Matthew 4:1-11; Luke 4:1-13).

It is clear from these passages that Jesus is presented as engaging in person-to-person spiritual combat. The devil is not depicted as merely the "dark side" or "shadow" of the human psyche (as with Carl Jung)[15] or a mythological personification of cosmic powers (as with Joseph Campbell).[16] Rather, he is an existing, intelligent being, the enemy of Jesus who tempts by twisting the meaning of the Bible itself. Yet Jesus resists his wiles, thus proving himself impervious to corruption, even under the most intensely intimidating circumstances imaginable. He is a man of integrity and power. But the final showdown with the devil was yet to come.

Jesus and His Kingdom

The claims and credentials of Jesus cannot be adequately addressed apart from his teaching on the kingdom of God, which forms the structure and provides the dynamics for his entire ministry. When Jesus began to preach, he proclaimed, "Repent, for the kingdom of heaven is near" (Matthew 4:17).

Jesus took elements of the traditional Jewish understanding of the kingdom of God and transformed them through his radical teaching and actions. He proclaimed the dynamic reign and rule of God as actively involved in his life and work. He said, "If I drive out demons by the

Spirit of God, then the kingdom of God has come upon you" (Matthew 12:28). It would not be inaccurate to say that Jesus preached the advent of a new age wherein God breaks into human history in unprecedented ways. The kingdom is inaugurated in the person of the King himself, Jesus. As F.F. Bruce notes:

> In Origen's great word, Jesus was the *autobasileia*, the kingdom in person; for the principles of the kingdom of God could not have been more completely embodied than in him who said to his Father, "not my will, but thine be done," and accepted the cross in that spirit.[17]

Jesus came as the very expression of the kingdom, "teaching in their synagogues, preaching the good news of the kingdom, and healing every disease and sickness among the people" (Matthew 4:23). As his ministry unfolds in the Gospels, his claims and credentials become clear.

Jesus was hailed as a master teacher. After the Sermon on the Mount, Matthew records that "the crowds were amazed at his teaching, because he taught as one who had authority" (Matthew 7:28,29). Although always on the theological hot seat, he was never burned by any questioner and often turned the tables on his questioners, exposing their dishonesty. But what exactly did Jesus teach?

Jesus' View of God

Jesus taught his disciples to pray in this manner: "Our Father in heaven, hallowed be your name, your kingdom come, your will be done on earth as it is in heaven" (Matthew 6:9,10). Jesus viewed God as a personal being, able to be personally addressed in prayer; the kingdom is administered by the King who *hears*. God, as a personal being, is fatherly. In teaching on prayer, Jesus said that the Father *sees* what one prays in secret and *knows* what we need even before we ask (Matthew 6:6-8). God will *forgive* us if we forgive others (Matthew 6:14) and *reward* those who fast in humility according to his will (Matthew 6:16-18).

From these teachings we learn that God is properly referred to as "Father," that he administers his kingdom, that he hears us, sees us, knows what we need, will forgive us and reward us. This kind of language cannot possibly refer to the impersonal energy, force, or principle so often emphasized in some circles. God is a personal being. Jesus speaks of the fellowship he had with God the Father "before the creation of the world" (John 17:24; cf. Mark 13:19). This indicates that Jesus' relationship was with a Person, and that God is prior to and distinct from the created universe. Jesus did not teach that everything was part of a divine unity.

Jesus said to pray that God's name be "hallowed," or revered as holy. He addressed God in prayer as "Holy Father" (John 17:11). He likewise taught that the heavenly Father is "perfect" (Matthew 5:48), and "God is spirit, and his worshipers must worship in spirit and in truth" (John 4:24). We discover that God is holy, not in an unqualified, nebulous sense of "the sacred," but as ultimate moral and spiritual perfection.

Jesus' View of Humanity

Jesus believed that humans are God's creatures. In dealing with the issue of divorce, he affirmed that "at the beginning of creation God 'made them male and female' " (Mark 10:6).

Jesus exalts humans above the animal world, assuring his listeners that they are "more valuable" than the birds of the air (Matthew 6:26). Furthermore, Jesus considers humans as spiritual beings with much to gain and much to lose in the spiritual realm: "What good will it be for a man if he gains the whole world, yet forfeits his soul? Or what can a man give in exchange for his soul?" (Matthew 16:26).

But is the soul divine? Jean Houston, popular New Age seminar leader and author, claims that Jesus taught that "God indwells every person. . . . [and] that the indwelling God, expressed as God-Son, Logos, Christ, or Chalice of Life, is the unique expression within us of the universal parent-being."[18] But consider Jesus' words to some of the Jews of his day who thought their national heritage assured them of a right standing before God:

> If God were your Father, you would love me, for I came from God and now am here. I have not come on my own; but he sent me. Why is my language not clear to you? Because you are unable to hear what I say. You belong to your father, the devil, and you want to carry out your father's desire (John 8:42-44).

Jesus refutes Houston. Because of their opposition to Jesus' teaching, some people are, ethically speaking, offspring of the devil (although all are created by God). Despite Jesus' high view of humanity, he never suggested we are ultimately one with God. Nor does he appeal to the Hindu doctrine of maya, which accepts only the appearance of finite, creaturely existence and affirms that the *only* reality is divine.

Yet several of Jesus' teachings are used by New Age interpreters to support the idea of the divinity of the soul.

First, Jesus' statement that "the kingdom of God is within you" (Luke 17:21) is often taken to teach that God is within each of us. But a glance at the context of Jesus' words brings this into question.

Jesus was addressing his religious opposition, the Pharisees, who had asked him when the kingdom of God would come. The nature of humanity was not at issue, but the timing of the manifestation of the kingdom. Jesus said, "The kingdom of God does not come visibly, nor will people say, 'Here it is,' or 'There it is,' because the kingdom of God is within you" (Luke 17:20,21). Jesus then turned to his disciples and discussed the events leading up to his second coming (verses 22-37). He is not addressing the nature of the soul.

It is unlikely that Jesus would ignore the heart of the Pharisees' statement on the timing of the kingdom and shift the subject to the nature of the soul. It is even more unlikely that he would tell the Pharisees, who opposed his teachings, that they were divine and then shift the subject back to the timing of the kingdom when talking to his disciples.

What did Jesus mean? Many scholars argue that the Greek word sometimes translated "within" is better translated "among" or "in your midst."[19] The New International Version lists "among" as an alternative reading. Understood in this light, Jesus was saying that the reign and rule of God is in the present; it is not something only to appear in the future. The kingdom was being expressed that very moment in Jesus' every thought, word, and deed.

Even if the verse is best rendered as "the kingdom of God is *within* you," this is not identical with saying "*God* is within you." Just as there is a simple difference between an earthly king and his kingdom, so is there a clear distinction between the kingdom of God and the God who is the King. Jesus is not teaching that God is within all of us.

Another statement of Jesus encourages some people to think he affirmed the deity of all people. Jesus' question "Is it not written in your Law, 'I have said you are gods'?" (John 10:34) is often used to support the New Age belief in the divine essence of humanity. John White asserts this:

> The Christian tradition, rightly understood, seeks to have us all become Jesuses, one in Christ. . . . Jesus himself pointed out that this is what the Judaic tradition, which he fulfilled, is all about when he said, "Is it not written in your Law, 'I said you are gods'?" (John 10:34).[20]

But is this what Jesus was talking about when he spoke these words?

During the Jewish Feast of Dedication, Jesus was in the temple. Some Jews asked him, "How long will you keep us in suspense? If you are the Christ, tell us plainly" (John 10:24). Jesus then asserted that he had already told them because his miracles speak for him. He then spoke of the greatness of the Father and affirmed, "I and the Father are one" (John 10:30).[21]

His audience then picked up stones to stone him, and Jesus asked them for which miracle they wished to stone him. They then answered that their anger was "for blasphemy, because you, a mere man, claim to be God" (John 10:33). Jesus then said:

> Is it not written in your Law, "I have said you are gods"? If he called them "gods," to whom the word of God came— and the Scripture cannot be broken—what about the one

whom the Father set apart as his very own and sent into the world? Why then do you accuse me of blasphemy because I said, "I am God's Son"? Do not believe me unless I do what my Father does. But if I do it, even though you do not believe me, believe the miracles, that you may learn and understand that the Father is in me, and I in the Father (John 10:34-38).

The issue at hand in this passage was Jesus' claim "I and the Father are one"—not a common claim in Jesus' day. His statement addressed the fact of his own uniqueness, not the essential divinity of all people. Our focus, though, will be primarily on Jesus' meaning of the phrase "you are gods."

First, Jesus quoted from Psalm 82, which begins, "God presides in the great assembly; he gives judgment among the 'gods'" (verse 1). God then upbraids these "gods" for not defending the cause of "the weak and fatherless" and not maintaining "the rights of the poor and oppressed" (verse 3). These "gods" know "nothing, they understand nothing. They walk about in darkness" (verse 5). In verse 6, God declares, "I said, 'You are "gods"; you are all sons of the Most High.'" Yet verse 7 announces, "But you will die like mere men; you will fall like every other *ruler*" (emphasis added).

It is clear that the "gods" are not divine beings in the theological sense of being supreme beings. The Hebrew word used for "gods" is *elohim*, which is sometimes used to refer to *humans* who, in certain limited respects, function in a divine capacity.[22] In this case the "gods" are "rulers" (verse 6) who have a God-given authority to govern justly—an authority they have failed to exercise. Therefore, they "will die like mere men" (verse 7). The word for "gods" (*elohim*) is not *Yahweh*, which is the personal name uniquely reserved for God.

When Jesus adds that "the Scripture cannot be broken" (John 10:35), he endorses the abiding truth of the Hebrew Scriptures as a whole and Psalm 82 in particular.[23] None of these Scriptures teaches the deity of the self. Jesus certainly recognized that the passage does not teach the divinity of all people. The text does not say that all people are "gods," but only the rulers in question. Secondly, the one true God judges these rulers ("gods") because of their injustice. Jesus also indicated that he was not referring to the rulers as divine in their own right when he said, "If he called them 'gods' *to whom the word of God came . . .*" (verse 35; emphasis added). These "gods" received and rejected the word of the true God.

Jesus was arguing from the lesser to the greater: If these inferior rulers can rightly be called "gods," how much more can Jesus, a truly righteous ruler sent from God and authenticated by his miracles, legitimately claim to be "one with the Father." Jesus has not reduced himself to being one member in a club of many gods. He is a righteous ruler and a true king (John 18:37).

When Jesus finished speaking, the crowd again tried to seize him. They understood him to have only amplified his earlier statement about being one with the Father. Now they were all the more belligerent to halt the "blasphemy." The issue at hand was not the divinity of all people, but Jesus' claim to be uniquely divine.[24]

It is also common in New Age circles to hear that Jesus taught that we are divine because he said that we would do "greater works" than he himself did. Commenting on this verse, John White says, "That is the human potential—the potential for growth into godhood."[25]

Jesus is here talking to his disciples shortly before the crucifixion. When asked concerning "the way," Jesus explained, "I am the way and the truth and the life. No one comes to the Father except through me" (John 14:6). When asked about the Father, Jesus said, "I am in the Father" and that "the Father is in me" (John 14:10). He then said "anyone who has faith in me will do what I have been doing. He will do even greater things than these, because I am going to the Father. And I will do whatever you ask in my name, so that the Son may bring glory to the Father" (John 14:12,13).

Whatever "things" Jesus had in mind—and we need not determine that here—they come from Jesus himself who alone is "the way and the truth and the life" (John 14:6).[26] The source of the power is not the divine self, as some claim. The works are derived from God and are to bring glory to the Father through the Son, not to the self.

Jesus' View of Sin

For Jesus, the soul is a perilous possession that can be forfeited because the heart is evil. Jesus presupposes this idea in the Sermon on the Mount and uses it for a premise of his argument: "If you, then, though *you* are evil, know how to give good gifts to your children, how much more will your Father in heaven give good gifts to those who ask him?" (Matthew 7:11; emphasis added). In a long and painful passage, Jesus zeros in on the inner engines of uncleanness:

> It is what comes out of a person that defiles, for it is from within, from the human heart, that evil intentions come:

> fornication, theft, murder, adultery, avarice, wickedness, deceit, licentiousness, envy, slander, pride, folly. All these evil things come from within, and they defile a person (Mark 7:20-23, NRSV).

Jesus lists multiple items of infamy residing in the human heart. For the Jewish mind, the heart was the core and center of one's being and stood for a person's "entire mental and moral activity, both the rational and the emotional elements. In other words the heart was used figuratively for the hidden springs of the personal life."[27] If the heart is corrupt, the self is not divine.

Jean Houston refers to sin as "unskilled behavior" that can be overcome through sacred rituals that enact the reality of the Christ within us all.[28] Many other New Age writers speak of this "unskilled behavior" as simply ignorance of the greatness within. The biblical Jesus moves in another moral world. It is psychologically taxing, to say the least, to imagine him calling theft, murder, adultery, greed, and so on "unskilled behavior," tantamount to a beginner's disappointing first round on the golf course. Many people, in fact, become quite skilled at these behaviors.

For Jesus, the issue of sin has eternal consequences. While "unskilled behavior" is nothing more than mere ignorance correctable through knowledge and practice, "evil" is something else entirely and a subject often on Jesus' lips. When Jesus was accused of casting out demons by demonic power, he responded:

> The good person brings good things out of a good treasure, and the evil person brings evil things out of an evil

treasure. I tell you, on the day of judgment you will have to give an account for every careless word you utter; for by your words you will be justified, and by your words you will be condemned (Matthew 12:35-37 NRSV; compare John 5:28,29).

For Jesus, sin is not simply an occasional mistake, but a deeply rooted disposition to disobey God. It is a condition of the heart, not an occasional flare-up of the will. Jesus warned, "I tell you the truth, everyone who sins is a slave to sin" (John 8:34). Jesus informed the most scrupulously religious leaders of his day that "not one of you keeps the [moral] law" (John 7:19).

The Ethics of Jesus

A discussion of Jesus' views on humanity and sin leads naturally into his view of ethics because, in Jesus' mind, sin is the violation of God's principles for life. When asked what was the "greatest commandment in the law," Jesus replied:

"Love the Lord your God with all your heart and with all your soul and with all your mind." This is the first and greatest commandment. And the second is like it: "Love your neighbor as yourself." All the Law and the Prophets hang on these two commandments (Matthew 22:37-40).

Jesus' ethical teachings are uncompromisingly elevated. Cutting through the religious formalism and hypocrisy of his day, Jesus went to the root of God's commands, revealing their deepest meaning. Not only should we not externally murder, we should not internally assassinate another through anger and defamation. Jesus warned, "Anyone who says, 'You fool!' will be in danger of the ·fire of hell" (Matthew 5:22). Not only should we not externally commit adultery, but "anyone who looks at a woman lustfully has already committed adultery with her in his heart" (Matthew 5:28). So serious are these ethical concerns that Jesus admonished:

> If your right eye causes you to sin, gouge it out and throw it away. It is better for you to lose one part of your body than for your whole body to be thrown into hell. And if your right hand causes you to sin, cut it off and throw it away. It is better for you to lose one part of your body than for your whole body to go into hell (Matthew 5:29,30).

These words put Jesus at variance with Joseph Campbell. Campbell interprets Jesus' teaching, "Do not judge, or you too will be judged" (Matthew 7:1), to mean that you should "put yourself back in the position of Paradise before you thought in terms of good and evil."[29] Campbell fails to notice that Jesus was not prohibiting all ethical discernment, as if such dualities dissipate when one is enlightened. Far from dismissing good and evil as moral categories, Jesus was warning of hypocrisy. He went on to say of those who don't consider their own sin before looking at another's, "You hypocrite, first take the plank out of your own eye, and then you will see clearly to remove the speck from your brother's eye" (Matthew 7:5, emphasis added). Specks and logs need to be removed, not ignored, in a world spoiled by sin (see also John 7:24). Campbell, believing he is agreeing with Jesus, continues, "One of the great challenges of life is to say 'yea' to that person or act or that condition which in your mind is the most abominable."[30] Jesus flatly rejected such amoralism; it has nothing to do with his message.

If Jesus had believed that people had the moral strength to achieve perfect obedience to these standards, he never would have said, "For I have not come to call the righteous, but sinners" (Matthew 9:13), or "For the Son of Man came to seek and to save what was lost" (Luke 19:10). When Jesus was pressed by a large crowd, "he had compassion on them, because they were like sheep without a shepherd. So he began teaching them many things" (Mark 6:34). The lost need a leader. Sinners need a Savior. Jesus believed he was that man. So strongly did he affirm this that he proclaimed that to disbelieve in him was sinful and disastrous.

In his farewell address to his disciples before the crucifixion, Jesus said that the Holy Spirit would come after he had returned to the Father and that the Spirit would "convict the world of guilt . . . because men do not believe in me" (John 16:8,9). So distressed was Jesus over the sin of his own people who would not accept him, he cried out, "O Jerusalem, Jerusalem, you who kill the prophets and stone those sent to you, how often I have longed to gather your children together, as a hen gathers her chicks under her wings, but you were not willing" (Matthew 23:37).

We have seen something of Jesus' early life and his teachings on God, humanity, and ethics. He does not fit the New Age mold, for he taught that God is personal, not impersonal; humans are creatures and not divine; sin is a reality; and that he, not the self, is the true focus of salvation.

Just why would Jesus expect anyone to see him as the one and only Christ that ever was, is, or will be? Can he back up his statement, "I am the way and the truth and the life" (John 14:6)? If Jesus inaugurated the kingdom of God, what does this involve, and what are his qualifications to be its herald? We take this up in the next chapter.

14

JESUS THE CHRIST:
HIS CLAIMS,
HIS CREDENTIALS

IN JESUS' LIFE and teaching, we find a stirring and stunning figure. He is *Jesus*—the one who saves others from sin. He is *the Christ* from birth—the uniquely anointed one of God—and he is appointed for a special mission "to seek and to save what was lost" (Luke 19:10). He spoke of the kingdom of God, or a new age, beginning with himself as King. He taught with authority, and his teachings do not harmonize with the new spirituality.

The Gospels tell us that Jesus' claims and actions set off shock waves 2000 years ago, and the Richter scale is still registering the responses. John White joins Ralph Waldo Emerson in lamenting that the religion *of* Jesus has become a religion *about* Jesus: "The religion *about* Jesus puts him on a pedestal, regards him as a parental Big Daddy in the Sky and childishly petitions him to be responsible for us."[1] The religion *of* Jesus "calls every human being to [attain] the same state of cosmic unity and wholeness which Jesus himself demonstrated."[2]

A careful look at the primary documents of Christianity is required in order to address adequately the controversy over Jesus' question: "Who do you say I am?" (Matthew 16:15). As we found in chapter 3, the New Testament should be received as worthy of close attention. In light of this, must we choose a "religion of Jesus" and reject a "religion about Jesus"? The answer hinges on Jesus' claims and credentials. We will further explore the New Testament in the hope of finding a satisfying answer.

The Gospels present a truly human Jesus, not a ghostly figure who only appeared to be flesh and blood. Jesus spoke of his own body (Mark 14:8), head (Luke 7:44-46), hands, feet, flesh, and bones (Luke 24:39), and blood (Matthew 26:28). He also displayed distinctly human feelings and qualities: He was moved by pity (Mark 1:41) and compassion (Mark 8:2). He was distressed (Mark 7:34; Luke 22:5; 8:24,25), angry (Mark 3:5), annoyed (Mark 10:14), surprised (Mark 6:6), disappointed (Mark 8:17; 9:19), hungry (Mark 11:12). He asked questions revealing his ignorance of some things (Mark 6:38; 8:29; 9:21; 10:18).[3]

Although he was born of a virgin, Jesus was a true human being. Yet after seeing Jesus calm a savage storm by simply "rebuk[ing] the winds and the waves," his disciples "were amazed and asked, 'What kind of man is this?'" (Matthew 8:27). This remains our question.

Jesus: Miracle Worker

All four Gospels relate that Jesus was hailed not only as a great teacher, but also as a worker of miracles, a man of power. His miracles single him out as a master of his circumstances and accredit him with a unique authority. These miracles were always centered on establishing his teaching, demonstrating his compassion, and demonstrating the kingdom of God. Before Jesus calmed the storm, he said to the disciples, "You of little faith, why are you so afraid?" (Matthew 8:26), thus challenging them to grow in their faith in him. Having calmed the storm, he proved that he was a proper object of their faith. None of Jesus' miracles were reckless or ostentatious demonstrations of cosmic clout. He even refused to perform miracles on command for those demanding a sign (Luke 11:16-28; Matthew 12:38-45).

Scholars have often noted that the miracle accounts in the Gospels differ markedly from other miracle stories in the ancient world. A.E. Harvey, for example, commented on the propriety and realism of Jesus' miracles in relation to other ancient literature:

> In general, one can say that the miracle stories in the Gospels are unlike anything else in ancient literature. . . . They do not exaggerate the miracle or add sensational details. . . . To a degree that is rare in the writings of antiquity, we can say, to use a modern phrase, that they tell the story straight.[4]

Nevertheless, Gospel accounts of Jesus' ministry explode with supernatural manifestations. Calming the sea (Mark 6:50,51), multiplying food for hungry crowds (Matthew 15:32-38; 14:15-21), changing water into wine (John 2:11)—all these mighty acts demonstrate his power over nature.[5] Jesus is a man of power.

Jesus was also an extraordinary healer. The Gospels overflow with cases of Jesus healing diverse physical infirmities—leprosy, dropsy, paralysis, fever, blindness, deafness, muteness, issues of blood—and all manner of human ills.

Although some healing may be psychosomatically explained, Jesus healed not only functional problems (in which the organism is intact, but dysfunctional) but deep organic maladies involving physical degeneration. For instance, he said to a man with a shriveled hand, "Stretch out your hand." The man obeyed, and his hand was completely restored (Matthew 12:13).

Jesus' healing power struck even at a distance. He was once addressed by a Roman military officer who spoke of his servant who was paralyzed and suffering terribly. Jesus immediately offered to heal the servant. The officer responded that he did not deserve to have Jesus come under his roof, but if Jesus would just say the word, his servant would be healed. Jesus, astonished at his great faith, said, " 'Go! It will be done just as you believed it would.' And his servant was healed at that very hour" (Matthew 8:5-13).[6]

The receiving of Jesus' miraculous potency was often related to a person's faith in him, and it was never a matter of making a withdrawal from the same impersonal cosmic bank account that Jesus used. Jesus, in harmony with the Father and the Spirit, was the source of healing. His credentials in this were unrivaled.

Although Jesus' enemies granted his ability to heal, they explained the power as coming from the devil, not God. But the character of Jesus gave no indication of demonic possession. Instead, he demonstrated his power by exorcising a host of demons in order to set captives free.

He proclaimed that his whole mission would be one of deliverance (Luke 4:18,19).

Jesus once encountered a demonized man who fell on his knees before him crying, "What do you want with me, Jesus, Son of the Most High God? Swear to God that you won't torture me!" When Jesus asked him his name, he replied, "My name is Legion . . . for we are many." Jesus then cast out the demons, and they entered a herd of pigs, causing them to drown. Even a legion of demons was no match for Jesus. The once-possessed man, who was "sitting there, dressed and in his right mind," then begged Jesus to let him go with him. But Jesus responded, "Go home to your family and tell them how much the Lord has done for you, and how he has had mercy on you" (Mark 5:1-19). Jesus' power—the power of the Lord—is released in mercy.

Jesus' most spectacular displays of authority involved reversing the universal decay that besets all earthly life. He raised the dead to life. The Gospels record three such cases, the most dramatic being the raising of Lazarus. When Jesus heard of Lazarus's illness, he said, "This sickness will not end in death. No, it is for God's glory so that God's Son may be glorified through it" (John 11:4). Jesus then mysteriously waited several days before reaching Lazarus. Upon arriving, he found that Lazarus had expired four days earlier. After comforting his sisters, Jesus asked them where Lazarus was buried. He was deeply moved and wept with them:

> Then Jesus looked up and said, "Father . . . I knew that you always hear me, but I said this for the benefit of the people standing here, that they may believe that you sent me." When he had said this, Jesus called in a loud voice,

"Lazarus, come out!" The dead man came out, his hands and feet wrapped with strips of linen, and a cloth around his face (John 11:41-44).

John then reports that many who had come to visit Mary, Lazarus's sister, "put their faith in him" (John 11:45). The mighty miracle did, indeed, validate Jesus' claim that he was sent from God (verse 42).

Jesus was "deeply moved" over human suffering. Yet Jesus was not helpless in the face of death. He raised the dead man to life, revealing the glory of God. The miracle provoked belief in Him. Another even more miraculous resurrection lay ahead.

The sheer number, power, and compassion of Jesus' miracles put him in a category by himself. What kind of a man is this? He is one of a kind. He has unique credentials as a miracle-worker.

Jesus was not a guru who tapped into cosmic power through yogic technique or occult initiation. Jesus' relationship to God is portrayed as an interaction with his Father—a Father he often consulted in prayer, even spending all night in personal communion with him (Luke 6:12).[7] His was not the spirituality of a Hindu sage who cultivates the divine through the arduous disciplines of yoga.

Neither were his miracles those of a shaman—the medicine man or witch doctor of tribal religions now experiencing something of a comeback in modern culture.[8] Anthropologist-cum-shaman Michael Harner describes a shaman as:

a man or woman who enters an altered state of consciousness—at will—to contact and utilize an ordinarily hidden reality in order to acquire knowledge, power, and to help other persons. The shaman has at least one, and usually more, "spirits" in his personal service.[9]

Jesus did not depend on entering altered states of consciousness, nor did he use exotic shamanic ritual materials or spirits (he drove them out!) for his healing. This also proves that he was not just another charismatic magician known to exist in the ancient world—as some in the Jesus Seminar have claimed. He did not rely on magical incantations or external props.[10] By his word and touch, people were made whole. The manifestation of the miraculous flowed out of his perfect obedience to his Father, his inspiration from the Holy Spirit, and his own personal potency as the Son. He did not serve as a catalyst for the activation of divine energy in others. He was the personal fountainhead of miraculous power.

Jesus did much more than this. He practiced his own preaching by loving his neighbor. He lived a life of openness to all who would listen. He found an especially attentive audience in the lowest class of his day, "the tax collectors and sinners," those who fell between the cracks of social and religious respectability. He was known as the friend of the downcast, and many of them believed in him. They knew Jesus as a true friend and recognized his credentials as a miracle-worker whose compassion brought deliverance to the captives.

Jesus: A Man of Authority

It should be obvious by now that Jesus yearned for people to *believe in him*. The religion *of* Jesus was also a religion *about*

Jesus. He is the object of faith for healing. He commands nature with a word. He raises the dead. He casts out demons with a word. This authority is resident within him as God's "beloved Son" and through his relationship to the Father and the Spirit, as was seen at his baptism. When his disciples were commissioned to move in his power, they received it from Jesus, not from themselves. The disciples cast out demons in Jesus' name, not in their own (Luke 10:17).

In Capernaum some resourceful people lowered a paralytic through an opening they made in the roof above Jesus. When Jesus recognized their faith, he said to the paralytic, "Son, your sins are forgiven." Some of the religious teachers responded, "Why does this fellow talk like that? He's blaspheming. Who can forgive sins but God alone?" Jesus countered:

> "Why are you thinking these things? Which is easier: to say to the paralytic, 'Your sins are forgiven,' or to say, 'Get up, take your mat and walk'? But that you may know that the Son of Man has authority on earth to forgive sins . . ." He said to the paralytic, "I tell you, get up, take your mat and go home." He got up, took his mat and walked out in full view of them all (Mark 2:8-12).

At a dinner at a Pharisee's house, a woman of ill repute came to Jesus and anointed his feet with perfume and her own tears. When the Pharisee objected to this behavior, Jesus told a parable to the effect that this woman loved Jesus much because she was forgiven much. Then Jesus said to her, "Your sins are forgiven." Again, those present were theologically scandalized and questioned, "Who is this who even forgives sins?" Jesus then said to the woman, "Your faith has saved you; go in peace" (Luke 7:48-50).

In both word and deed, Jesus was claiming the uniquely divine prerogative to forgive sins. It is one thing for me to forgive myself for something or to forgive you for offending me; it is quite another for me to forgive someone else for offending you! Imagine, then, someone claiming to forgive your *every* sin.

Jesus valued faith in him. He never deemed faith to be an independent tool capable of plugging into a universal energy current, as many today teach. Jesus honored and encouraged faith in Jesus—a faith that heals and saves, *a faith about Jesus.*

Jesus also provoked faith in many by the confidence with which he spoke of himself and his role. As E. Stanley Jones put it, "He never used such words as 'perhaps,' 'maybe,' 'I think so.' Even his words had a concrete feeling about them. They fell upon the soul with the authority of certainty."[11]

This "authority of certainty" is manifest in the fact that he never had to apologize or hesitate, whether in word or deed. He issued challenging moral absolutes such as "love your enemies" (Matthew 5:44) without reservation. He made grand promises without caution, such as "Blessed are those who hunger and thirst for righteousness, for they will be filled" (Matthew 5:6) and "If you hold to my teaching, you are really my disciples. Then you will know the truth, and the truth will set you free" (John 8:31,32). He confidently asserted that "heaven and earth will pass away, but my words will never pass away" (Matthew 24:35). He warned his hearers that their eternal destiny depended on their response to him (Mark 8:38). He foretold the future in no uncertain terms, not for curiosity's sake or date-setting, but because of its bearing on the present (Matthew 24).[12]

Jesus not only warned his hearers of the judgment day, but he also proclaimed himself the Judge of the world. In warning of false prophets to come in his name, Jesus declared that he will say to them on the day of judgment, "I never knew you. Away from me, you evildoers!" (Matthew 7:23). Jesus stated that "the Father judges no one, but has entrusted all judgment to the Son" (John 5:22), and "Whoever hears my word and believes him who sent me has eternal life and will not be condemned; he has crossed over from death to life" (John 5:24).

Yet not all will respond to his word in saving faith. Speaking of his authority as the Son of Man to judge, Jesus continued:

> Do not be amazed at this, for a time is coming when all who are in their graves will hear his voice and come out— those who have done good will rise to live, and those who have done evil will rise to be condemned (John 5:28,29).

The Son of Man will divide humanity on that day:

> When the Son of Man comes in his glory, and all the angels with him, he will sit on his throne in heavenly glory. All the nations will be gathered before him, and he will separate the people one from another as a shepherd separates the sheep from the goats (Matthew 25:31,32).[13]

He added that the goats "will go away to eternal punishment, but the righteous to eternal life" (Matthew 25:46), all on the basis of how they responded to Jesus during their one life on earth. He did not teach reincarnation.[14]

The Uniqueness of Jesus, the Christ

Jesus' authority makes perfect sense if, as we noted in the last chapter, he and the Father "are one" (John 10:30). He knows the Father and the Father knows him in a unique way. Jesus said, "All things have been committed to me by my Father. No one knows the Son except the Father, and no one knows the Father except the Son and those to whom the Son chooses to reveal him" (Matthew 11:27). Jesus placed his own knowledge of the Father on the same level as the Father's knowledge of the Son, thus asserting his unique equality with the Father.[15] William Craig comments that this verse

> tells us that Jesus claimed to be the Son of God in an *exclusive* and *absolute* sense. Jesus says here that His relationship of sonship to God is unique. And He also claims to be the only one who can reveal the Father to men. In other words, Jesus claims to be the absolute revelation of God.[16]

When challenged about his activities on the Sabbath, Jesus responded, "My Father is always at his work to this very day, and I, too, am working" (John 5:17). John notes, "For this reason the Jews tried all the harder to kill him; not only was he breaking the Sabbath, but he was even calling God his own Father, making himself equal with God" (John 5:18). Jesus healed on the Sabbath on several occasions and once used the opportunity to proclaim, "The Son of Man is Lord even of the Sabbath" (Mark 2:28). The Lord of the Sabbath can be no less than the Lord of creation who made the Sabbath (Genesis 2:2).

When Jesus' disputants said, "Who do you think you are?" (John 8:53), Jesus concluded his response by saying, "I tell you the truth . . . before Abraham was born, I am!" (verse 58). John notes: "At this, they picked up stones to stone him, but Jesus hid himself, slipping away from the temple grounds" (verse 59). Jesus affirmed his existence as God, the "I Am" (Exodus 3:14), from before Abraham's day. Although some claim that this statement is a reference to *reincarnation* (Jesus previously existing as another human), it makes more sense to see it as a reference to Jesus' *pre-incarnation* identity as divine. That is how his audience interpreted it. We should follow their lead.

Jesus also expressed his uniqueness by saying, "For God so loved the world that he gave his one and only Son, that whoever believes in him shall not perish but have eternal life" (John 3:16). He affirmed that he alone is the agent of redemption as God's "only Son." He further underscored this when he claimed, "I am the way and the truth and the life. No one comes to the Father except through me" (John 14:6). In these passages Jesus is asserting something about himself by using the personal, first-person pronoun "I." He does not say, "The God already within you is the way, the truth and the life," or "We are the way, the truth and the life." These ideas are emphatically excluded.

Nevertheless, some interpreters of Jesus miss this point entirely. When the Buddhist monk and author Thich Nhat Hanh discusses Jesus' statement, "I am the way," he claims that the "I" is not Jesus as the only Lord and Savior but "life itself." This life, Hanh claims, can be discovered by practicing "deeply the life and teachings of Buddha or the life and teachings of Jesus" such that "life eternal presents itself to us."[17] Hanh emphasizes the divine self rather than the objective reality of Jesus Christ. He says that "we are of the same reality as Jesus" because he is "our Self."[18] Jesus' straightforward statement, "I am the way and the truth and the life," is distorted to mean that we have the way, truth, and life within us already—with or without Jesus.

Jesus singled himself out of the crowd by his words and deeds. The particulars of his life were His unique credentials that cannot be accredited to divinity-in-general—an impersonal force that is everything in general and nothing in particular. His claims could be made by anyone, but they could only be substantiated by Jesus. For the Gospel writers, God is focused in Jesus of Nazareth.[19] John declares that Jesus has made the Father known (John 1:18).

Jesus knew the Father as his "Abba" (Mark 14:36), an Aramaic term of tender endearment used of intimate knowledge and affection for one's father. The English word *papa* comes close to capturing the meaning. Throughout the Gospels we find Jesus in prayerful communion with the Father. He hears the Father's voice and does the Father's will. Jesus is involved in a relationship with a personal God. Jesus' oneness with the Father (John 10:30) does not mean the dissolution of Jesus or the Father as persons. They are one in essence and substance, yet this oneness is not a featureless uniformity of being (impersonal monism) but a living relationship between persons. This can be seen throughout John's account of Jesus' long prayer to the Father before his crucifixion. Jesus says that the Father glorifies the Son and the Son glorifies the Father (John 17:4,5). This is the language of reciprocal communion, not impersonal oneness.

Jesus glorified the Father as no one else could. Therefore, he can make strong demands on God's creatures. We hear the ring of exclusivity in Jesus' warning:

> Enter through the narrow gate. For wide is the gate and broad is the road that leads to destruction, and many enter through it. But small is the gate and narrow the road that leads to life, and only a few find it (Matthew 7:13,14)

Jesus also said: "I tell you the truth, I am the gate for the sheep. All who ever came before me were thieves and robbers, but the sheep did not listen to them. I am the gate; whoever enters through me will be saved" (John 10:7-9).

The Gospel of John catalogs several other of Jesus' "I am" statements that accentuate his uniqueness: "I am the bread of life" (6:48), and "I am the living bread that came down from heaven. If a man eats of this bread, he will live forever. This bread is my flesh, which I will give for the life of the world" (6:51). "I am the light of the world. Whoever follows me will never walk in darkness, but will have the light of life" (8:12). "I am the good shepherd. The good shepherd lays down his life for the sheep" (10:11). "I am the resurrection and the life. He who believes in me will live, even though he dies" (11:25).[20]

Jesus the Christ

In the last chapter we discussed the term *Christ* as a title given to Jesus at his birth, but it is crucial to witness how it functioned in his ministry.

Christ is the Greek equivalent of the Hebrew word *Messiah*. So whenever Jesus is called "the Christ," he is being referred to as the Messiah. He openly admitted this to the Samaritan woman who said to him, " 'I know that Messiah' (called Christ) 'is coming. When he comes, he will explain everything to us.' Then Jesus declared, 'I who speak to you am he' " (John 4:25,26). Jesus likewise admitted to being the Christ when he said to his disciples, "I tell you the truth, anyone who gives you a cup of water in my name because you belong to Christ will certainly not lose his reward" (Mark 9:41; see also Matthew 23:10; John 17:3).

Originally, in the Old Testament, *Messiah* could refer to various people specially "anointed" by God for specific tasks performed in his service. Through various prophecies the concept was narrowed down to the person of the Messiah— one uniquely equipped by God for a divine mission.

Several strands made up the messianic expectation of the Old Testament. One was political. The Messiah would rule on David's throne in righteousness. Another was apocalyptic: The Son of Man would come from heaven to judge evil. The last was that of the suffering servant who bears the sin of his people.[21]

Jesus of Nazareth fulfilled all three expectations, although in ways not expected by many. In so doing he fulfilled scores of prophecies concerning his life, teaching, death, and resurrection, only a few of which we will address.[22] He did not set up an earthly political rule but, nevertheless, viewed himself as King. He did not bring apocalyptic judgment at his Incarnation, but promised that it will come when he returns at the end of the age. As the suffering servant, the Christ must go to the cross.

The Death of Christ

Jesus explained to the disciples that he must go to Jerusalem to suffer many things, be killed, and be raised to life on the third day (Matthew 16:21,22). We have seen that on several occasions crowds wanted to stone him, but Jesus narrowly escaped because the time had not yet come. Opposition from the religious establishment was building and would soon reach a critical point. Jesus faced his crucifixion not as an accident or a mistake, but as a necessary part of his mission. B.B. Warfield has aptly commented that:

> He came into the world to die, and every stage of the road that led to this destiny was determined not for Him but by Him. He was never the victim but always the Master of circumstance, and pursued His pathway from the beginning to the end, not merely in full knowledge from the start of all its turns and twists up to its bitter conclusion, but in complete control of them and of it.[23]

As the hour approached, Jesus becomes more explicit:

> We are going up to Jerusalem, and the Son of Man will be betrayed to the chief priests and the teachers of the law. They will condemn him to death and will turn him over to the Gentiles to be mocked and flogged and crucified. On the third day he will be raised to life! (Matthew 20:18,19).

We will not give all the details of the last days of Jesus' life, although it is important to remember that "one-third of Matthew, one-third of Mark, one-fourth of Luke, and one-half of John are devoted to the last hours of Jesus. Thus about one-third of the material making up the four Gospels relates to the last week of Jesus."[24] We will sample a few key events and statements to better understand the death of Jesus in light of alternative teachings about him.

Jesus' sense of his impending death harmonizes with his sense of mission. We noted that he said, referring to himself, "The good shepherd lays down his life for the sheep" (John 10:11). When explaining that his disciples should not jockey for power and prestige, but rather serve their neighbors, Jesus used himself as the supreme example by saying, "The Son of Man did not come to be served, but to serve, and to give his life as a ransom for many" (Matthew 20:28). Jesus would give his life for many. He also said, "For the Son of Man came to seek and to save what was lost" (Luke 19:10).

Shortly before Jesus' betrayal, he was in great agony over his coming death and prayed, "Abba, Father . . . everything is possible for you. Take this cup from me. Yet not what I will, but what you will" (Mark 14:36). Soon after this, when Jesus was arrested, someone tried to protect him by the sword. Jesus responded by rebuking the deed and saying, "Do you think I cannot call on my Father, and he will at once put at my disposal more than twelve legions of angels? But how then would the Scriptures be fulfilled that say it must happen in this way?" (Matthew 26:53,54).

Later the Jewish religious leaders said, "Tell us if you are the Christ, the Son of God." Jesus replied, "Yes, it is as you say. . . . But I say to all of you: In the future you will see the Son of Man sitting at the right hand of the Mighty One and coming on the clouds of heaven" (Matthew 26:63,64). At this the high priest ripped his clothes, evidencing his response to the blasphemy of someone equating himself with God in this way. Jesus was then beaten and handed over to the Roman political officials, who further beat him, taunted him, spit upon him . . . and had him crucified.

Yet New Age teaching either denies that Jesus was crucified and killed or denies that his death was for the forgiveness of sin. The pulsating heart of the Gospel accounts is surgically removed by some revisionist views.

According to Mark L. and Elizabeth Clare Prophet, "The doctrine of vicarious atonement for sin through the crucifixion of Jesus Christ is simply not what Jesus taught." This and other such pronouncements make up what they call "the lost teachings of Jesus."[25] In another book they refer to the idea of a blood sacrifice of Jesus as "an erroneous doctrine" that is "a remnant of pagan rite long refuted by the Word of the Lord" and never taught by Jesus himself.[26] In contrast, the Gospel stories are charged with the idea of sacrifice, as we have shown and as we will further demonstrate.

Although crucifixion was the most gruesome form of execution in the ancient world, the Gospel writers give us few details of the act. We find that Jesus was savagely scourged before being crucified, and he carried the cross partway to Golgotha before another man was constrained to shoulder it the rest of the way (John 19:17; Mark 15:21). Jesus was nailed between two common criminals. In the midst of the suffering of the cross, Jesus cried, "Father, forgive them, for they do not know what they are doing" (Luke 23:34). Jesus loved his enemies, even to the end, but did not deny their need for divine forgiveness.

Jesus' last words on the cross were, "My God, my God, why have you forsaken me?" (Mark 15:34). After this:

> With a loud cry, Jesus breathed his last. The curtain of the temple was torn in two from top to bottom. And when the centurion, who stood there in front of Jesus, heard his cry and saw how he died, he said, "Surely this man was the Son of God!" (verses 37-39).

The crucifixion and its meaning was revealed hundreds of years before the fact. Jesus himself often quoted from Isaiah 53 that said of the Messiah: "He poured out his life unto death, and was numbered with the transgressors. For he bore the sin of many, and made intercession for the transgressors" (Isaiah 53:12). It was fulfilled to the letter.

Isaiah speaks of one "despised and rejected by men, a man of sorrows, and familiar with suffering" (verse 3). "Surely he has borne our griefs and carried our sorrows; yet we esteemed him stricken, smitten by God, and afflicted. But he was wounded for our transgressions, he was bruised for our iniquities; upon him was the chastisement that made us whole, and with his stripes we are healed" (verses 4,5). Although "all we like sheep have gone astray . . . the Lord has laid on him the iniquity of us all" (verse 6). He was "like a lamb" led to the slaughter (verse 7), for he was "stricken for the transgression of my people" (verse 8). And although "he had done no violence nor was any deceit in his mouth" (verse 9), the Lord "makes himself an offering for sin" (verse 10). Isaiah concludes the chapter by saying,

"Yet he bore the sin of many, and made intercession for the transgressors" (verse 12).

It takes little imagination to see Jesus as the Christ who is the suffering servant. But the suffering servant is also the risen Lord.

The Resurrection of Jesus

After Jesus' death on the cross, he was buried in a tomb donated by Joseph of Arimathea. His disciples were crushed and left desolate, although Jesus had promised he would rise from the dead on the third day.

Then two women followers of Jesus reported that the tomb was empty. Although first met with disbelief, this report was confirmed by several disciples. Jesus himself then appeared to the disciples several times over a 40-day period as the Lord of life. On one occasion, Jesus demonstrated the tangible reality of his resurrected body by saying, "Look at my hands and my feet. It is I myself! Touch me and see; a ghost does not have flesh and bones, as you see I have" (Luke 24:39).

The resurrected Jesus elicited the faith of his doubting disciple Thomas when he appeared and said, "Put your finger here; see my hands. Reach out your hand and put it into my side. Stop doubting and believe" (John 20:27). Thomas then exclaimed, "My Lord and my God!" (verse 28). Jesus was demonstrated to be God in the flesh, crucified as the Christ had to be, but now risen from the dead as Lord.

The resurrected Jesus said, "This is what is written: The Christ will suffer and rise from the dead on the third day, and repentance and forgiveness of sins will be preached in his name to all nations" (Luke 24:46,47). On this basis did Christianity permeate the ancient world.[27]

The Jesus of the Gospels and More

The Jesus of Christianity is the Jesus of the four Gospels. He is a man of wisdom, power, and compassion. Yet he is more than a man. He is God in human form.

The preface to John's Gospel declares:

> In the beginning was the Word, and the Word was with God, and the Word was God. He was with God in the beginning. Through him all things were made; without him nothing was made that has been made. In him was life, and that life was the light of men. The light shines in the darkness, but the darkness has not understood it. (John 1:1-5)

Later John states that the Word has invaded human history:

> The Word became flesh and lived for awhile among us. We have seen his glory, the glory of the one and only Son, who came from the Father, full of grace and truth (verse 14).

The word John uses for "Word" is the Greek *logos*. While the term has been used in Greek philosophy to mean the *impersonal* ordering principle of the universe, John uses it to refer to the *personal* God of the universe who has taken on human nature to dispel the darkness of sin.[28]

Jesus is not a man who attained an impersonal Christ consciousness, but is the Christ to whom the Old Testament pointed with great expectation. He is the suffering servant who declares he will die so that others may live free from sin and guilt. He is the resurrected one who commissions his followers to proclaim the gospel in *his name.*

Jesus highlighted his uniqueness and supremacy when he affirmed that:

> All authority in heaven and on earth has been given to me. Therefore go and make disciples of all nations, baptizing them in the name of the Father and of the Son and of the Holy Spirit, and teaching them to obey everything I have commanded you. And surely I am with you always, to the very end of the age (Matthew 28:18-20).

Besides a reference to Isaiah 53, this chapter has only referred to the Gospels for testimony concerning Jesus. The rest of the New Testament abundantly confirms what is said in the Gospels and further elaborates on the meaning of Jesus and his mission.

After Jesus' ascension, Peter became a great preacher and the "fisher of men" that Jesus had promised he would be. When standing before the rulers and elders of the Jews in Jerusalem, Peter proclaimed, "Salvation is found in no one else, for there is no other name under heaven given to men by which we must be saved" (Acts 4:12).

The apostle John in his letter to the early church writes, "That which was from the beginning, which we have heard, which we have seen with our eyes, which we have looked at and our hands have touched—this we proclaim concerning the Word of life" (1 John 1:1). He later says, "He is the atoning sacrifice for our sins, and not only for ours but also for the sins of the whole world. We know that we have come to know him if we obey his commands" (2:2,3). He states that Jesus "appeared so that he might take away our sins. And in him is no sin" (3:5). John also notes triumphantly, "The reason the Son of God appeared was to destroy the devil's work" (3:8).

The apostle Paul, not one of the original disciples but one later transformed by Jesus, also accentuates the uniqueness and supremacy of Jesus. "For there is one God: there is also one mediator between God and humankind, Christ Jesus, himself human, who gave himself as a ransom for all" (1 Timothy 2:5,6, NRSV).

According to the New Testament, *the religion of Jesus* is also *the religion about Jesus.* Jesus encouraged belief in him when he said, "The work of God is this: to believe in the one he has sent" (John 6:29; cf. John 3:16). He is the center of redemption who makes exclusive claims and backs them up with his credentials as a teacher, wonder-worker, healer, man of compassion, suffering servant, and risen Lord.

Although New Age proponents may praise Jesus, they do not bow in worship. John White maintains that Jesus must not be put on a pedestal. Yet we find biblical warrant that he was not placed upon a pedestal by any human being. He is rightfully on the pedestal of the universe, but only through lowering himself by becoming the servant of all, the lamb who was willing to be sacrificed on the cross to give life to those who come to him in faith.[29] The apostle Paul writes that Christ Jesus,

> Who, being in very nature God,
> did not consider equality with God something to be grasped,

but made himself nothing,
taking the very nature of a servant,
being made in human likeness.
And being found in appearance as a man,
he humbled himself
and became obedient to death—
even death on a cross!
Therefore God exalted him to the highest place
and gave him the name that is above every name,
that at the name of Jesus every knee should bow,
in heaven and on earth and under the earth,
and every tongue confess that Jesus Christ is Lord,
to the glory of God the Father (Philippians 2:6-11;
cf. Isaiah 45:23).

This exaltation makes Jesus the Christ of cosmic dimensions. Yet how does this view of Jesus square with other notions of the Cosmic Christ? We explore this in the next chapter.

15

JESUS AND THE COSMIC CHRIST

MANY WHO HAVE caught the New Age vision have rejected orthodox Christianity, yet remain attracted to, if not entranced by Jesus. The new spirituality is hospitable to Jesus as a Gnostic Revealer, a well-traveled, mystical magus, an Essene initiate, or a Christ-conscious master. Yet "old age" orthodox views of Jesus are often rejected as "dogmatic," "narrow," or "anthropomorphic." Christ consciousness cannot, they say, be chained to one solitary incarnation.

Many spiritual seekers yearn for no less than a Cosmic Christ. David Spangler declared, "Naturally, any old Christ will not do, not if we need to show that we have something better than the mainstream Christian traditions. It must be a Cosmic Christ, a universal Christ, a New Age Christ."[1] He goes on to say that these concepts take us beyond "purely anthropomorphic associations and thought-forms about the Christ."[2]

For Spangler and the New Age in general, the Christ is a universal presence working within all humanity to raise it to a higher level of evolutionary attainment. Christ is not as much a person as "a cosmic principle, a spiritual presence whose quality infuses and appears in various ways in all the religions and philosophies that uplift humanity and seek unity with spirit."[3] The second coming has already occurred in the "inner planes of Earth" through the Christ life impregnating and inspiring evolutionary advancement. This second coming "is not a person; it is a life which quickens a comparable Christ life within each of us."[4]

Matthew Fox, once a controversial Roman Catholic priest who became an Episcopalian priest after being defrocked, has heralded "the coming of the Cosmic Christ." While claiming to be within the orthodox orbit, Fox decries what he calls "Jesus-olatry" in which people "concentrate so much on Jesus that they miss the Cosmic Christ and the divinity within the creation."[5] Jesus, for Fox, is one of many manifestations of divine wisdom.[6] In fact, when Jesus identified himself as the "I am" of Exodus 3:14 (John 8:58), Fox claims he "shows us how to embrace our own divinity" because "the Cosmic Christ is the 'I am' of every creature."[7] Fox claims, "We are Cosmic Christs."[8]

Likewise, Teilhard de Chardin (1881–1955) wrote of Christ as the spiritual dynamo for evolutionary advancement. Highly influential in New Age circles, the Jesuit paleontologist and philosopher focused not on Jesus as a particular person, but on Christ as a universal energy that would eventually perfect the universe at the omega point, which Teilhard sometimes viewed as the second coming. He says, "Christ is the great source of power and energy which is drawing all things toward itself."[9] Teilhard foresaw a New Age of global religious and political unity emerging through cosmic evolution.[10]

What Spangler, Fox, Teilhard de Chardin, and others yearn for is a total explanation for reality and a comprehensive significance for existence that gives us hope. In Spangler's system of thought, Jesus plays a crucial role in tuning into the Christ consciousness and releasing evolutionary powers into the divine realm. However, the Christ consciousness is an *impersonal* principle, operative not only in Jesus but in all people and religions to varying degrees. Fox's vision is similar, though couched in more orthodox terms. Is this estimation of Christ "something better" than the Christ of biblical Christianity?

Jesus: Uniting the Personal and the Cosmic

The "cosmic" refers to the entire cosmos. If something is cosmic, it has a universal or comprehensive meaning, significance, and value. The cosmic is the opposite of the pedestrian, the mundane, or the constricted.

Many have taken the biblical teaching of the Incarnation to be a limited view of God: Christ is contained in one person, not universalized as the inner reality of all people. While the New Age Christ is an impersonal cosmic process or principle, historic Christianity unites both the cosmic and the personal in Jesus Christ. The New Testament does reveal a Cosmic Christ.

The introduction to John's Gospel reads:

In the beginning was the Word, and the Word was with God, and the Word was God. He was with God in the beginning.

Through him all things were made; without him nothing was made that has been made. In him was life, and that life was the light of men (John 1:1-4).

The "Word became flesh" (John 1:14) is the personal Incarnation of God in Jesus. "Word," both here and in John 1:1, is from the Greek word *Logos*, from which we derive our word *logic* and all words ending in "-ology," such as *psychology, theology,* and *sociology.* In Greek philosophy it generally referred to an immanent and *impersonal* ordering principle in the cosmos that provided coherence. Logos make the world a *universe* instead of a *multiverse.* R.C. Sproul notes that "the Apostle John dropped a theological bombshell on the philosophical playground of his day by looking at Jesus and talking about Him not as an impersonal concept, but as the incarnation of the eternal Logos."[11] John harnesses a word so rich in philosophical meaning for a unique purpose. Jaroslav Pelikan explains:

> "Logos of God" when applied to Jesus Christ meant far more than "Word of God," more even than divine revelation; there were many other Greek vocables that would have sufficed to express that much and no more, and several of them were being used in the New Testament and in other early Christian literature. Employing the specific name Logos implied in addition to this that what had come in Jesus Christ was also the *Reason and Mind of the cosmos.*[12]

John borrows a term, but does not parrot its previous meaning. God is the Logos. God is uncreated reason in his very being. As such he provides the order, regularity, law, and intelligibility to the cosmos—not as some impersonal world soul, but as the cosmos's personal Creator. Paul says of Christ: "Through *him* all things were *made*; without *him* nothing was *made* that has been *made*" (John 1:3; emphasis added). The Maker is not one with the made; yet the Maker, the Logos, ensures that the cosmos will not sink into chaos. To put it another way, the Logos is the cosmic or universal support system for all the qualities and quantities of creation. More vividly, "In him was life, and that life was the light of men" (1:4). John further affirms, "The true light that gives light to every man was coming into the world" (John 1:9).

The divine Logos has cosmic significance. The Logos is not provincial, pedestrian, or constricted. Carl Henry powerfully puts this into perspective: "The Logos of the Bible is personal and self-revealed, transcendent to man and the world, eternal and essentially divine, intrinsically intelligible, and incarnate in Jesus Christ."[13] The Logos is "the foundation of all meaning, and the transcendent personal source and support of the rational, moral, and purposive order of created reality."[14] The Logos is indispensably involved with the entire cosmos, but it is not the cosmos itself, as Matthew Fox and others have taught.[15]

Why do mathematical constructs relate to external reality so successfully? How can we calculate the trajectory of a spaceship all the way to the moon and back? Because of the Logos. Why do chemical reactions occur uniformly under similar conditions? Because of the Logos. Why do all societies affirm, in one form or another, the golden rule in morality?[16] Because of the Logos. Why have all societies throughout history had some understanding of a spiritual realm surpassing the physical world? Because of the Logos.

Although Paul does not use the term *Logos*, his thinking also centers on this concept in the book of Colossians where he presents the Cosmic Christ:

> He is the image of the invisible God, the firstborn over all creation. For by him all things were created: things in heaven and on earth, visible and invisible, whether thrones or powers or rulers or authorities; all things were created by him and for him . . . And he is the head of the body, the church; he is the beginning and the firstborn from among the dead, so that in everything he might have the supremacy. For God was pleased to have all his fullness dwell in him (Colossians 1:15-19).

By "firstborn," Paul refers to Christ's exalted cosmic status, as the firstborn Jewish male had an exalted social status; that is, Paul is referring to Christ's theological priority, not to his being the first thing created. No, he himself created all things for himself. Not only that, he is "the firstborn from among the dead" through his resurrection—the final proof of his supremacy (Romans 1:4).

The writer of Hebrews speaks of the same Cosmic Christ: "The Son is the radiance of God's glory and the exact representation of his being, sustaining all things by his powerful word" (Hebrews 1:3). The Son is equal to God: He is the heir of all things and the agent of creation who also sustains the entire cosmos without *being* the cosmos.

All of the biblical writers unmistakably unite the Cosmic Christ with the personal Jesus. They are not praising an impersonal and abstract principle. They are exalting a Cosmic Person, who, though eternally divine, was born as a human, lived a perfect life, died for others, was raised from the dead, and now is enthroned as "King of kings and Lord of lords." Jesus himself announced his cosmic rule shortly before his ascension. Matthew tells us that Jesus said, "All authority in heaven and on earth has been given to me" (Matthew 28:18). We have seen in chapters 13 and 14 that Jesus repeatedly affirmed his deity. These are cosmic affirmations uttered from the human lips of Jesus.

If God originally created humans "in his image and likeness," human personality is a fitting mode for the supreme divine manifestation. Because we had become blinded and could not "recognize Him as ordering and ruling creation as a whole,"[17] God made himself even more tangible, available, and recognizable in the Incarnation. The early church theologian Athanasius expands on this:

> He takes to Himself for [his] instrument a part of the whole, namely a human body, and enters into that. Thus he ensured that men should recognize Him in the part who could not do so in the whole, and that those who could not lift their eyes to His unseen power might recognize and behold Him in the likeness of themselves. For, being men, they could naturally learn to know His Father more quickly and directly by means of a body that corresponded to their own and by the Divine works done through it.[18]

The Cosmic Christ appeared in the person of Jesus just when the cosmos was ripe for the revelation. Paul says that "when the time had fully come, God sent his Son" (Galatians 4:4). Not only did Jesus, the Christ, fulfill a manifold of Jewish prophecies concerning his life, death, and resurrection,[19] he also appeared when the message of the gospel could have free rein in the ancient world.

First, the Roman Empire provided a highly efficient and comprehensive system of roads, facilitating ease of travel throughout all provinces controlled by Rome.[20] Good news could spread easily.

Second, because of the *Pax Romana,* or Peace of Rome, travelers could move from one province to another with little concern for anything such as a passport or visa. The general ambiance of peace provided a fit medium for the dissemination of new ideas across borders.[21]

Third, prior to the Roman conquest, Alexander the Great had brought Greek to his empire. By the time of the Roman Empire, Koine Greek had become the world language. This was a common form of Greek spoken by the masses and the language in which the New Testament was written. A.T. Robertson notes that inscriptions in Koine have been found throughout Asia, Egypt, Greece, Italy, Sicily, and on various islands. The Roman senate and imperial governor had their decrees translated into this language to be distributed throughout the empire: "It was really an epoch in the world's history when the babel of tongues was used in the wonderful language of Greece."[22] The world was ready for the Revelation.

How can Christianity affirm both the Cosmic Christ and the personal Jesus? Is not the insistence on Christ being incarnate once-for-all in the person of Jesus more limiting than the expansive claims of the new spirituality that the impersonal Christ consciousness is equally accessible to everyone?

Despite the central focus on this particular Jesus as *the* Christ, as the sole Savior and Lord, Jesus himself proclaimed a universal message. It was not universal in the vague sense that all religious aspirations lead equally to God. Rather, Jesus' message was universal in that the Incarnation is meant for all people. The gospel must penetrate the entire planet. Jesus was born in ancient Palestine and began his outreach to the Jews, but he also reached out to others, such as the Roman centurion who amazed Jesus with the strength of his faith (Luke 7:1-10). When asked if only a few people would be saved, Jesus replied, "Make every effort to enter through the narrow door, because many, I tell you, will try to enter and will not be able to" (Luke 13:24). He then said that many of his own people will be cast out because they rejected their Messiah, but people "will come from east and west and north and south, and will take their places at the feast in the kingdom of God" (Luke 13:29).

The universality of Jesus' message is seen when he said to his disciples, "You will receive power when the Holy Spirit comes on you; and you will be my witnesses in Jerusalem, and in all Judea and Samaria, *and to the ends of the earth*" (Acts 1:8, emphasis added; cf. Luke 24:46-48). Jesus also proclaimed:

> Come to me, *all* you who are weary and burdened, and I will give you rest. Take my yoke upon you and learn from me, for I am gentle and humble in heart, and you will find rest for your souls. For my yoke is easy and my burden is light (Matthew 11:28-30, emphasis added).

Jesus, the personal Incarnation of God, was not a vessel too small for the Cosmic Christ. As Paul said, "For God was pleased to have *all* his fullness dwell in him" (Colossians

1:19, emphasis added). In Jesus Christ, "all things hold to-gether" (Colossians 1:17).

Myth Becomes Fact in Jesus

Throughout the history of the world, human beings have enshrined their weariness, burdens, and hopes in their sym-bols, religions, and myths. The human condition is subject to pain from which we seek deliverance. Humanity's spiri-tual awareness, at whatever level, is due to the quickening power of God, the Logos. He reveals something of himself even in the midst of a fallen world—a world where humans made in the divine image nevertheless choose to disobey their Creator (see Romans 1-2).

William James noted that all religions share two com-mon themes: They recognize that the human situation is not the way it ought to be, and that this must in some sense be rectified.[23] From a biblical viewpoint, this can be ex-plained in terms of human sinfulness. Humans know that they have fallen short of their standards and that their con-science has been defiled. Guilt is a universal problem. Something is wrong. Something must be done about it.

Any fair-minded analysis of world religions and mythologies will reveal that the way in which the human problem is described and the solution that is prescribed dif-fer significantly.[24] Yet there are similarities in the themes ad-dressed and basic concerns voiced. From the vantage point of the Logos doctrine, this is no surprise. God has built us so that even in our rebellion against him, our need for re-demption is revealed. The Logos makes it so. John Warwick Montgomery's analysis is worth quoting in full:

Suppose that the fallen race had kept a primordial realization of its separation from God through sinful self-centeredness and of its specific need for redemption through the divine-human conquest of the evil powers arrayed against it. Suppose within each human heart this realization were etched beyond effacement. The sinner would, of course, repress this knowledge, for his sin would be too painful to bear and his egotism would not want to face redemption apart from works-righteousness. Though "the invisible things of God are clearly seen," so that men are "without excuse," they become "vain in their imagination" and their "foolish hearts are darkened" (Romans 1:20-21). The darkening of the heart would quite naturally take the form of a repression of the natural knowledge of God's redemptive plan to the subconscious level, where it could be ignored consciously; but its eradication from the psyche could never occur. Under these circumstances, redemptive knowledge would surface not in a direct fashion but by way of symbolic patterns—visible not only to the sensitive psychoanalyst but also to the folklorist whose material "bubbles up" collectively from the subconscious of the race.[25]

In viewing Christ as the Logos, we can explain the universal patterns of human thought throughout the ages: the quest for a lost paradise, the reality of dark forces both within and without, the need for forgiveness and restoration, and the desire for a redeemer to make that restoration a reality. Even though human sin may cloud the meaning behind the universe, its witness is inextinguishable.

As C.S. Lewis noted, the Cosmic Christ fulfills these human desires in concrete historical and personal fashion. The mythic themes of human history find their answer in Jesus. Lewis says:

The heart of Christianity is a myth which is also a fact. The old myth of the Dying God, *without ceasing to be myth,* comes down from the heaven of legend and imagination to the earth of history. It happens—at a particular date, in a particular place, followed by definable historical consequences. We pass from a Balder or an Osiris, dying nobody knows when or where, to an historical Person crucified (it is all in order) *under Pontius Pilate.* By becoming fact it does not cease to be myth: that is the miracle.[26]

It should be clear that by "myth" Lewis means the deep, universal, and provocative themes of religion, literature, and symbolism that disclose the depths of the psyche. They evidence the incorrigibly human concern with spiritual matters. Yet myth became fact. The blurry longing became particular in a way more shockingly real and alive than anyone could have imagined.[27] Christ lived among us, died, and rose again from the dead.[28] The riddle of redemption is solved, the scattered pieces of the jigsaw puzzle are brought together in Christ, the Logos.

Jesus' Resurrection and the Cosmic Christ

We now turn to the greatest reason to believe that Jesus is the Cosmic Christ: his singular defeat of death itself through resurrection. Belief in Christ's resurrection need not be a blind leap of faith in the dark. There are solid reasons of which we can lay hold.

First, the New Testament considers the resurrection as a matter of paramount significance to everything else it says.

It is no incidental item or cosmic hiccup. Bernard Ramm notes that:

> The resurrection with the incarnation and atonement is planted at the very heart of the gospel and plan of redemption. So crucial is the resurrection to the writers of the New Testament that Peter attributes all the blessings of redemption to it (1 Peter 1:3); Paul avows that without it the work of Christ is undone (1 Corinthians 15:7), and that the confession of the resurrection is integral to salvation (Romans 10:9-10).[29]

The New Testament reverberates and glistens with the reality of Jesus' resurrection. The Gospels record Jesus' teaching that he must be betrayed, killed, and rise again. Then they all testify that his tomb was empty and that he appeared to his disciples as he said. The book of Acts records the preaching of the resurrected Christ as its central fact. The various New Testament letters and the book of Revelation would melt into nothingness without a resurrected Jesus. The resurrection is attested to by four separate Gospels, the history of the early church (Acts), by the letters of Paul, Peter, John, James, Jude, and the letter to the Hebrews. There is a diversity of credible witnesses. Since the New Testament volumes show considerable fitness in terms of historical reliability (see chapter 3), this is a good initial reason to accept the resurrection as an objective reality.

Second, we discover solid historical evidence for the empty tomb of Jesus. Luke, whom we have found to be a trustworthy historian, tells us that the early church began to preach the resurrection in Jerusalem about seven weeks

after Jesus' death. The preaching was heard by those familiar with Jesus and his crucifixion. If Jesus' tomb had not
been empty, the apostles' preaching could have been
stopped dead in its tracks simply by producing Jesus' body.
Both the Jewish religious leadership and the Roman political leadership would have had a vested interest in doing so
in order to stop a threatening movement. They did not.
The apostles feared nothing of the sort and boldly proclaimed a risen Jesus as the central theme of all the sermons
recorded in Acts.[30] Furthermore, the Jewish concept of resurrection would not allow for any non-bodily, spiritual resurrection. A Jesus with rigor mortis was not a resurrected
Jesus.[31]

If Jesus had in fact been killed and buried, it would be
very likely that his tomb would be venerated as that of a
saint, as was the custom in that day. In the Palestine of Jesus'
day, there were at least 50 such venerated tombs (see Luke
11:47,48). Luke tells us that women followed Joseph of Arimathea to the tomb of Jesus, probably to mark the spot for
later tribute. Yet the church commemorates an empty
tomb, not an occupied one.[32]

The early Jewish argument against the Christians pre-
supposed an empty tomb. The New Testament itself records
that the Jews spread the word that the disciples stole the
body (Matthew 28:11-15). The notion of a corpse heist was
highly implausible because of the skilled guard set around
the tomb, the difficulty in identifying the disciples as the
thieves if they somehow sneaked past the guards without
getting caught, and because we could only find it ludicrous
that these thieving disciples would then flatly preach a blatant lie seven weeks later in Jerusalem.[33]

Third, there is good historical evidence for the postcrucifixion appearances of Jesus. Probably the earliest written account of the resurrection comes from the apostle Paul in 1 Corinthians 15, where he says:

> For what I received I passed on to you as of first importance: that Christ died for our sins according to the Scriptures, that he was buried, that he was raised on the third day according to the Scriptures, and that he appeared to Peter, and then to the Twelve. After that, he appeared to more than five hundred of the brothers at the same time, most of whom are still living, though some have fallen asleep. Then he appeared to James, then to all the apostles, and last of all he appeared to me also, as to one abnormally born (verses 3-8).

We noted in chapter 3 that verses 3 and following are thought by most scholars to be an early Hebrew-Christian creed. Jewish New Testament scholar Pinchas Lapide lists eight separate "linguistic items" that "speak in favor of the fact that Paul in this oldest faith statement about the resurrection does not pass on his own thoughts but indeed delivers what he himself has 'received' from the first witnesses."[34]

These features of Paul's passage would date the original creed for the burial and resurrection of Jesus during the A.D. 30s, considerably before the writing of Paul's letter at approximately the A.D. mid-50s.[35] The affirmation of the death and resurrection of Christ was so firmly established just a few years after his death as to be formulated in a creed—a brief summary and confession of the community's essential beliefs. This disproves the notion of the resurrection as a legendary development of a later period, especially when we remember that Paul speaks of those *now living* who had seen the resurrected Jesus. The witnesses were alive and available. This is either one of the greatest bluffs in the history of religion or a confident assertion of substantiated fact.

Although it may not strike us as strange, the fact that the Gospels report that women first witnessed the crucifixion and saw the risen Jesus firms up the historicity of these accounts. This is because women were not considered reliable witnesses in that culture[36] (which is likely why Paul did not insert them in his list in 1 Corinthians 15). Therefore, the accounts that list women as primary eyewitnesses to the resurrection have the ring of authenticity, not contrivance.[37] It is unlikely that if the disciples had faked the story, they would have given the women disciples the crucial roles of witnesses of the risen Jesus.

We should also remember that all the reports of the resurrected Jesus in the Gospels, while possibly later than Paul's list of eyewitnesses, are still too close to the events at hand to admit legendary additions.[38]

Thus far, we have dealt with *documentary evidence* for the resurrection—reasons based on various written sources claiming to present accurate information about the primary events themselves. Yet there is also strong *circumstantial evidence* for the historicity of the resurrection that appeals to certain events that are best explained by the resurrection.

First, if this resurrection did not actually occur, how can we account for the origin and rapid spread of Christianity across the face of the ancient world? How did the same disciples—who could not pray but one hour for their Lord before his crucifixion and who scattered after his capture—be

the same evangelists who braved persecution and martyrdom for a resurrected Jesus?

Christianity was born out of the afterglow of the resurrection of Jesus. This was the fire of its motivation and the
fiber of its courage. The uniqueness of the infant Christian
message was rooted in the resurrection. Noting that the origin of Christianity cannot be explained without the resurrection, C.F.D. Moule affirmed that "the birth and rapid
rise of the Christian church *therefore remain an unsolved
enigma for any historian who refuses to take seriously the only explanation offered by the Church itself.*"[39] Lapide has called the
resurrection "the birth certificate of the church."[40]

We discover another line of evidence in the religious
practices of the early church. The symbol of baptism is
based on the analogy that just as Jesus died and was raised
to life, the believer dies to sinful ways and is raised to a new
life in Christ (see Romans 6:3,4). Baptism presupposes and
is meaningless without the resurrection. Another sacra-
ment is that of the Lord's Supper as a symbol of Jesus' life
given for the believer. Michael Green notes that this was no
"memorial feast in honor of a dead founder"; believers
"broke bread with *agalliasis,* exultation (Acts 2:46) because
they believed the risen Lord was in their midst as they took
the tokens of His death for them."[41] Both practices, he adds,
"would have been a complete travesty had the earliest Christians not believed that Jesus rose from the dead."[42]

Very quickly after the death of Jesus, the early church
also began meeting on Sunday, the first day of the week
(Acts 20:7). This went against the religious grain of Jewish
observance that honored Saturday, the seventh day, as the
Sabbath. The Gospels do not record Jesus advocating a new

holy day, yet the church began to meet on Sunday in honor of the risen Lord. This deep change in spiritual observance is best explained by the resurrection itself.

Is it likely that despite these lines of evidence, the purported eyewitnesses of the risen Jesus were sincerely deceived? The most common defense of this notion is that the resurrection appearances were hallucinations and not objectively real. Does this make sense?

The New Testament certainly presents all the appearances as objective, physical realities. It is impossible to defend the idea that such a diversity of persons, at different times and places, were all subject to the same hallucination. Hallucinations are not a group phenomenon, but are individual aberrations. They also are occasioned through intense wish fulfillment. But the disciples gave Jesus up for dead and were quite shocked at the first reports of his resurrection (Luke 24:1-11; John 20:24-26).[43] The hallucination theory also leads to the unlikely conclusion that the very existence of Christianity is based on mental illness and that its earliest converts preached, quite literally, a message of madness.[44] Lapide tellingly comments:

> If the defeated and depressed group of disciples overnight could change into a victorious movement of faith, based only on autosuggestion or self-deception—without a fundamental faith experience—then this would be a much greater miracle than the resurrection itself.[45]

Although Lapide remains a non-Christian Jew,[46] he affirms the reality of the resurrection and says "the resurrection

belongs to the category of the truly real and effective occurrences, for without a fact of history there is no act of true
faith."[47]

Some attempt to deny the resurrection by accusing the
early church of perpetuating a belief they knew to be a lie.
They were not deceived, but willful deceivers. What logical
motive could account for such a lie? Blaise Pascal puts the
lie to the lie theory:

> The hypothesis that the Apostles were knaves is quite ab-
> surd. Follow it out to the end and imagine these twelve men
> meeting after Jesus' death and conspiring to say that he
> had risen from the dead. This means attacking all the pow-
> ers that be. The human heart is singularly susceptible to
> fickleness, to change, to promises, to bribery. One of them
> had only to deny this story under these inducements, or
> still more because of possible imprisonment, tortures and
> death, and they would all have been lost. Follow that out.[48]

We can follow this out by listening to Watergate conspir-
ator Charles Colson. In a fascinating chapter called "Watergate and the Resurrection" from his book *Loving God*
(1983), Colson recounts the desperate efforts involved in
trying to cover up the Nixon administration's wrongdoing
surrounding the Watergate break-in. He says: "With the
most powerful office in the world at stake, a small band of
hard-picked loyalists, no more than ten of us, could not hold
a conspiracy together for more than two weeks."[49] Despite
the fact that these men's and President Nixon's reputations
were at stake, and that they had tremendous power and

privileges at their fingertips, "after just a few weeks the natural human instinct for self-preservation was so overwhelming that the conspirators, one by one, deserted their
leader."[50] The lie could not be perpetuated under the
pressures that were brought to bear.

Colson argues that if the Watergate conspirators de-
fected at the risk of ruined careers and possible imprison-
ment, there would have been far more incentive for Jesus'
disciples to confess their fraud in the face of even worse
consequences such as beatings, poverty, and even martyrdom. Nor would they have had the social power to deceive
that was at the disposal of the Watergate conspirators. However, there is no record of any such confession of fraud.
There is no reason to believe the disciples had conspired to
perpetuate belief in a resurrection that never happened.
Colson sums this up cogently:

> Take it from one who was inside the Watergate web look-
> ing out, who saw firsthand how vulnerable a cover-up is:
> Nothing less than a witness as awesome as the resurrected
> Christ could have caused those men to maintain to their
> dying whispers that Jesus is alive and Lord.[51]

When taken together, these multiple lines of evidence,
both documentary and circumstantial, lead us to a Christ-
less tomb, a dead man found alive, and a dynamic group of
followers who turned the ancient world upside down. In
light of this firm foundation, any exotic speculations about
Jesus' burial in India must be dismissed as mere romantic
legends. The burden of proof simply presses the life out of
such claims.[52]

Resurrection, Not Reincarnation

The fact of Jesus' resurrection also nails shut the possibility of reincarnation. He did not teach it, and he did not live it. Jesus taught the bodily resurrection of the dead at the end of history, not a process of multiple incarnations of one soul in many bodies (John 5:24-29; Matthew 25:46). His reference to John the Baptist being Elijah (Matthew 11:14; 17:3) should be recognized in its context as a figure of speech meaning that John had a ministry like Elijah's. John himself denied being literally Elijah (John 1:21); and the Old Testament prophet himself never died (2 Kings 2:9-18), so he could not have come back in the body of John.[53]

Jesus rose from the dead, according to Paul, as "the first-born from among the dead, so that in everything he might have the supremacy" (Colossians 1:18) as cosmic Lord. He also says that Jesus Christ "was declared with power to be the Son of God by his resurrection from the dead" (Romans 1:4). When the ascended Jesus appeared to his disciple John, he announced, "I was dead, and behold I am alive for ever and ever!" (Revelation 1:18). Jesus was not reincarnated. He was incarnated, once for all. Jesus will not reincarnate, because he is resurrected and now enthroned forever (Ephesians 1:21-23). He will reappear in his glory at the end of the age. He promises his followers not a gradual salvation through the school of reincarnation, but a resurrected life through faith in him: "I am the resurrection and the life. He who believes in me will live, even though he dies; and whoever lives and believes in me will never die" (John 11:25,26).

Only the Cosmic Christ can credibly make such claims—one who himself defeated death by passing through it bruised, bloody, and broken only to reverse its reality through resurrection. No other world religion boldly claims a founder resurrected in literal, physical form as the cornerstone of its faith. Wilbur Smith notes that the millions and millions of Jews, Buddhists, and Muslims "agree that their founders have never come up out of the dust or the earth in resurrection."[54]

The significance of Jesus' bodily resurrection is not exhausted by the idea of a resuscitated corpse. Those whom Jesus raised from the dead eventually died again. Jesus was raised immortal in a resurrected body, freed from all the constraints of a fallen world, just as his followers one day will be at his physical return (Acts 1:8; 1 Corinthians 15:12-58). Hebrews says:

> Because Jesus lives forever, he has a permanent priesthood. Therefore he is able to save completely those who come to God through him, because he always lives to intercede for them. Such a high priest meets our need—one who is holy, blameless, pure, set apart from sinners, exalted above the heavens (Hebrews 7:24-26).

The Cross, Not a Secret Code

The Cosmic Christ is not the discovery of Gnostic illumination. The Cosmic Christ is the concrete Jesus. The resurrected Jesus is available to everyone who seeks him. The Christian message is the clear and direct message of Jesus himself. Jesus kept no secrets, ultimately. He had a perfect sense of timing and did not divulge everything about himself or his mission at once. He came to earth to make the

Father known (John 1:18) and to regather lost sheep (Matthew 9:36), not to befuddle the masses with a message that only the esoterically initiated could fathom.[55] Though Paul sometimes used the word *mystery* to refer to what cannot be completely grasped by finite beings, he also used it to refer to what is now in fact *revealed* for human benefit, as when he said that God "*made known* to us the mystery of his will according to his good pleasure, which he purposed in Christ" (Ephesians 1:9; emphasis added; cf. 3:3-9; Romans 16:25).[56]

In essence, there is no esoteric Christianity. What you see in the biblical Jesus in his life, death, and resurrection is what you get—or what you reject. His message is universal and applicable to all. By virtue of the biblical record which we have consulted and defended in this book, esoteric Christianity must be judged to be a contradiction in terms. It is a concept invented by those outside the Christian orbit in the hope of finding a worldview entirely alien to the biblical documents. The Bible nowhere gives any indication of being written in a mystical code. Few human documents, outside of military intelligence, can be accurately understood or handled as coded messages.[57] The New Testament presents not a code, but a cross—and a resurrection.

This cross is the key to unlocking the message of Jesus and to entering the new age he promised to inaugurate in history and finally consummate at the end of history. It is not a new age of sleeping gods and goddesses awakening to the Christ consciousness, but of erring creatures coming to the cross of Christ for forgiveness and new life in him. It is a new age of a growing community of Jesus' followers willing to live for him and to lay down their lives for others, just as

Jesus laid down his life for them. It is a community of people willing to take up their own crosses in their pursuit of his kingdom, all the while depending on Christ himself for both the power and peace that comes from redemption. It is a community of those united, not in their deity, but in their experience of forgiveness and new life in Jesus the Christ. It is, finally, a community of those awaiting Christ's second coming. This is not the reincarnation of Jesus or the collective unleashing of humanity's true deity, but the resurrected Lord's triumphant return to earth at the end of the age, when all shall be brought to culmination (Acts 1:11; 3:21; Philippians 3:20,21).

One vital question remains unanswered. If Jesus is who we have claimed he is, how can we come to know him as our spiritual liberator? What does it mean to come to terms with Jesus Christ?

1 6

COMING TO TERMS
WITH JESUS

THE COLLECTION OF Jesus images that we have encountered in these pages do not all ring true. Jesus is not an ambiguous ink blot upon which we project our pet theories, hopes, or fears. He is a living reality who can be mastered by no one, since he is the Master of the universe. He challenges every counterfeit with his genuineness, every distortion with his veracity.

Jesus is not the talking head of the Jesus Seminar, who emerges out of the prejudicial preferences of self-selected critics. Jesus will not be domesticated to suit modern secular sensibilities. The New Testament that the Seminar disassembles, edits, and reassembles according to its skeptical and antisupernatural views is sturdy enough to survive these attacks and to provide us with an accurate account of Jesus of Nazareth.

Neither is Jesus a Gnostic revelator who spurns the physical world and seeks to ignite the divinity within the souls of others. The Gnostic Jesus is an after-the-fact fabrication of those who rejected his message but wanted to co-opt his image. The Gnostics wanted a Jesus with neither cross nor gospel; yet the cross remains a fact of history, and the gospel continues to be the only means of setting people free (John 8:31,32).

Those who paint Jesus in the image of an Essene and/or mystical world traveler have only spattered their canvasses with vanity and folly. The Jesus of the Gospels cannot be so understood. His singularity as the sinless Savior and living Lord cannot be assimilated into alien frameworks. It is only by devaluing the most reliable records and elevating the most suspect that such a pseudo-Jesus can be presented. Such a one is not worthy of belief or trust.

Likewise unworthy of belief are the various new messages about Jesus said to originate from the spiritual realm. These channeled revelations—whether claimed to have issued from ascended masters, assorted spirits, extraterrestrials, or even Jesus himself—invariably substitute for the real Jesus one that is without biblical, logical, or historical foundation. They are channels of deception.

Although the resurrection of Jesus from the dead inaugurated a new era in world history, Jesus was not a herald of the New Age in the modern sense. Although he spoke of and always lived within the spiritual realm, he did not teach that we are all divine. When he raised the dead and healed the sick, he was not harnessing an impersonal power through a magical technique. He was exercising his authority as the Son of God in perfect harmony with his heavenly Father and the Holy Spirit. Jesus never presented himself, nor did his apostles present him, as one among many gurus, swamis, yogis, masters, avatars, sages, or prophets who all resonate with the same divine energy. All of his words and all of his actions accentuated his uniqueness and ascendancy.

Stephen Mitchell insists, "*Once the sectarian passages [of the Gospels] are left out,* we can recognize that Jesus speaks in harmony with the supreme teachings of all the great religions: the Upanishads, the Tao Te Ching, the Buddhist sutras, the Zen and Sufi and Hasidic Masters."[1] However, when we grasp the big picture of the Gospels as real-life narratives of Jesus' complex but integrated personality, and when we recognize their historical trustworthiness, we can rightly reject any such attempt to place Jesus in a crowd of equals. When the full teachings of the Gospels and the rest of the New Testament are left in their original form, Jesus' particularity and supremacy are unmistakable.

Buddhist monk Thich Nhat Hanh agrees that Jesus is unique, but relativizes that uniqueness by saying, "But who is not unique? Socrates, Muhammad, the Buddha, you, and I are all unique." He claims that the idea that Jesus is the only way of salvation "does not help."[2] Jesus' uniqueness, however, is not merely that of an individual who differs from others. His uniqueness lies in his preeminence and finality. His uniqueness is that of God's one and only Son who vindicated his claim to be "the way and the truth and the life" (John 14:6) through his perfect life, his miraculous power, his agonizing death on the cross, his death-defeating resurrection, and his ascension to the right hand of the Father. His uniqueness puts him in a category entirely different from that of Muhammad, Buddha, you, me, or anyone else. And only his uniqueness can guarantee our liberation from wrong living and eternal death.

Several recent spiritual fads have sidetracked many spirituality seekers. The angel craze, fascination with near-death experiences, and interest in goddess religion have obscured the real Jesus for many. Before we explore how our spirituality can be grounded in Jesus himself, we need to address these matters briefly.

Jesus and the Angels

In the last several years angels seem to have come out of hiding. Dozens of books on angels fill bookstore shelves; television programs interview those touched by angels; and workshops are held for the purpose of contacting angels for health, peace, and prosperity. A recent issue of *Life* magazine told of an "angel circle," where people gather around and lay hands on a hurting person in order to call out to ministering angels for assistance. One woman acts as a spokesperson for the angels, assuring the woman being attended to that her needs will be met by the angels.[3] For these angel-intoxicated souls, angels clearly replace Christ as the spiritual focus.

I was on a live, call-in radio program with a woman who claimed to have had several experiences with angels, which led her to open a shop called "Angels for All Seasons." The store features angel literature, calendars, artwork, and other assorted items. The owner believes her store has a spiritual mission. Yet when she was asked by a caller if she believed that Jesus is the only way to God, she equivocated and refused to answer.

The angel craze signals a desire for spiritual contact, protection, and guidance. Most Americans are familiar with the concept of angels and feel at ease with the idea of guardian angels. Much of the interest in angels, however, is uninformed by a biblical understanding of their nature and purpose. Worse yet, much of the material written about and even supposedly communicated from the angels themselves (mediumship) is spiritually deceptive. George Colt perceptively notes that "today's angels seem to spend a lot less time praising God than serving us."[4] He goes on to ask:

> But why angels? Why not God? One reason may be that among the vast numbers of people who yearn for spiritual growth are many who feel alienated from traditional religious worship. They are uncomfortable fearing God, and they are drawn to the comfy, pliable nature of the 1995 angel: a kind of God-lite.[5]

God-lite spirituality also often includes a New Age emphasis. A Maryland woman claims she has been selected by angels to use their energies to help unlock negative patterns from people's past lives (reincarnation). Chery Welch-Charrier says, "I introduce people to their guardian angels and then function as a channel so they can ask questions for their angel."[6] Many messages channeled from angels proclaim that a New Age is dawning. Terry Lynn Taylor says that the "main lesson the angels have for us is that we are love, we are God on earth, and it is time to love ourselves and open our hearts."[7] Another supposedly angelic communication tells us that "the more you are infused with the energy of your divine mind, the greater the restoration of the chord of wisdom."[8]

The Bible speaks often of angels, and we find angels present in the life of Jesus: announcing his birth (Luke 2:8-15), ministering to him after his temptation in the wilderness (Matthew 4:11), declaring his resurrection (Matthew 28:1-7), and commenting on his ascension into heaven (Acts 1:9-11). Nevertheless, angels never take center stage in the biblical drama. That role is reserved for Jesus Christ alone. The apostle Paul warns of those distracted by visions of angels (Colossians 2:18-19), and affirms that there is but one mediator between a holy God and sinful humans, Jesus Christ (1 Timothy 2:5). The book of Hebrews makes clear that Jesus "became as much superior to the angels as the name he has inherited is superior to theirs," because he alone is God's first-born Son (Hebrews 1:4-6). The angels are instructed to worship Christ, who has an authority far higher than any angel (Hebrews 1:6-14; see also Revelation 5:11,12).

As we found in chapter 12, Jesus also warned of fallen angels or demons who, led by the devil, rebelled against God's authority and set themselves against his purposes (Jude 6; Matthew 25:41). These corrupt spiritual creatures often disguise themselves as benign beings intent on inspiring needy humans (2 Corinthians 11:14). The apostle John teaches us to test the spirits by discerning their views on Christ, because "every spirit that does not acknowledge Jesus is not from God" (1 John 4:3). Any angel who misrepresents Jesus must be rejected as a fallen angel unworthy of allegiance. The Christian need not cower before these deceiving spirits, however: "You, dear children, are from God and have overcome them, because the one who is in you [Christ] is greater than the one who is in the world [the devil]" (1 John 4:4; see also Colossians 2:8-10).

Jesus and the Near-Death Experience

Another spiritual trend is creating bestselling books, making instant celebrities—and causing much confusion about Jesus and the afterlife. Since the publication of Raymond Moody's ground-breaking book *Life After Life* (1975), the idea of the near-death experience (or NDE) has become part of the spiritual landscape. Through interviews with people who had clinically died or come close to death, Moody found that many people who lose vital bodily functions—such as heartbeat, breathing, and possibly brain waves—report spiritual experiences of various kinds. These experiences often involve feeling a sense of peace, leaving one's body, going through a tunnel, seeing deceased relatives and spiritual beings, having a review of one's life, meeting a being of light (who often was identified as Jesus), and returning to the body. Moody's work was more anecdotal than scientific, but other writers such as Kenneth Ring, Michael Sabom, and Melvin Morse have conducted more scientific studies that verify Moody's basic idea that these experiences are not contrived and are somewhat common.[9]

Books such as Betty Eadie's *Embraced by the Light* (1992), Dannion Brinkley's *Saved by the Light* (1994), and a host of other bestsellers (usually with the word *light* in the title) have heralded the NDE as a revelation of the nature of the afterlife and spiritual reality. Eadie claims that during her NDE she was embraced by none other than Jesus himself, who revealed to her many surprising truths.

Since I have evaluated the NDE at length in *Deceived by the Light* (1995), in this chapter I will only summarize some matters that bear on our relationship with Jesus. Although some people dismiss the experience as merely the hallucinations of a brain in crisis, I do not believe that every aspect of every NDE can be explained in purely physical terms. Many people who have had a near-death experience seem to have a spiritual experience of some kind. In light of Jesus' teachings concerning spiritual error and deception, however, we know that an experience can be spiritual (of the spiritual realm) without being truthful.

Although people who experience NDEs develop a variety of impressions of the spiritual world, several common themes often convey a deceptive message First, those who have had a near-death experience often understand the being of light to be Jesus—even when the being communicates things at odds with the Jesus of the New Testament. For example, Betty Eadie learned from her being of light that she was worthy of being accepted by Jesus and that God accepts all religions whether or not they exalt Jesus as Lord. She also downplays the reality of sin and claims that no one will end up in hell. Eadie mentions nothing about Jesus' death on the cross as the sufficient sacrifice for sin. Her overall worldview is a combination of Mormon and New Age ideas.[10] Many other NDE reports also depict Jesus as a being of light who welcomes everyone into heaven and condemns no one.

Second, many who return from an NDE become involved in occult practices and belief systems and may even develop psychic abilities through these experiences, as Dannion Brinkley claims to have done. Many adopt the New Age beliefs that humans are divine, all is one, there is no sin, all religions are from God, we are reincarnated at death, and humanity is poised on the verge of a New Age of spiritual evolution. One near-death experiencer spoke of God as "a tremendous source of energy. . . . I think that God is in every one of us; we are God."[11]

Third, the general impression given by many NDEs is that death is nothing to be feared, eternal hell is an illusion, and all roads lead to a blissful afterlife. The Christian emphasis on the stark, eternal realities of heaven and hell is rejected as dogmatic and negative.[12]

Although some NDEs have a Christian message and others recount hellish experiences of various kinds, the most popular versions of the NDE usually undermine the reality of Jesus Christ as our only hope in life and death. Instead of trusting in Jesus' work on the cross for us, those entranced by NDEs tend to place their hope on a vague sense of spiritual optimism. A warm and welcoming light awaits us all after death. This assumption is unfounded, however, because the NDE is not an experience of actual death; it is a *near*-death experience. Unlike Jesus, those who write and lecture about their near-death experiences have not been resurrected from the dead. Moreover, the theological content of the various NDEs often conflicts. Some are Mormon-oriented, some are New Age, some speak of hell, some exclude God altogether, others match up well with the biblical understanding of the afterlife. Since these diverse reports cannot all be true, we must appeal to an external standard by which to judge them.

Of course, if one were to die and then rise from the dead three days later in a deathless body as the Lord of life, such a person would be in a unique position to declare the truth about life and death, heaven and hell. This describes the biography of Jesus Christ—and no one else. His Word is the dependable standard for judgment on matters of eternity, life, and death, and Jesus never consoled us that our inherent goodness would win us heaven or that we would have repeated chances to get it right through reincarnation (Matthew 25:46; John 5:24-29; see also Hebrews 9:27). On the contrary, he proclaimed that he alone was the resurrection and the life, and that whoever would believe in him would pass from death to life and experience eternal life (John 5:24; 11:25,26).

Jesus and the Goddess

Another obstacle hinders many souls from trusting in Jesus as their hope for this life and the next. Many modern women have felt the anguish of being treated as second-class citizens in a man's world. They have been stereotyped and marginalized by men who fail to see their real abilities and understand their real desires. Because many women have been discriminated against unfairly because of their gender, they justifiably complain of the sting of sexism.

Christians should be sensitive to these problems, since God calls us to respect everyone equally on the basis of the truth that we are all created in the image of God (Genesis 1:27), to love our neighbor as ourselves (Matthew 19:19), and to recognize our unity and equality in Christ (Galatians 3:26-29). Yet sadly, many women see the Bible itself as justifying the mistreatment of half the human race.

A few years ago I wrote an essay for a campus newspaper that responded to an editorial by a young goddess worshiper named Lia Salciccia. The woman's article was provocatively titled "Christianity Fails to Honor Women,"[13] and represented the thinking of scores of people who reject the gospel because they believe the Bible is sexist.

Several charges are often leveled against the God of the Bible. Many non-Christian feminists claim that the God of the Bible is male. If God is male, then men are more like God than women. Therefore, men have a godlike authority over women in a way analogous to God's authority over his creation. This devalues and disempowers women who, because of their gender, will never have the privileged status of men. Salciccia wonders how Christian women put up with it. "Do they enjoy following a religion governed by a book that says they are inferior?" she asks. "When these woman pray to God is it a man's face that they see?"[14] Some feminists also complain that since the Incarnation of God occurred in the form of a man, Jesus, this God cannot properly relate to women's experiences. Because of these problems with Christianity, they say, women must turn to a feminine understanding of the divine, the goddess. Hence the bumper sticker "Thank Goddess."

Goddess religion takes many forms. Generally speaking, it rejects male-dominated religious practices and centers on ancient pagan practices that revere the earth and its energies, often drawing on unreliable prehistoric sources to fashion a suitable spirituality for women today.[15] Goddess religion rejects the notion of God as a distant Creator who sends his male emissary (Jesus) to the world. Instead, it worships the goddess as the divine power and presence that permeates the universe. Salciccia says, "If I can choose my own deity . . . I will choose one I can relate to, one which is reflected by all living things, including my very female self."[16] The goddess, however, is not a personal deity. Despite the references to "She" and "Mother," this deity is really nothing more than an impersonal force, principle, or source that is embedded in nature. The goddess is more of a metaphorical or poetic idea than a literal or actual being.

In rebutting these charges against the God of the Bible, I will highlight several points that pertain to Jesus.[17] Those drawn to the goddess must come to terms with the real Jesus, not a sexist caricature. First, the God of the Bible is not male in any sense. God is not a sexual being. Jesus taught that God is spirit (John 4:24) and not one who brings things into existence through procreation. God is not to be represented as either a male or a female (Exodus 20:4; Deuteronomy 4:16). The Bible does refer to God as our Father, but as theologian Alister McGrath explains:

> To speak of God as father is to say that the role of the father in ancient Israel allows us insights into the nature of God, not that God is a male human being. Neither male or female sexuality is to be attributed to God. Indeed, sexuality is an attribute of the created order that cannot be assumed to correspond directly to any such polarity within the creator God himself.[18]

Scripture refers to God as "he" and Jesus called God his Father, not to emphasize masculinity against femininity, but to highlight that God is a personal and powerful being. Unlike the idea of the goddess, the biblical God is a knowing, willing, holy, and loving personal agent who reveals himself in the Bible and through becoming a human being in Jesus Christ. In the cultures to which the Bible originally came, men had more authority than women. Although the Bible does not sanction sexism or the marginalization of women, it used the terms and concepts that would best communicate God's position of prestige and his role as our protector and provider.

Nevertheless, the Bible uses feminine imagery when it speaks of God as giving birth to Israel (Deuteronomy 32:18) and to the Christian (James 1:18). Jesus said he longed to gather rebellious Israel to himself as a mother hen gathers her chicks (Matthew 23:37-39). These kinds of metaphors reveal that although God is not a sexual being, he possesses all the qualities that we appreciate in both men and women, because God is the giver of every good and perfect gift (James 1:17).

Second, Jesus did not set up a male-dominated religious system in which women would be permanently subjugated. He surprised his followers by teaching theology to women in private and in public (John 4:7-27; 11:21-27; Luke 10:38-42) at a time when women were excluded from such affairs. Although he esteemed the family, Jesus stipulated that a woman's principal purpose in life is not reducible to motherhood and domestic work but is found in knowing and following God's will (Luke 10:38-42; 11:27,28). Jesus also appeared to Mary after his resurrection and appointed her as a witness to his world-changing event—in a time when the witness of a woman was not respected (John 20:17,18; Matthew 28:5-10). His model of leadership was based on mutual service and sacrifice, not hierarchical authority structures:

> You know that the rulers of the Gentiles lord it over them, and their high officials exercise authority over them. Not so with you. Instead, whoever wants to become great among

you must be your servant, and whoever wants to be first must be your slave—just as the Son of Man did not come to be served, but to serve, and to give his life as a ransom for many (Matthew 20:25-28).

In addition, in the early church, women served as prophets (Acts 2:17,18; 21:9) and teachers (Acts 18:24-28). Paul clearly articulated the equality of believers when he said, "You are all sons of God through faith in Christ Jesus, for all of you who were baptized into Christ have clothed yourselves with Christ. There is neither Jew nor Greek, slave nor free, male nor female, and you are all one in Christ Jesus" (Galatians 3:26-28).[19]

Third, the Incarnation of God in Jesus does not imply that God is male or that God excludes or devalues women. For God to manifest himself in person as a human being, he would have to be either a male or a female. He could not be both simultaneously. However, the most important fact about Jesus was not his maleness (although maleness enabled him to gain respect in ancient, patriarchal Jewish culture), but his holy humanity and identification with the entire human race. As McGrath says, "The fact that Jesus was male, the fact that he was a Jew ... all these are secondary to the fact that God took upon himself human nature, thereby lending it new dignity and meaning."[20]

Jesus understands us all from the inside out: "For we do not have a high priest who is unable to sympathize with our weaknesses, but we have one who has been tempted in every way, just as we are—yet without sin" (Hebrews 4:15). Although Jesus lived in perfect harmony with the Father and the Holy Spirit, when he joined the human family he knew what it was like to suffer and feel pain, even as we do:

> During the days of Jesus' life on earth, he offered up prayers and petitions with loud cries and tears to the one who could save him from death, and he was heard because of his reverent submission. Although he was a son, he learned obedience from what he suffered and, once made perfect, he became the source of eternal salvation for all who obey him (Hebrews 5:7-9).

Those who gravitate toward the goddess because of the problems they perceive with the God of the Bible should realize that Jesus Christ died for the sins of the world, including the sins that men commit against women. Jesus neither endorses nor excuses any sin, but calls everyone to repent of sin and accept him as Savior, Master, and Friend (John 15:15). An impersonal principle, power, or presence romantically called the goddess can be no one's friend, let alone Savior. Despite the sentimental use of feminine language, one cannot relate personally to an impersonal power.

While goddess religion is speculatively reconstructed from the dark recesses of prehistory, the drama of Jesus is enshrined in datable, space-time, human history. God has a human face—the visage of Jesus. His story has spoken to countless millions of women and men worldwide for the last 2000 years—and continues to speak to us today.

Knowing the Living Christ

Throughout this book I have argued that the historic Christian confession of Jesus Christ as Lord and Savior meets the various challenges offered by those who would abandon the Scriptures in order to fashion another Jesus. My labor is not a merely academic exercise, but comes out of 20 years of Christian experience and ministry to those involved in non-Christian spiritualities. I would do my readers a disservice not to explain how one can come to terms with the living Christ and know him as the Lord and Savior that he is. A few words about my story may be appropriate.

Although my parents believed in God and were nominally Christian, our family did not attend church together. I attended a Presbyterian Sunday school class for a few years as a child, but was allowed to drop out when I became too bored. As a teenager, I became fascinated by many of the Eastern mystical ideas that influenced some of my favorite rock and jazz musicians. I thought there was something of significance there, but I could not quite tell what it was. When I entered college in 1975, I began to pursue my spiritual interests more earnestly through taking classes in philosophy and religion and by reading material on the occult and Eastern religions. I also made some attempt to practice meditation with the hopes of entering an altered state of consciousness. Jesus had little to do with my pursuits at this time. This, however, would soon change.

While visiting a friend at a nearby campus, I came across two young Christian women who fearlessly challenged me to consider the claims of Christ. I resisted, thinking that I was too hip to resort to such a traditional and old-fashioned spirituality. However, I began to wonder if they might be right. During this time I was reading the Christian philosopher Soren Kierkegaard for one of my philosophy classes. His book *The Sickness Unto Death* explained the state of the soul in rebellion against God. Although I did not want to believe that I was a creature at odds with my Creator,

Kierkegaard's analysis was penetrating and memorable. He offered faith in Christ as the only solution to the human problem of sin against a holy God.

The summer after my first year in college, I returned home to find that many of my high school friends had become Christians. I spent many hours talking with them, reading the Bible, reading my occult books, and also interacting with non-Christian friends who were worried that I, too, would become "a Jesus freak" (as young Christians then were often labeled). There was a battle raging for my soul, and I knew I had to choose sides.

I was impressed by the change in my Christian friends' lives. Several had given up drug abuse and other unfruitful behavior. They were excited about their new Christian faith and were sharing it everywhere. I was also deeply challenged by the Jesus of the Gospels. Although I knew little of the New Testament, I soon realized that Jesus could not be put in the comfortable category of another spiritual guru. He claimed to be our only hope and demanded our ultimate allegiance. I was beginning to see that I had to accept him for who he is or reject him to pursue my own way.

In 1976 at the age of 19 before a large group of young Christians, I prayed to become a Christian by asking Jesus to forgive my sins and be the Lord of my life. Shortly after that I was baptized. Unlike many of my friends, I did not feel any differently after that prayer. Nevertheless, over the next several months I gained a stability, direction, and peace in my life that I had not known before. This period of time was not without its struggles, but I came to realize that Jesus was the source of my life and that I could trust him to lead me. I have never regretted coming to Jesus Christ.

Since then I have acquired three degrees in philosophy and have researched numerous non-Christian worldviews, both secular and spiritual. Although some Christians seem to fear the challenge of alternative beliefs, my Christian life has involved an ongoing dialogue with other religions and belief systems. Through this dialogue—which arises out my deep conviction that the Christian message is objectively true and of ultimate consequence for everyone—I have grown in my assurance that Jesus is who he said he was. Out of this intellectual and spiritual confidence has come the book now in your hands.

I resonate with the apostle Paul who said that in Christ "are hidden all the treasures of wisdom and knowledge" (Colossians 2:3). As Pascal noted, Christ is the key to life:

> Not only do we only know God through Jesus Christ, but we only know ourselves through Jesus Christ; we only know life and death through Jesus Christ. Apart from Jesus Christ we cannot know the meaning of our life or our death, of God or of ourselves.
>
> Thus without Scripture, whose only object is Christ, we know nothing, and can see nothing but obscurity and confusion in the nature of God and in nature itself.[21]

The confidence that I share with other Christians can belong to anyone who recognizes his or her spiritual need and comes to Jesus on his terms. Christianity need not be a blind leap of faith in the dark. There are, as I have tried to highlight, many reasons to believe (1 Peter 3:15,16). Although this book is filled with various facts and arguments, the way of coming to know Christ is not complex or confusing; but it does require honesty and humility to realize that we need to be forgiven and restored through Jesus Christ.

Those who create a Christ in their own image attempt to eliminate the need for divine forgiveness and rebirth. Stephen Mitchell, in his recent poetic "translation" of the Gospels uses a scissors-and-paste method to create a different Jesus: He eliminates all the scriptural passages that do not fit with his preceptions claiming, for example that Jesus never taught that he forgave sin because he accepts all without needing to forgive them.[22] In commenting on Jesus' instruction in Matthew 6:12 to pray, "forgive our wrongs" (as Mitchell translates it), he states that "God, whose very being is forgiveness, cannot forgive a wrong that we commit against a particular person; only that person can. Here the meaning is, 'Once we have righted the wrong, help us forgive ourselves.'"[23]

Mitchell's amendment utterly avoids the actual text, which clearly calls us to pray to God for his forgiveness of our sins. Nor can Mitchell face up to what Jesus told his disciples after his resurrection: "This is what is written: The Christ will suffer and rise from the dead on the third day, and repentance and forgiveness of sins will be preached in his name to all the nations" (Luke 24:45-47). Those who forgive themselves apart from divine forgiveness may feel good about themselves, but only for a time, because a day of reckoning is coming.

Without repentance and forgiveness, there is no gospel and no hope of a spiritual life infused with the presence and power of the risen Christ. Repentance is the natural and logical response when we begin to apprehend the holiness of God in relation to our moral wrongdoing. We must

turn away from our old pattern of life and turn toward the
grace and forgiveness offered us through Jesus. This requires the willingness to esteem him as our authority and
obey him as our leader in all things. The riches of Christ
can only be received by trusting in the sufficiency of his
work to secure our complete acceptance before God. Paul
makes this evident when he says, "For it is by grace you have
been saved, through faith—and this is not from yourselves,
it is the gift of God—not by works, so that no one can boast"
(Ephesians 2:8). He also speaks of the Christian as having
been justified by God's grace (Titus 3:7). We are made right
with God through the work of Christ, plus nothing. This is
not a process of becoming good enough to be accepted by
God. It is only because Christ alone was good enough that
his righteousness can become ours—if we trust in him.[24]
Paul's Lord put it in these justly famous words:

> For God so loved the world that he gave his one and only
> Son that whoever believes in him shall not perish but have
> eternal life. For God did not send his Son into the world to
> condemn the world, but to save the world through him.
> Whoever believes in him is not condemned, but whoever
> does not believe stands condemned already because he
> has not believed in the name of God's one and only Son
> (John 3:16-18).

In Christ we find our destiny and dignity as sinful creatures who have been reconciled to God through his Son.
Pascal states it well: "Jesus is a God whom we can approach
without pride and before whom we can humble ourselves
without despair."[25] Those who have humbled themselves

before Jesus can stand with confidence and without presumption, because "in all things God works for the good of those who love him, who have been called according to his purpose" (Romans 8:28). As Pascal observes:

> Knowing God without knowing our own wretchedness makes for pride.
>
> Knowing our own wretchedness without knowing God makes for despair.
>
> Knowing Jesus Christ strikes the balance because he shows us both God and our wretchedness.[26]

If we claim to know God without Christ, we presume that we are acceptable to God apart from the work of a mediator. This leads to pride. Lamenting over our broken lives and uneasy consciences without a knowledge of God's love in Christ leads to despair. However, if we grasp that we are doomed to divine punishment without Jesus because of our sinfulness, and recognize that God entered the human race with the express purpose of setting us right with himself, we rejoice in God's ability to save us and his love for us. Despite our lack of moral perfection, we can know that "there is now no condemnation for those who are in Christ" (Romans 8:1). Jesus taught that without him we can do nothing of lasting value (John 15:1-8), yet through him we can do all things God inspires us to do (Philippians 4:13).

It is my genuine and passionate hope that any reader who has yet to repent of wrong living and trust in Jesus Christ for a new and eternal life will take that step of faith. As the apostle John promised of his Lord:

If we claim to be without sin, we deceive ourselves and the truth is not in us. If we confess our sins, he is faithful and just and will forgive us our sins and purify us from all unrighteousness. If we claim we have not sinned, we make him out to be a liar and his word has no place in our lives (1 John 1:8-10).

Yet to all who received him, to those who believed in his name, he gave the right to become children of God (John 1:12).

Appendix

THE NEW TESTAMENT CANON

IN A SENSE the following brief discussion of how the 27 books of the New Testament were recognized as canonical Scripture (as divinely inspired) is unnecessary. We have argued in chapter 6 that the entire New Testament has historical *integrity*, and we've shown that the Gospels, Acts, and several key writings of Paul have *authenticity* and *veracity* as well. This alone should lead us to trust reports concerning Jesus of Nazareth as reliable. We need not understand every detail of the historical process that led to the inclusion of all the New Testament books into our Bible in order to trust the documents themselves.

Nevertheless, misconceptions linger on this issue. For instance, *The Other Bible* (1984) consists of what it calls "ancient esoteric texts" from Gnosticism, the Kabala, and a variety of other nonbiblical sources. The introduction deems these nonbiblical texts to be inspired works that were not included in the Bible for merely historical or political reasons. Thanks to *The Other Bible*, "today, free of doctrinal strictures, we can read the 'greater bible' of the Judeo-Christian world."[1] This attitude completely ignores the facts surrounding the formation of the biblical canon and assumes that all the religious books of the ancient world were equal. In light of this, we will highlight a few important facts.

We have already noted in chapter 3 that the church fathers from early on quoted many New Testament books. In many cases, they even put them on the same level as the Old Testament itself. So intoxicated with the New Testament were the early church fathers (through the third century) that nearly the entire New Testament can be reproduced from their writings. J. Harold Greenlee writes that "these quotations are so extensive that the New Testament could virtually be reconstructed from them without the use of the New Testament manuscripts."[2]

The process of formally recognizing these documents as Scripture inspired by God was not one of *creating* a Bible, but rather of *discovering* what was already functioning as the authoritative rule in the historic church. This cannot be emphasized enough. The idea of a power-hungry, or simply incompetent bunch of ignorant clerics arbitrarily including and excluding books into the New Testament is a pervasive but historically indefensible notion.

The voting members who induct members into baseball's Hall of Fame do not create the candidate's batting, fielding, and pitching statistics. They rather recognize a previous greatness worthy of sporting fame. The inclusion of our four Gospels into the official canons of the fourth century was probably as automatic and uncontroversial as Willie Mays's induction into the Hall of Fame as soon as he was eligible. In fact the Gospels, Acts, and the major epistles of Paul (the sources from which we derive virtually all our knowledge of Jesus' life) were never a matter of dispute.

Although the final official recognition of our New Testament did not occur until the end of the fourth century, all of the books included were several centuries old by then and had long been in circulation. The Muratorian Fragment, referred to in chapter 3, dates at the end of the second century and lists 21 of the 27 New Testament books as authoritative. Justin Martyr, writing in the early second century, speaks of Christians congregating on Sunday when "the memoirs of the apostles or the writings of the apostles are read, as long as time permits,"[3] thus putting the Gospels on the same level as the Old Testament Scriptures.

Even earlier than this, when Polycarp writes to the Philippian church, he hopes that they are "well versed in the Sacred Scriptures." He continues, "It is declared in these Scriptures, 'Be ye angry, but sin not,' and 'Let not the sun go down upon your wrath.' "[4] The first reference can refer to either Psalm 4:4 from the Old Testament or to its quotation by Paul in Ephesians 4:26 in the New Testament. But although the second quotation is not found in the Old Testament, it is found in Paul's writings. Polycarp sees both references equally as sacred Scripture. There are also many other examples from the church fathers that illustrate this point.

We also see a recognition of New Testament writings as Scripture even in the New Testament itself. In 1 Timothy 5:18 a quotation of Jesus (Luke 10:7) is put side by side with an Old Testament passage (Deuteronomy 25:4), and both are referred to as Scripture. Second Peter 3:16 speaks of Paul's writings as Scripture.

Even the early protests of the Gnostics indirectly testified to an authoritative body of written teaching. The previously mentioned Gnostic document, the *Gospel of Truth*, dating from the mid-second century and likely written by Valentinus, shows an acquaintance with the Gospels, the Pauline letters, Hebrews, and Revelation and traces of Acts, 1 John, 1 Peter, and perhaps other New Testament books as well.[5] John Wenham notes that the writer's language is "permeated by [the New Testament books], because for him the language of these books is the language of the church."[6] W.C. van Unnik shows the significance of this:

> Before the [New Testament] Books could be used in the way they are used in the Gospel of Truth, they must have already enjoyed authority for a considerable time. To treat them as a collection was not a discovery of a few months before.[7]

Wenham also comments that "this evidence alone gives us the New Testament in the middle of the first half rather than the second half of the second century."[8] At the very least, the *Gospel of Truth* shows us that several New Testament books were handled as authoritative early on even by the heretics, whether or not the entire New Testament was so considered.[9]

Irenaeus agrees when he states that the Gospels are so securely established "that the very heretics themselves bear witness to them, and, starting from these [documents], each one of them endeavors to establish his own peculiar doctrine."[10]

The fact that the church did not officially recognize the canon until the fourth century can be understood in light of several historical contingencies. First, communication and transportation were less rapid than today, "hence, it took much longer for the believers in the West to become fully aware of the evidence for the books first written and circulated in the East, and vice versa."[11] Teleconferences on the canon were not possible. Second, because of widespread persecutions until A.D. 325 (including the destruction of biblical manuscripts), the church lacked the resources and circumstances needed for such universal and definitive decisions.[12] Shortly after, theological peace prevailed with Constantine, the councils of Hippo (A.D. 393) and Carthage (A.D. 397) were held, and our New Testament was officially recognized.[13] Third, it was not necessary to define a precise canon until various other unorthodox or deficient documents vied for attention.[14] The Gnostic challenge was a major prod in that direction.

The official recognition of the New Testament documents was not haphazard or politically charged, akin to the selection of a presidential candidate at the political party's convention. Documents were recognized as authoritative and deemed canonical on the basis of their apostolic authorship or approval, their antiquity, doctrinal content, universality of acceptance (or catholicity), traditional use and inspiration. While the selection process took time and did not lack some debate on certain books, it was not haphazard.[15]

Bruce Metzger's summary of this situation deserves full quotation:

> The slowness of determining the final limits of the canon is testimony to the care and vigilance of early Christians in receiving books purporting to be apostolic. But, while the collection of the New Testament into one volume was slow,

the belief in a written rule of faith was primitive and apostolic. . . . In the most basic sense neither individuals nor councils created the canon; instead they came to perceive and acknowledge the self-authenticating quality of these writings, which imposed themselves as canonical upon the church.[16]

The canon of the New Testament is not an inauthentic collection of material created to suppress legitimate documents that present a New Age version of Jesus. No one should reject the biblical presentation of Jesus on the basis that the books of the New Testament were merely a result of political or theological prejudice. That idea simply does not bear historical scrutiny.

Bibliography

This bibliography is not exhaustive, but it will direct the reader toward some core books on the topics addressed in this book. Since some books fit nicely into several of the categories below, I have tried to note this in the annotation. Those seeking more specifics on references and other sources should consult the footnotes throughout the chapters, which give specific page numbers and list articles as well as books.

General Analysis of the New Age Movement

Chandler, Russell. *Understanding the New Age.* Waco, TX: Word, 1988. Extensive, fair, but critical treatment by a thoughtful journalist.

Clark, David, and Geisler, Norman. *Apologetics in the New Age: A Christian Critique of Pantheism.* Grand Rapids, MI: Baker Books, 1990. A careful analysis of the worldview of pantheistic monism.

Groothuis, Douglas. *Unmasking the New Age.* Downers Grove, IL: InterVarsity Press, 1986. Examines the New Age worldview, its effect on society, and offers a biblical critique.

————. *Confronting the New Age.* Downers Grove, IL: InterVarsity Press, 1988. Aimed at meeting New Age challenges biblically and logically.

Hoyt, Karen, ed. *The New Age Rage.* Old Tappan, NJ: Fleming H. Revell Company, 1987. A collection of worthy critical essays.

Mangalwadi, Vishal. *When the New Age Gets Old.* Downers Grove, IL: InterVarsity Press, 1992. An excellent overview that treats subjects not mentioned in other critiques.

Miller, Eliot. *A Crash Course on the New Age.* Grand Rapids, MI: Baker Book House, 1989. A thoughtful and critical overview.

North, Gary. *Unholy Spirits.* Fort Worth: Dominion Press, 1986. A large, indepth, but sometimes idiosyncratic treatment.

Rhodes, Ron. *The Counterfeit Christ of the New Age Movement.* Grand Rapids, MI: Baker Books, 1991. A solid assessment of the relevant material.

Snyder, Tom. *Myth Conceptions: Joseph Campbell and the New Age.* Grand Rapids, MI: Baker Books, 1995. A biblical and logical assessment.

Angels and the New Spirituality

Kinnaman, Gary. *Angels: Dark and Light.* Ann Arbor, MI: Servant Books, 1994. Good overview of biblical and unbiblical views of angels.

Rhodes, Ron. *Angels Among Us.* Eugene, OR: Harvest House, 1995. A biblical study that examines unbiblical views.

Near-Death Experiences

Abanes, Richard. *Embraced by the Light and the Bible: Betty Eadie and Near-Death Experiences in the Light of Scripture.* Camp Hill, PA: Horizon Books, 1994. A journalistic investigation of note.

Groothuis, Doug. *Deceived by the Light.* Eugene, OR: Harvest House, 1995. An analysis of near-death experiences from a logical and biblical viewpoint.

Jesus Christ: Biblical Perspectives

Anderson, Norman. *Jesus Christ: The Witness of History.* Downers Grove, IL: InterVarsity Press, 1985. Explains the biblical meaning of Jesus and gives reasons to believe it is historically true. Good material on the resurrection also.

Ankerberg, John; Weldon, John; and Kaiser, Walter. *The Case for Jesus the Messiah.* Chattanooga, TN: The John Ankerberg Evangelistic Association, 1988. Presents and explains many Old Testament prophecies for Jesus as the Messiah.

Ankerberg, John, and Weldon, John. *The Facts on the "Last Temptation of Christ."* Eugene, OR: Harvest House, 1988. Revealing booklet on the controversial movie and book.

Athanasius, St. *The Incarnation of the Word of God.* New York: Macmillan, 1946. A classic from the fourth century.

Buell, Jon A., and Hyder, O. Quentin. *Jesus: Ghost, God or Guru?* Grand Rapids, MI: Zondervan, 1978. Helpful introductory treatment of the biblical Jesus.

Erickson, Millard. *The Word Became Flesh: A Contemporary Incarnational Christology.* Grand Rapids, MI: Baker Books, 1991. A major treatment by a well-recognized scholar.

Fernando, Ajith. *The Supremacy of Christ.* Wheaton, IL: Crossway Books, 1995. A compelling defense of the incomparability of Jesus Christ.

Gallup, George, and O'Connell, George. *Who Do Americans Say That I Am?* Philadelphia: Westminster, 1986. Interesting survey material with some comment.

Green, Michael. *The Empty Cross of Jesus.* Downers Grove, IL: InterVarsity Press, 1984. A solid treatment of the meaning of the cross and the resurrection.

Harper, Michael. *The Healings of Jesus.* Downers Grove, IL: InterVarsity Press, 1986. Explains the meaning, methods, and kinds of Jesus' healing.

Jones, E. Stanley. *The Christ of the Indian Road.* New York: Grosset & Dunlap, 1925. A classic by a missionary on how Jesus relates to a largely Hindu culture.

Kreeft, Peter. *Socrates Meets Jesus.* Downers Grove, IL: InterVarsity Press, 1987. The important issues about Jesus are discussed in an engaging and entertaining dialogue format.

Lockyer, Herbert. *Everything Jesus Taught.* San Francisco: Harper and Row, 1984. Summary of Jesus' teaching.

Machen, J. Gresham. *The Virgin Birth of Christ.* New York: Harper and Brothers Publishers, 1930. A classic defense of the doctrine with a strong refutation of the notion that Christianity got the idea of the virgin birth from Buddhism.

Mangalwadi, Vishal. *World of the Gurus,* second edition. Chicago, IL: Cornerstone Press, 1992. A look at contemporary Hindu gurus in relation to Jesus. Written by an Indian.

Ramm, Bernard. *An Evangelical Christology.* Nashville: Thomas Nelson Publishers, 1985. Christology from a veteran theologian very conversant with modern theology.

Speer, Robert E. *The Finality of Jesus Christ.* Westwood, NJ: Fleming H. Revell Company, 1933. A classic statement defending the uniqueness of Jesus.

Sproul, R.C. *Who Is Jesus?* Wheaton, IL: Tyndale House, 1988. A concise and informative booklet.

Stott, John R.W. *Christ the Controversialist.* Downers Grove, IL: InterVarsity Press, 1972. A balanced, biblical analysis.

————. *The Cross of Christ.* Downers Grove, IL: InterVarsity Press, 1987. A masterful treatment of the atonement.

Warfield, B.B. *The Person and Work of Christ.* Philadelphia: The Presbyterian and Reformed Publishing Company, 1950. A collection of important essays from a leading American theologian from two generations ago.

Wells, David F. *The Person of Christ.* Westchester, IL: Crossway Books, 1984. A scholarly, but readable perspective.

Wright, N.T. *Who Was Jesus?* Grand Rapids, MI: Eerdmans, 1992. An assessment of three popular views of Jesus by Barbara Thiering, A.N. Wilson, and John Spong that contradict the New Testament.

Jesus Christ: New Age Perspectives

Campbell, Joseph. *The Power of Myth.* New York: Doubleday, 1988. Although not specifically about Jesus, Campbell often comments on Jesus and Christianity from a neo-Gnostic point of view.

The Christ. *New Teachings for an Awakening Humanity.* Santa Clara, CA: Spiritual Education Endeavors Company, 1986. Purportedly channeled material with the channeler not listed.

Fox, Matthew. *The Coming of the Cosmic Christ.* San Francisco: Harper and Row, 1988. While retaining some orthodox points, Fox's view of Jesus is in many important ways closer to the New Age vision than to the biblical picture.

Gruber, Elmar R., and Kersten, Holger. *The Original Jesus: The Buddhist Sources of Christianity*. Rockport, MA: Element Books, 1995. Speculations on the supposedly Buddhist teachings of the original Jesus.

Hanh, Thich Nhat. *Living Buddha, Living Christ*. New York: G.P. Putnam, 1995. An unsuccessful attempt to reconcile opposing worldviews.

Hall, Manly P. *The Mystical Christ*. Los Angeles: The Philosophical Research Society, 1951. Developed treatment by an influential New Age writer.

Hassnain, Fida. *A Search for the Historical Jesus: From Apocryphal, Buddhist, Islamic, and Sanskrit Sources*. Bath: United Kingdom: Gateway Books, 1994. An uncritical collection of discredited sources are employed to defend unorthodox ideas about Jesus.

Houston, Jean. *Godseed: The Journey of Christ*. Amity, NY: Amity House, 1988. Meant primarily as a manual for sacred rituals, it also gives a neo-Gnostic portrait of Jesus.

Lewis, H. Spencer. *The Mystical Life of Jesus*. San Jose, CA: Supreme Grand Lodge of AMORC, 1974. A Rosicrucian perspective appealing to an esoteric tradition.

———. *The Secret Doctrines of Jesus*. San Jose, CA: Supreme Grand Lodge of AMORC, 1981.

MacLaine, Shirley. *Going Within*. New York: Bantam, 1989. Not specifically about Jesus, but mentions some New Age interpretations, including Jesus as an Essene.

Mitchell, Stephen. *The Gospel According to Jesus: A New Translation and Guide to His Essential Teachings for Believers and Unbelievers*. New York: Harper-Perennial, 1991. Takes a scissors-and-paste view of the Gospels and interprets what is left in an essentially New Age fashion.

Spangler, David. *Reflections on the Christ*. Glasgow, Scotland: Findhorn, 1978. An influential New Age treatment.

Steiner, Rudolf. *Christianity As a Mystical Fact*. New York: Anthroposophic Press, 1972. A reinterpretation of Jesus along neo-Gnostic lines.

Williamson, Marianne. *A Return to Love: Reflections on the Principles of "A Course in Miracles"*. New York: HarperCollins Publishers, 1992. A very popular presentation of the ideas of *A Course in Miracles*.

Gnosticism

Brown, Harold O.J. *Heresies*. Garden City, NY: Doubleday, 1984. Includes a helpful chapter comparing Gnosticism with orthodoxy.

Dart, John. *The Jesus of Heresy and History*. San Francisco: Harper and Row, 1988. A thoughtful journalist's treatment of the Nag Hammadi find and its meaning. Sympathetic to Gnosticism.

Helmbold, Andrew. *The Nag Hammadi Gnostic Texts and the Bible*. Grand Rapids, MI: Baker Book House, 1967. An early Christian analysis.

Irenaeus. *Against Heresies*. In *Ante-Nicene Fathers*. Edited by Alexander Roberts and James Donaldson. Grand Rapids, MI: Wm. B. Eerdmans, 1987. The classic orthodox response to Gnosticism. Still quite relevant today.

Jonas, Hans. *The Gnostic Religion*. Boston: Beacon Press, 1963. A landmark study by a philosopher in the existentialist tradition.

Layton, Bentley. *The Gnostic Scriptures*. Garden City, NY: Doubleday & Company, 1987. Layton's introductions and annotations make the Gnostic materials more accessible.

Meyer, Marvin W. *The Secret Teachings of Jesus*. New York: Random House, 1984. A small selection of Nag Hammadi texts with commentary.

Nash, Ronald. *Christianity and the Hellenistic World*. Grand Rapids, MI: Zondervan, 1984. Contains several helpful chapters on Gnosticism, defending the originality and authenticity of Christianity in confrontation with Gnosticism.

Pagels, Elaine. *The Gnostic Gospels*. New York: Random House, 1979. A watershed book that opened Gnosticism to the masses. Quite sympathetic to Gnosticism.

Robinson, James M. *The Nag Hammadi Library*. San Francisco: Harper and Row, 1988. The standard reference work with introductory materials but no annotation.

Rudolph, Kurt. *Gnosis*. San Francisco: Harper and Row, 1987. A comprehensive major work by a German scholar.

Summers, Ray. *The Secret Sayings of the Living Jesus*. Waco, TX: Word, 1968. An early Christian analysis of the *Gospel of Thomas*.

Wenham, David, ed. *The Jesus Tradition Outside the Gospels.* Gospel Perspectives Series, vol. 5. England: JSOT Press, 1985. Contains two excellent scholarly articles on the authenticity of biblical Christianity in relation to Gnosticism. The entire "Gospel Perspectives" series presents a scholarly defense of the reliability of the New Testament against criticism.

Winterhalter, Robert. *The Fifth Gospel.* San Francisco: Harper and Row, 1988. A New Age devotional commentary on the *Gospel of Thomas.*

The Historical Reliability of the New Testament

Archer, Gleason L. *Encyclopedia of Biblical Difficulties.* Grand Rapids, MI: Zondervan Publishing House, 1982. Defends the noncontradictory character of the Bible by explaining many difficult passages.

Barnett, Paul. *Is the New Testament History?* Ann Arbor, MI: Servant, 1986. A simple but compelling case for the New Testament as reliable history.

Blomberg, Craig. *The Historical Reliability of the Gospels.* Downers Grove, IL: InterVarsity Press, 1987. An excellent treatment of the trustworthiness of the Gospels in light of modern scholarship.

Bruce, F.F. *The New Testament Documents—Are They Reliable?* sixth ed. Grand Rapids, MI: Eerdmans, 1987. A classic defense.

———. *The Canon of Scripture.* Downers Grove, IL: InterVarsity Press, 1988. A clear and scholarly treatment by a seasoned scholar.

———. *Jesus and Christian Origins Outside the New Testament.* Grand Rapids, MI: Eerdmans, 1982. Careful treatment of nonbiblical sources on Christianity.

———. *Paul: Apostle of the Heart Set Free.* Grand Rapids, MI: Eerdmans, 1979. Shows, among other things, the harmony of Paul with the Gospels.

Corduan, Winfried. *Reasonable Faith: Basic Christian Apologetics.* Nashville, TN: Broadman and Holman Publishers, 1993. Has several fine chapters on the reliability of the New Testament and the uniqueness of Jesus.

Dunn, James D.G. *The Evidence for Jesus.* Philadelphia: Westminster, 1985. More liberal than most books in this category, but still provides helpful insights, particularly on Gnosticism.

France, R.T. *The Evidence for Jesus.* Downers Grove, IL: InterVarsity Press, 1986. Helpful look at the historical evidence for the biblical Jesus.

Geisler, Norman L., and Nix, William E. *A General Introduction to the Bible.* Chicago: Moody Press, 1986. A comprehensive treatment of biblical reliability and inspiration.

Guthrie, Donald. *New Testament Introduction,* rev. ed. Downers Grove, IL: InterVarsity Press, 1990. Especially helpful in dealing with the authorship of New Testament books and the relationship between the Gospels.

Habermas, Gary. *The Verdict of History.* Nashville: Thomas Nelson Publishers, 1988. Excellent resource for material on Jesus and early Christianity culled from nonbiblical sources.

Hagerty, Cornelius. *The Authenticity of the Sacred Scriptures.* Houston: Lumen Christi Press, 1969. A Roman Catholic defense of biblical authority with many good insights.

Juedes, John P. "George Lamsa: Christian Scholar or Cultic Torchbearer?" *Christian Research Journal* (Fall 1989), pp. 9-14. Lamsa's translation of the Bible is popular in some New Age circles. This article shows the inadequacies of Lamsa's translation, his scholarly deficiencies, and the unbiblical beliefs of Lamsa himself.

Moreland, J.P. *Scaling the Secular City.* Grand Rapids, MI: Baker Book House, 1987. Contains a very instructive chapter on biblical reliability and another on the historicity of the resurrection of Christ.

Phillips, J.B. *The Ring of Truth.* New York: The Macmillan Company, 1967. A small, often insightful testimony to the New Testament's truth.

Robinson, John A.T. *Can We Trust the New Testament?* London and Oxford: Mowbrays, 1977. He answers yes and gives reasons to date the books quite early, despite some less-than-orthodox positions.

Wenham, John. *Christ and the Bible.* Leicester: InterVarsity Press, 1984. Deals with both Christ's view of the Bible and with the reliability of the Bible.

Yamauchi, Edwin. *The Stones and the Scriptures.* London: InterVarsity Press, 1973. Discusses the relevance of archaeology to the Bible.

The Jesus Seminar

Borg, Marcus. *Meeting Jesus Again for the First Time.* San Francisco: Harper-SanFrancisco, 1994. A member of the Jesus Seminar gives an essential New Age view of Jesus.

Boyd, Gregory A. *Cynic Sage or Son of God? Recovering the Real Jesus in an Age of Revisionist Replies.* Wheaton, IL: Victor Books, 1995. An indepth response to the views of Burton Mack and Dominic Crossan.

————. *Jesus Under Siege.* Wheaton, IL: Victor Books, 1995. An introductory response to the Jesus Seminar.

Funk, Robert, Hoover, Roy W. and the Jesus Seminar. *The Five Gospels: The Search for the Authentic Words of Jesus.* New York: Macmillan Publishing Company, 1993. The Jesus Seminar's translation and commentary.

Johnson, Luke Timothy. *The Real Jesus: The Misguided Quest for the Historical Jesus and the Truth of the Traditional Gospels.* San Francisco: Harper-SanFrancisco, 1996. A sharp and telling critique of the Jesus Seminar.

Wilkins, Michael and Moreland, J.P., eds. *Jesus Under Fire: Modern Scholarship Reinvents the Historical Jesus.* Grand Rapids, MI: Zondervan, 1995. A collection of essays by top evangelical scholars.

Witherington, Ben. *The Jesus Quest: The Third Quest for the Jew of Nazareth.* Downers Grove, IL: InterVarsity Press, 1995. A survey of ·recent scholarship by a noted evangelical scholar.

Biblical Interpretation

Barker, Kenneth, ed. *The NIV Study Bible.* London: Hodder and Stoughton, 1987. An excellent study Bible, by a team of biblical scholars, based on the New International Version.

Fee, Gordon D., and Stuart, Douglas. *How to Read the Bible for All Its Worth.* London: Scripture Union, 1983. Very important work for reliably interpreting the biblical documents.

Keener, Craig S. *The IVP Bible Background Commentary*. Downers Grove, IL: InterVarsity Press, 1993. An in-depth study of what the Scriptures mean in light of their original cultural settings.

Kline, William W., Blomberg, Craig L., and Hubbard, Robert L. *Introduction to Biblical Interpretation*. Dallas, TX: Word Publishing, 1993. A comprehensive treatment.

Sire, James. *Scripture Twisting*. Downers Grove, IL: InterVarsity Press, 1980. Explains 20 ways in which religious groups misinterpret the Bible. Very helpful in spotting faulty interpretations.

The Lost Years of Jesus

Beskow, Per. *Strange Tales About Jesus: A Survey of Unfamiliar Gospels*. Philadelphia: Fortress Press, 1985. An invaluable aid in evaluating many unconventional views of Jesus. His treatment of the Essene Jesus of Szekely and the Aquarian Christ of Levi are also very helpful. Written by a New Testament scholar as an update on Goodspeed's work (see below).

Bock, Janet. *The Jesus Mystery*. Los Angeles: Aura Books, 1984. Reproduces Notovitch's "The Life of Saint Issa" and defends the lost years' idea in the context of promoting the Hindu mysticism of Indian guru Sai Baba.

Goodspeed, Edgar J. *Modern Apocrypha*. Boston: The Beacon Press, 1956. A classic, critical treatment not only of the Notovitch materials, but also of the Aquarian Christ and other controversial claims.

Kersten, Holger. *Jesus Lived in India*. Shaftesbury: Element Books, 1986. Uses and adds to the Notovitch and Levi material in the context of Indian legends.

Notovitch, Nicholas. *The Unknown Life of Jesus Christ*. Translated by J.H. Connelly and L. Landsberg. New York: R.F. Fenno & Company, 1890. Notovitch's book went through several American editions. This incorrectly lists the copyright date as 1890 when, in fact, the first publication in the United States was not until some five years later. See Goodspeed, *Modern Apocrypha*, 4.

Prophet, Elizabeth Clare. *The Lost Years of Jesus*. Livingston, MT: Summit University Press, 1984. The most thorough defense of the "lost years" thesis. Includes the text of *The Unknown Life of Christ* by Notovitch and other accounts of the "Life of Saint Issa."

Jesus and the Essenes

Bruce, F.F. *Second Thoughts on the Dead Sea Scrolls*. Exeter: Paternoster Press, 1966. Careful treatment of a sometimes misunderstood phenomenon.

——. *New Testament History*. London: Pickering and Inglis, 1969. Valuable background material to the New Testament environment.

Charlesworth, James H. *Jesus Within Judaism*. New York: Doubleday, 1988. Useful information on recent studies on Jesus and Essenism and other ancient writings. Not a conservative treatment.

Cook, Edward M. *Solving the Mystery of the Dead Sea Scrolls: New Light on the Bible*. Grand Rapids, MI: Zondervan, 1994. An introductory update on recent developments.

Cross, Frank Moore. *The Ancient Library of Qumran and Modern Biblical Studies*. Grand Rapids, MI: Baker Book House, 1961. A careful treatment by a world-renowned scholar.

Graystone, Geoffrey. *The Dead Sea Scrolls and the Originality of Christ*. New York: Sheed & Ward, 1956. A short and early treatment which, nevertheless, puts many important issues in clear focus.

LaSor, William Sanford. *The Dead Sea Scrolls and the New Testament*. Grand Rapids, MI: Eerdmans, 1969. A helpful introduction.

Pfeiffer, Charles F. *The Dead Sea Scrolls and the Bible*. Grand Rapids, MI: Baker Book House, 1984. A simple but insightful overview.

Szekely, Edmond Bordeaux. *The Essene Jesus*. San Diego: Academy Books, 1977. Distills materials from his supposed manuscript finds.

——. *The Essene Gospel of Peace: Book One*. USA: International Biogenic Society, 1981.

———. *The Essene Gospel of Peace: Book Two.* San Diego: Academy Books, 1977.

———. *The Essene Gospel of Peace: Book Three.* San Diego: Academy Books, 1977.

———. *The Discovery of "The Essene Gospel of Peace."* San Diego: Academy Books, 1975. The romantic story of a highly questionable document.

Thiering, Barbara. *Jesus and the Riddle of the Dead Sea Scrolls: Unlocking the Secrets of His History.* San Francisco: HarperSanFrancisco, 1992. Speculations about the Gospels as coded documents.

Vermes, G. *The Dead Sea Scrolls in English.* London: Penguin Books, 1988. His introductory comments are very helpful in separating fact from fiction on the beliefs of the Essenes as revealed in the scrolls.

Jesus and Channeling

Alnor, William M. *UFOs in the New Age: Extraterrestrial Messages and the Truth of Scripture.* Grand Rapids, MI: Baker Books, 1992. A careful analysis of the spiritual implications of UFO phenomena.

A Course in Miracles. 3 vols. Farmington, NY: Foundation for Inner Peace, 1981. Voluminous material purportedly received from Jesus.

Alexander, Brooks. *Spirit Channeling.* Downers Grove, IL: InterVarsity Press, 1988. A concise but brilliant analysis of modern channeling.

Ankerberg, John, and Weldon, John. *The Facts on Spirit Guides.* Eugene, OR: Harvest House, 1988. Helpful booklet on the essential issues involved.

Cayce, Edgar. *Edgar Cayce's Story of Jesus.* Jeffrey Furst, ed. New York: Berkeley Books, 1976. Material collected and summarized from the Cayce readings.

———. *Edgar Cayce on Jesus and His Church.* Edited by Hugh Lynn Cayce. New York: Paperback Library, 1970. Another collection similar to the above.

Downing, Levi. *The Aquarian Gospel of Jesus the Christ.* Marina Del Rey, CA: Devorss & Co., 1981. An influential New Age treatment supposedly transcribed from the Akashic Records.

Klimo, Jon. *Channeling.* Los Angeles: Jeremy P. Tarcher, 1987. A thorough, sympathetic treatment.

Perry, Robert. *An Introduction to "A Course in Miracles."* USA: Miracle Distribution Center, 1989. Introductory booklet.

Ramtha, with Mahr, James Douglas. *Voyage to the New World.* New York: Fawcett Gold Medal, 1985. Material channeled through J.Z. Knight on assorted subjects.

Swihart, Philip. *Reincarnation, Edgar Cayce and the Bible.* Downers Grove, IL: InterVarsity Press, 1975. Insightful Christian booklet.

The Urantia Book. Chicago: The Urantia Foundation, 1955. A massive volume supposedly channeled from extraterrestrial sources.

Jesus, the Resurrection, and the Cosmic Christ

Albrecht, Mark. *Reincarnation: A New Age Doctrine.* Downers Grove, IL: InterVarsity Press, 1987. A careful defense of the biblical doctrine of resurrection over reincarnation.

Craig, William Lane. *Knowing the Truth About the Resurrection.* Ann Arbor, MI: Servant Books, 1988. A readable but thorough defense of the resurrection of Jesus which is very knowledgeable of modern scholarship.

———. *Assessing the New Testament Evidence for the Historicity of the Resurrection of Jesus.* England: The Edwin Mellen Press, 1989. An extremely thorough and scholarly analysis of all the New Testament evidence for the resurrection.

Henry, Carl F.H. *God, Revelation, and Authority,* vol. 3. Waco, TX: Word Books, 1979. A large, astute section on Jesus as the Logos makes this especially significant.

Lapide, Pinchas. *The Resurrection of Jesus: A Jewish Perspective.* Minneapolis: Augsburg, 1983. A fascinating affirmation of the physical resurrection of Jesus by a non-Christian, Jewish New Testament scholar.

Miethe, Terry L., ed. *Did Jesus Rise from the Dead?* San Francisco: Harper and Row, 1987. The record of a debate on the issue with the case for the resurrection presented by Gary Habermas.

Montgomery, John Warwick, ed. *Myth, Allegory and Gospel.* Minneapolis: Bethany Fellowship, Inc., 1974. A collection of essays on the relation of the biblical message to literature. Montgomery's introductory essay is especially provocative on the latent truths embedded in mythologies and literature and how they relate to the Christian message.

Pelikan, Jaroslav. *Jesus through the Centuries.* San Francisco: Harper and Row, 1987. A masterful survey of how Jesus has been seen through the centuries, which discusses the Cosmic Christ as understood by early Christian theologians.

Publications

Christian Research Journal. P.O. Box 500, San Juan Capistrano, CA 92693-0500. Deals with cults, the occult, ethics, and the new spirituality. Published quarterly.

Spiritual Counterfeits Project Journal. P. O. Box 4308, Berkeley, CA 94704. Focuses on issues related to the new spirituality, occultism, and cultural criticism.

Notes

Chapter 1—Who Do You Say That I Am?

1. "Who Was Jesus?" *Life,* December 1994, 67.
2. Robert Funk in *Forum* 1/1, 1985, 12; quoted in Luke Timothy Johnson, *The Real Jesus: The Misguided Quest for the Historical Jesus and the Truth of the Traditional Gospels* (San Francisco: HarperSanFrancisco, 1996), 8.
3. Quoted in the *Atlanta Constitution,* September 30, 1989; quoted in Johnson, 15.
4. Quoted in "Who Was Jesus?" *Life,* December 1994, 72.
5. Emmet Fox, *The Sermon on the Mount* (New York: Harper and Brothers, 1938), 1.
6. Ibid., 2.
7. Quoted in "Who Was Jesus?" 71.
8. Stephen Mitchell, *The Gospel According to Jesus: A New Translation and Guide to His Essential Teachings for Believers and Unbelievers* (New York: HarperPerennial, 1991), 7–8.
9. Cited in John Leo, "A Holy Furor," *Time,* August 15, 1988, 35.
10. Ibid.
11. Ibid., 36.
12. Michael Grosso, "Testing the Images of God," *Gnosis,* Winter 1989, 42.
13. Ibid., 41.
14. Ibid., 42.
15. Bertrand Russell, *Why I Am Not a Christian* (New York: Simon and Schuster, 1957),15–16.
16. Nietzsche even entitled one of his books *The Antichrist.*
17. George Gallup, Jr., and George O'Connell, *Who Do Americans Say That I Am?* (Philadelphia: Westminster Press, 1986), 19.
18. Ibid., 20.

19. Ibid., 19.
20. Ibid., 89.
21. Ibid., 62.
22. Ibid., 64.
23. Blaise Pascal, *Pensees* (New York: Penguin, 1966), # 739/864, 256.

Chapter 2—The Demoted Deity of the Jesus Seminar

1. J.D. Crossan quoted in *Boston Sunday Globe,* July 26, 1992; quoted in Gregory Boyd, *Jesus Under Siege* (Wheaton, IL: Victor Books, 1995), 19.
2. Quoted in *Los Angeles Times,* Feb. 24, 1994, View section; quoted in Luke Timothy Johnson, *The Real Jesus: The Misguided Quest for the Historical Jesus and the Truth of the Traditional Gospels* (San Francisco: HarperSanFrancisco, 1996), 7.
3. Quoted in Kenneth L. Woodward, "The Death of Jesus," *Newsweek,* April 4, 1994, 49.
4. The way the votes were weighted may be prejudiced against the more positive colors. See Ben Witherington, III, *The Jesus Quest: The Third Search for the Jew of Nazareth* (Downers Grove, IL: InterVarsity Press, 1995), 45–46.
5. Robert Funk, Roy Hoover, and the Jesus Seminar, *The Five Gospels: The Search for the Authentic Words of Jesus* (New York: Macmillan Publishing Company, 1993), 37.
6. Quoted in Woodward, 54.
7. Johnson, 21.
8. D.A. Carson, "Five Gospels, No Jesus," *Christianity Today,* April 25, 1994, 32.
9. Interestingly, the popular and conservative *NIV Study Bible,* Kenneth Baker, ed. (Grand Rapids, MI: Zondervan Publishers, 1985) does not color this red but takes it as a paraphrase of Jesus' teaching given by John.
10. Funk, et al., 5.
11. Quoted in Russell Watson, "A Lesser Child of God," *Newsweek,* April 4, 1994, 54.
12. Marcus Borg, *Meeting Jesus Again for the First Time* (San Francisco: HarperSanFrancisco, 1994). Borg's views differ somewhat from what is presented in *The Five Gospels* in that he thinks Jesus was a social reformer and movement founder. See 20–45.
13. Ibid., 37.
14. Ibid., 32.

15. Ibid., 32–33.
16. Ibid., 34.
17. Ibid., 131.
18. For a thorough analysis of Borg's view of Jesus, see R. Douglas Geivett, "Is Jesus the Only Way?" in *Jesus Under Fire: Modern Scholarship Reinvents the Historical Jesus,* Michael J. Wilkins and J.P. Moreland, eds. (Grand Rapids, MI: Zondervan Publishing House, 1995), 177–205.
19. Robert Funk, "The Issue of Jesus," *Forum* 1/1 (1985), 8; quoted in Johnson, 6.
20. Johnson, 10; emphasis in the original.
21. Robert Funk, quoted in *U.S. News and World Report,* July 1, 1991; quoted in Johnson, 7.
22. Johnson, 2.
23. Witherington, 43.
24. Johnson, 3.
25. Craig L. Blomberg, "The Seventy-four 'Scholars': Who Does the Jesus Seminar Really Speak For?" *Christian Research Journal* (Fall 1994), 34.
26. Ibid.
27. Richard Hays, "The Corrected Jesus: A Review of The Five Gospels," *First Things* (May 1994), 47.
28. Funk, et al., 3.
29. Carson, 30.
30. Blomberg, 35.
31. See Darrell L. Bock, "The Words of Jesus in the Gospels: Live, Jive, or Memorex?" in *Jesus Under Fire,* 73–99.
32. Funk, et al., 3.
33. This will be addressed in more detail in chapter 3.
34. Funk, et al., 3.
35. Ibid.
36. Witherington, 116–36.
37. Funk, et al., 4.
38. Ibid., 4–5.
39. Carson, 30.
40. Blomberg, 37.
41. Gregory Boyd, *Jesus Under Siege* (Wheaton, IL: Victor Books, 1995), 34; underscore in the original.
42. Ibid., 122–23; Gregory A. Boyd, *Cynic Sage or Son of God? Recovering the Real Jesus in an Age of Revisionist Replies* (Wheaton, IL: Victor Books,

1995), 144. For instance, the healing of the centurion's servant (Matthew 8:5–13; Luke 7:1–10) is from Q, as are other supernatural accounts.

43. Ibid., 144–45.

44. Boyd, *Jesus Under Siege,* 35.

45. C.S. Lewis, "Modern Biblical Criticism," in *Christian Reflections* (Grand Rapids, MI: Wm. B. Eerdmans Publishing Company, 1967), 157.

46. See Boyd, *Cynic Sage or Son or God,* 163; and Boyd, *Jesus Under Siege,* 121-124.

47. On this see C. Stephen Evans, "Can the New Jesus Save Us?" *Books and Culture: A Christian Review* (November/December, 1995), 8.

48. According to a poll reported in *U.S. News and World Report,* April 4, 1994, 48.

49. Ibid., 50.

50. On the legitimacy of admitting the supernatural into historical explanations, see William Lane Craig, *Reasonable Faith: Christian Truth and Apologetics* (Wheaton, IL: Crossway, 1994), chapter 5, and Norman L. Geisler, *Miracles and the Modern Mind* (Grand Rapids, MI: Baker Books, 1992), chapter 7.

51. Funk, et al., 2.

52. For instance, see J.P. Moreland, ed., *The Design Hypothesis* (Downers Grove, IL: InterVarsity Press, 1994). This is a collection of essays by scientists and philosophers in support of the belief in God as Creator of the universe and life on earth.

53. For more developed argumentation, see J.P. Moreland, *Scaling the Secular City* (Grand Rapids, MI: Baker Books, 1987).

54. Thomas Morris, ed., *God and the Philosophers* (Oxford: Oxford University Press, 1994).

55. Kelly James Clark, ed., *Philosophers Who Believe: The Spiritual Journeys of 11 Leading Thinkers* (Downers Grove, IL: InterVarsity Press, 1993).

56. See, for example, James Charlesworth, *Jesus Within Judaism* (New York: Doubleday, 1988).

57. On this see F.F. Bruce, *Jesus and Christian Origins Outside the New Testament* (Grand Rapids, MI: Wm. B. Eerdmans Publishing Company, 1974), 22–31.

58. See Carson, 32.

59. Critics have also noted that the Seminar does not even employ this criterion consistently because it eliminates certain unique statements

on the basis of their implications about Jesus' status as Messiah. See Bock, 91.

60. Funk, et al., 5.
61. Witherington, 57.
62. Ibid., 56.
63. See chapter 3 and chapter 8.
64. Hays, 46.
65. Johnson, 53. The idea that myths were added to an originally non-supernatural Jesus is taken up in chapter 3.

Chapter 3—The New Testament Witness to Jesus

1. Elmar R. Gruber and Holger Kersten, *The Original Jesus: The Buddhist Sources of Christianity* (Rockport, MA: Element Books, 1995). This book relies on many of the questionable assumptions used by the Jesus Seminar, which were criticized in chapter 2.
2. This follows the breakdown of Cornelius Hagerty, *The Authenticity of the Sacred Scriptures* (Houston: Lumen Christi Press, 1969), 225–26.
3. Bruce M. Metzger, *Manuscripts of the Greek Bible* (New York: Oxford University Press, 1981), 54.
4. Ibid.
5. Kurt Aland and Barbara Aland, *The Text of the New Testament* (Grand Rapids, MI: Eerdmans, 1987), 84.
6. Ibid., p. 87. See also Bruce Metzger, *The Text of the New Testament* (New York: Oxford University Press, 1964), 36–42.
7. Metzger, *Text,* 36–42.
8. Ibid., 42–61.
9. Ibid., 47–48.
10. Metzger, *Manuscripts,* 54.
11. Metzger, *Text,* 61–66.
12. Ibid., 30–31.
13. Ibid., 68–86.
14. See the illustrative chart in J.P. Moreland, *Scaling the Secular City* (Grand Rapids, MI: Baker Book House, 1987), 135.
15. Richard Ostling, "Who Was Jesus?" *Time,* August 15, 1988, 37.
16. Hagerty, 303.
17. John Wenham, *Christ and the Bible* (Grand Rapids, MI: Baker, 1984), 177.

18. Stephen Neill and Tom Wright, *The Interpretation of the New Testament 1861–1986* (Oxford: Oxford University Press, 1988), 86.

19. Although he does not come to orthodox conclusions, it is interesting to note that Wilson believes the manuscript evidence for the Gospels is very good. See Ian Wilson, *Jesus: The Evidence* (San Francisco: Harper and Row, 1984), 29–31. He says, "On the whole, errors and textual variations are relatively minor, and the canonical gospels can be judged to be very much as their authors wrote them" (p. 31).

20. We have argued that every New Testament book has historical integrity. Detailed arguments for the veracity and authenticity of books I do not discuss can be found in Donald Guthrie's *New Testament Introduction,* revised edition (Downers Grove, IL: InterVarsity Press, 1990).

21. Paul Barnett, *Is the New Testament History?* (Ann Arbor, MI: Servant Publications, 1986), 38–39.

22. Ibid.

23. Ibid. Robinson dates 1 Clement at A.D. 70. See John A.T. Robinson, *Redating the New Testament* (Philadelphia: Westminster, 1976), 335; see his whole discussion of the dating of postapostolic writings, 312–35. Robinson's thesis is that every book of the New Testament was written before A.D. 70.

24. Corinthians by Clement (A.D. 95) and The Epistle of Pseudo-Barnabas (A.D. 130–38) also mention various New Testament books. See Gary Habermas, *The Verdict of History* (Nashville: Thomas Nelson, 1988), 141–42, 144–45.

25. Although Polycarp, Ignatius, and Clement do not refer to every New Testament book, this does not necessarily mean they were not in existence at that time; to argue otherwise would be "the argument from silence" (fallacy). It could be that the other books simply did not warrant the writers' attention or that they did not know of their existence.

26. On this entire issue, known as the "synoptic problem," see Guthrie, 136–208.

27. The view of the early church was that Matthew predated Mark and Luke, but this is the minority opinion among modern scholars. Even if Matthew did not predate Mark or Luke, the dating of Acts still gives us the approximate date for Luke.

28. I am here following the general argument of J.P. Moreland, 151–54. See also Guthrie, 355–61.

29. Lewis Foster, "Introduction: Acts of the Apostles," in *The NIV Study Bible*, Kenneth L. Barker, ed. (Grand Rapids, MI: Zondervan, 1985), 1641.

30. Moreland, 154. Even if Luke does not depend on Mark and Matthew, the argument just given still gives us a very early date for Luke and Acts. Early dates can be argued for Mark and Matthew along other lines as well. On this see Guthrie, *New Testament Introduction*.

31. In logical terms, the argument we are using to this point is called the "denial of the consequent." Abstractly put, it runs as follows: If *A* (the antecedent), then *B* (the consequent). Not *B*. Therefore, not *A*. In our terms: If *a later date for Acts* then (likely) x, y, z. But we do not find x, y, z. Therefore, (likely) no *later date for Acts*.

32. "Toward a More Conservative Faith: Interview with William F. Albright," *Christianity Today*, January 18, 1963, 3.

33. F.F. Bruce, *The New Testament Documents: Are They Reliable?* sixth ed. (Grand Rapids, MI: Eerdmans Publishers, 1987), 12.

34. Ibid., 14.

35. Ibid., 30–46.

36. Ibid., 45.

37. Ibid., 45–46.

38. Ibid., 46; see also Craig Blomberg, *The Historical Reliability of the Gospels* (Downers Grove, IL: InterVarsity Press, 1987), 31–33.

39. Bruce, *New Testament Documents*, 46. For a discussion of the reliability of the New Testament witnesses in terms of legal evidence and reasoning, see John Warwick Montgomery, *Human Rights and Human Dignity* (Grand Rapids, MI: Zondervan Publishers, 1986), 131–60.

40. Barnett, 40.

41. Ibid., 41.

42. Ibid.

43. Eusebius, *Ecclesiastical History*, 6.14.7.

44. Irenaeus, *Against Heresies*, 3.1.1.

45. See Leon Morris, *The Gospel of John* (Grand Rapids, MI: Eerdmans, 1971), 32; see 30–35 for his argument for early dating. See also Barnett, 61–66.

46. Blomberg, 26.

47. Ibid., 27.

48. For the entire discussion of this issue, see Ibid., 25–31, and Moreland, 142–44.

49. A.N. Sherwin-White, *Roman Society and Roman Law in the New Testament* (Oxford: Clarendon, 1963), 188–91; cited in William L. Craig, *Knowing the Truth about the Resurrection* (Ann Arbor, MI: Servant, 1988), 96. See also, Julius Mueller, *The Theory of Myths, in Its Application to the Gospel History, Examined and Confuted* (London: John Chapman, 1844), 26; cited in Craig, 95.

50. J.B. Phillips, *The Ring of Truth* (New York: The Macmillan Company, 1967), 77.

51. Ibid.

52. Habermas, 154–55.

53. Bruce, *New Testament Documents*, 94.

54. R.T. France, *The Evidence for Jesus* (Downers Grove, IL: InterVarsity Press, 1986), 147.

55. Ibid. 149–50.

56. Ibid., 151–52.

57. W.M. Ramsay, *The Bearing of Recent Discovery on the Trustworthiness of the New Testament* (London: Hodder and Stoughton, 1915), 222; cited in Bruce, *New Testament Documents*, 91.

58. See Habermas, 152–53.

59. Barnett, 64; on archaeological insights on Jesus and his day, see also James H. Charlesworth, *Jesus within Judaism* (New York: Doubleday, 1988), 103–30.

60. For a review of these, see Habermas, 164–69. The entire book is dedicated to uncovering extrabiblical evidence for the life of Jesus.

61. Hagerty, 230.

62. Eusebius, 3.39.16.

63. See Bruce Metzger, *The Canon of the New Testament* (Oxford: Clarendon Press, 1987), 51–56. For a discussion of Papias's reference to John the Elder, which some have thought to be different from John the apostle, see Guthrie, 278–81.

64. See Metzger, *Canon*, 153–56, on Irenaeus's view of Scripture.

65. Irenaeus, 3.1.1.

66. Justin Martyr, *The First Apology of Justin Martyr,* chapter 66, in *The Apostolic Fathers,* 185; emphasis added.

67. Justin Martyr, *Dialogue with Trypho* in *The Apostolic Fathers,* chapter 103, 185.

68. Cited in F.F. Bruce, *The Canon of Scripture* (Downers Grove, IL: InterVarsity Press, 1988), 159.

69. Ibid. The extant text is mutilated at the beginning and only names Luke and John. We can legitimately surmise that the original mentioned the first and second Gospels as well.

70. See Hagerty, 234–36.

71. Ibid., 234.

72. Guthrie, 52.

73. Ibid., 53.

74. Homer A. Kent, "Introduction: The Gospel According to Matthew," in *The Wycliffe Bible Commentary,* Charles F. Pfeiffer and Everett F. Harrison, eds. (Chicago: Moody Press, 1977), 929.

75. Guthrie, 52.

76. For a defense of Matthew's authorship against some modern criticisms see Guthrie, 43–53, and Hagerty, 252–58.

77. See Barnett, 85–86.

78. Ibid., 84.

79. Ibid., 83–84.

80. Ibid., 57.

81. Ibid., 58–59. See also Bruce, *New Testament Documents,* 47–48.

82. On the importance of eyewitness testimony see Barnett, 49–55, and Moreland, 137–42.

83. See John A.T. Robinson, *Can We Trust the New Testament?* (London and Oxford: Mowbrays, 1977), 8.

84. David Wells, *The Person of Christ* (Westchester, IL: Crossway Books, 1984), 14.

85. France, 103.

86. Will Durant, *Caesar and Christ,* vol. 2, The Story of Civilization (New York: Simon and Schuster, 1944), 557.

87. Joseph Campbell, *The Power of Myth* (New York: Doubleday), 211.

88. See especially Blomberg, 113–89. See also Gleason Archer, *Encyclopedia of Biblical Difficulties;* and Robert L. Thomas and Stanley N. Gundry, *A Harmony of the Gospels with Explanations and Essays* (San Francisco: Harper and Row, 1978), 265–337.

89. See the sections on authorship for the other epistles in Guthrie.

90. Bruce, *New Testament Documents,* 76.

91. Moreland, 136–37, and Phillips, 39.

92. Moreland, 148.

93. Ibid., 149.

94. Bernard Ramm, *An Evangelical Christology* (Nashville: Thomas Nelson Publishers, 1985), 114.

95. Ibid. On the early creeds and hymns see also Habermas, 120–27.

96. This accusation is leveled by Holger Kersten in *Jesus Lived in India* (Longmead, England: Element Book Ltd., 1986). This book will be critiqued in chapter 8.

97. See Barnett, 131.

98. Bruce, *New Testament Documents,* 79. See also Barnett, 125–36. For a more detailed treatment of Paul's view of Jesus see F.F. Bruce, *Paul: Apostle of the Heart Set Free* (Grand Rapids, MI: Eerdmans, 1979), 95–112. For a defense of Paul's fidelity to the historical Jesus and the nonsyncretistic nature of his theology see J. Gresham Machen, *The Origin of Paul's Religion* (Grand Rapids, MI: Eerdmans, 1976), particularly 117–69, and Ronald Nash, *Christianity in the Hellenistic World* (Grand Rapids, MI: Zondervan, 1984), especially 57–79, 183–99, 241–50.

99. We have specifically dealt with only the Gospels and several of Paul's writings as passing all three tests of integrity, authenticity, and veracity. We have, though, shown that all the New Testament documents have integrity and were early recognized by the church as authoritative. For a more full-orbed defense of the entire New Testament, see Bruce, *The New Testament Documents* and *The Canon of Scripture;* Barnett, *Is the New Testament History?;* Hagerty, *The Authenticity of the Sacred Scriptures;* John Wenham, *Christ and the Bible;* and Guthrie, *New Testament Introduction.*

Chapter 4—Jesus and the New Spirituality

1. Barbara Kantrowitz, et al., "In Search of the Sacred," *Newsweek,* November 28, 1994, 54.

2. Eugene Taylor, "Desperately Seeking Spirituality," *Psychology Today,* November/December 1994, 55ff.

3. Deepak Chopra, *The Seven Spiritual Laws of Success* (San Raphael, CA: Amber-Allen Publishing/New World Library, 1994), 1–2.

4. Ibid., 3.

5. For a critique of this book, see the Douglas Groothuis book review in *The Christian Research Journal,* Fall 1995, 51ff.

6. Thomas Moore, *The Care of the Soul: A Guide for Cultivating Depth and Sacredness in Everyday Life* (New York: HarperPerennial, 1992), 4, 268, 273, 281.

7. Ibid., 133–34.

8. Ibid., 133.

9. Ibid., 239, 246.

10. Ibid., 66, 99–100, 107, 233.

11. Ibid., 229, 290.

12. On this mind-set, see Douglas Groothuis, "The Smorgasbord Mentality" in *Christianity That Counts: Being a Christian in a Non-Christian World* (Grand Rapids, MI: Baker Books, 1994), 97–101.

13. Cited in Gene Edward Veith, *Postmodern Times: A Christian Guide to Contemporary Thought and Culture* (Wheaton, IL: Crossway Books, 1994), 175–76.

14. He should not be confused with the Christian writer of the same name who has written many books for InterVarsity Press.

15. John White, "Jesus and the Idea of a New Age," *The Quest,* Summer 1989, 14.

16. Ibid., 16.

17. Ibid., 15.

18. Ibid., 17.

19. Ibid., 14; emphasis in the original.

20. Ibid.; emphasis in the original.

21. Ibid., 17; emphasis in the original

22. Ibid., 18; emphasis in the original.

23. Ibid., 22; emphasis in the original.

24. Ibid., 18.

25. Cited by Michael Grosso, "Testing the Images of God," *Gnosis,* Winter 1989, 43.

26. David Spangler, *Reflections on the Christ* (Glasgow, Scotland: Findhorn Foundation, 1977), 103.

27. Kathy Korpi; quoted in *What Do We Mean When We Say God?,* compiled by Deidre Sullivan (New York: Doubleday, 1990), 89.

28. John Beverly Butcher, *The Tao of Jesus: A Book of Days for the Natural Year* (San Francisco: HarperSanFrancisco, 1994), dedication page.

29. Janet Bock, *The Jesus Mystery* (Los Angeles: Aura Books, 1984), 112.

30. Thich Nhat Hanh, *Living Buddha, Living Christ* (New York: G.P. Putnam, 1995), 6–7, 100.

31. Stephen Mitchell, *The Gospel According to Jesus: A New Translation and Guide to His Essential Teachings for Believers and Unbelievers* (New York: HarperPerennial, 1991), 9.

32. Hahn, 31.

33. Ibid., 35.

34. Quoted in Mark O'Keefe, "The Jesus Wars," *The Sunday Oregonian,* February 4, 1996, L1.

35. See the discussion of Borg's beliefs in chapter 2.

36. Otto Friedrich, "New Age Harmonies," *Time,* December 7, 1987, 66.

37. Joseph Campbell, *The Power of Myth* (New York: Doubleday, 1988), 57.
38. Elizabeth Clare Prophet, *The Lost Years of Jesus* (Livingstone, MT: Summit University Press, 1984), flyleaf.
39. Shirley MacLaine, *Going Within* (New York: Bantam Books, 1989), 178.
40. Ibid., 181.
41. White, 18.
42. Ibid., 19; emphasis in the original.
43. Ibid., 17.
44. Campbell, 56.
45. These verses will be evaluated in depth in chapter 13.
46. Mitchell, 10.

Chapter 5—Jesus and Secret Knowledge: Gnosticism

1. Joseph Campbell, *The Power of Myth* (New York: Doubleday, 1988), 210.
2. Elaine Pagels, "Introduction," in Thich Nhat Hanh, *Living Buddha, Living Christ* (New York: G.P. Putman's Sons, 1995), xxii–xxiii.
3. Ibid., xxvii.
4. Don Lattin, "Rediscovery of Gnostic Christianity," *San Francisco Chronicle,* April 1, 1989, A-5.
5. Ibid., A-4.
6. Ibid., A-5.
7. Stephen A. Hoeller, "Wandering Bishops," *Gnosis,* Summer 1989, 24.
8. Patrick Henry, *New Directions in New Testament Study* (Philadelphia: Westminster Press, 1979), 94.
9. "The Gnostic Jung: An Interview with Stephen Hoeller," *The Quest,* Summer 1989, 85.
10. C.G. Jung, *Psychological Types* (Princeton, NJ: Princeton University Press, 1976), 11.
11. C.G. Jung, *Memories, Dreams, and Reflections* (New York: Vintage Books, 1973), 192. The *Seven Sermons to the Dead* is reprinted on 378–90. On Jung's Gnostic and pagan perspectives, see Richard Noll, *The Jung Cult: Origins of a Charismatic Movement* (New York: Princeton University Press, 1994); and Charles Strohmer, "Jung: Man of Mystic Proportions," *Spiritual Counterfeits Project Journal,* 9, no. 2, (1990), 32–44.
12. See Richard Smith, "The Modern Relevance of Gnosticism," in James M. Robinson, ed., *The Nag Hammadi Library* (San Francisco: Harper and Row, 1988), 53-49.

13. "Gnosticism," *Critique,* June-September 1989, 66.

14. For the full story of these events see John Dart, *The Jesus of History and Heresy* (San Francisco: Harper and Row, 1988), 1–49.

15. Elaine Pagels, *The Gnostic Gospels* (New York: Random House, 1979), xxxv.

16. For an able summary of this controversy see Ronald Nash, *Christianity in the Hellenistic World* (Grand Rapids, MI: Zondervan, 1984), 203–61.

17. Kurt Rudolph, *Gnosis: The Nature and History of Gnosticism* (San Francisco: Harper and Row, 1987), 57ff.

18. Robinson, 154.

19. In reviewing the movie *The Last Temptation of Christ,* Michael Grosso clearly affirms this idea when he rejects the perfect God of orthodoxy for an imperfect God who "would have to throw in his lot with us. Our fortunes would rise and fall together. The divine adventure would be the mirror image of the human adventure. *It would not only be that God is our Savior; we would ourselves become the Saviors of God*—it's the title of a book by Kazantzakis" (Michael Grosso, "Testing the Images of God," *Gnosis,* Winter 1989, 44, emphasis added).

20. Some of our information comes not from primary documents but from writings of the early Christian apologists (heresiologists) who sought to refute the so-called Gnostics ("those who claim to know").

21. See Dart, 162–92, for a plausible reconstruction of the original order of the sayings.

22. Robinson, 126.

23. F.F. Bruce, *Jesus and Christian Origins Outside the New Testament* (Grand Rapids, MI: Eerdmans, 1974), 112–13.

24. Robinson, 126.

25. Ibid., 134.

26. Pagels, 124.

27. Ibid., 126.

28. Christopher Farmer, "An Interview with Gilles Quispel," *Gnosis,* Fall/Winter 1985, 28.

29. Stephen A. Hoeller, "Valentinus: A Gnostic for All Seasons," *Gnosis,* Fall/Winter 1985, 24.

30. Ibid., 25.

31. Robinson, 130.

32. Ibid., 263.

33. Ibid., 150.

34. Ibid., 135.

35. Ibid., 377.

36. Ibid., 265.
37. Dart, 97.
38. Layton, 317.
39. See "Treatise on the Resurrection" in Robinson, 56.
40. Pagels, 11.
41. Irenaeus, *Against Heresies,* 3.16.5.
42. Ibid., 3.18.5.
43. Ibid., 3.18.2.
44. Ibid., 3.3.4.
45. *The Epistle of Polycarp,* chapter 8, in *The Apostolic Fathers,* A. Cleveland Coxe, ed. (Grand Rapids, MI: Eerdmans, 1987), 35.
46. E. Stanley Jones, *The Christ of the Indian Road* (New York: Grosset & Dunlap, 1925), 194.
47. See Norman L. Geisler, "I Believe . . . in the Resurrection of the Flesh," *Christian Research Journal,* Summer 1989, 21–22.
48. For a discussion of how the apostle understood this psalm to predict the resurrection, see Walter C. Kaiser, *The Uses of the Old Testament in the New* (Chicago: Moody Press, 1985), 25–41.
49. For a detailed and convincing defense of this interpretation, see William Lane Craig, "The Bodily Resurrection of Jesus," *Gospel Perspectives,* vol. 1, R.T. France and David Wenham, eds. (Sheffield: JSOT Press, 1980), 47–74. Pagels wrongly believes that the apostle Paul taught a nonphysical view of resurrection.
50. For a review of this phenomenon, see Dart, 60–74.
51. Robinson, 117.
52. Ibid., 209.
53. Ibid., 210.
54. Ibid., 224–25.
55. See John Ankerberg, John Weldon, Walter Kaiser, The *Case for Jesus, the Messiah* (Chattanooga, TN: John Ankerberg Evangelistic Association, 1989), 62–65.
56. The apostle Paul explicitly refers to Jesus as righteousness in Romans 3:21–26.
57. For more on the Messiah as divine, see Jon A. Buell and O. Quentin Hyder, *Jesus: God, Ghost, or Guru?* (Grand Rapids, MI: Zondervan, 1978), 113–19.
58. Campbell, 31.
59. Ibid., 49.
60. Ibid.

61. For a further critique of the idea of experiencing and expressing the ineffable, see Keith E. Yandell, *The Epistemology of Religious Experience* (New York: Cambridge University Press, 1993), chapters 3–5 and Irenaeus, 1.11.3–4.

62. See Hoeller, 24.

63. Pheme Perkins, "Popularizing the Past," *Commonweal* 9 (November 1979):634.

64. Kenneth Pitchford, "The Good News About God," *Ms.*, April 1980, 32–35.

65. Kathleen McVey, "Gnosticism, Feminism and Elaine Pagels," *Theology Today*, January 1981, 500. For the primary sources, see *Against Heresies* 1.1.1–8 and the *Apocryphon of John* in Robinson, 104–23.
    One may note that the male Creator is not directly accused of creating matter in this case, but this simply shows the diversity within the basic Gnostic orbit.

66. Robinson, 138. Bruce Chilton notes that "Thomas is notoriously antisexual; within this Gospel, sexual polarities are part of the evil which it is the business of salvation to overcome" (Bruce Chilton, "The Gospel According to Thomas As a Source of Jesus' Teaching," *Gospel Perspectives*, vol. 5, David Wenham, ed. [Sheffield: JSOT Press, 1985], 169).

67. Ann Belford Ulanov, "The God You Touch," *Parabola*, August 1987, 24.

68. See for instance, *The Book of Thomas, the Contender*, in Robinson, 205.

69. See Layton, 17.

70. F.F. Bruce, *The Canon of Scripture* (Downers Grove, IL: InterVarsity Press, 1988), 277.

Chapter 6—Jesus and the Gnostic Gospels

1. Harold W. Attridge and George W. MacRae, "Introduction: The Gospel of Truth" in James M. Robinson, ed., *The Nag Hammadi Library* (San Francisco: Harper and Row, 1988), 38.

2. Wesley W. Isenberg, "Introduction: The Gospel of Philip," in Robinson, 139.

3. Bentley Layton, *The Gnostic Scriptures* (Garden City, NY: Doubleday and Company, Inc., 1987), 325.

4. Joseph Fitzmyer, "The Gnostic Gospels According to Pagels," *America*, February 16, 1980, 123.

5. F.F. Bruce, *Jesus and Christian Origins outside the New Testament* (Grand Rapids, MI: Eerdmans, 1974), 154.

6. Ibid., 155.
7. Robinson, 434.
8. Ibid., 435. See the discussion of supposed "Gnostic feminism" in the previous chapter for more on this theme.
9. This follows the breakdown of Cornelius Hagerty, *The Authenticity of the Sacred Scriptures* (Houston: Lumen Christi Press, 1969), 225–26, who uses it only in discussing the New Testament documents, as we did in chapter 3.
10. Robinson, 2.
11. Ibid.
12. Ibid.
13. Ibid.
14. Ibid.; emphasis added.
15. Certainly it is granted that some of the canonical books or portions of books in the Old Testament do not readily tell us their author. This need not necessarily disqualify a document from being historically reliable, but it is one factor to be considered along with the two others to be mentioned.
16. Marvin W. Meyer, "Introduction: The Letter of Peter to Philip," in *Nag Hammadi,* 433.
17. See Ray Summers, *The Secret Sayings of the Living Jesus* (Waco, TX: Word Books, 1968), 14; and Craig Blomberg, *The Historical Reliability of the Gospels* (Downers Grove, IL: InterVarsity Press, 1987), 209.
18. Michael Grosso, "Testing the Images of God," *Gnosis,* Winter 1989, 43.
19. Wesley W. Isenberg, "Introduction: The Gospel of Philip," Robinson, 141. Although Bentley Layton doesn't hazard a guess as to the date of composition, he refers to Philip as an instance of "Valentinian pseudepigraphy" (Layton, 326).
20. Blomberg, 208.
21. Ibid.
22. Such as Gilles Quispel, "An Interview," *Gnosis,* Fall/Winter 1985, 28; and Bentley Layton, 251.
23. Such as Stephen Hoeller, "Valentinus: A Gnostic for All Seasons," *Gnosis,* Fall/Winter, 1985, 25.
24. Robinson, 38.
25. Layton, 251.
26. Ibid.
27. Ibid.

28. C.M. Tuckett, "Synoptic Tradition in the Gospel of Truth and the Testimony of Truth," *Journal of Theological Studies,* n.s. 35 (1984): 145.

29. Blomberg, 213–14.

30. Andrew K. Hembold, *The Nag Hammadi Texts and the Bible* (Grand Rapids, MI: Baker Book House, 1967), 89.

31. Christopher Tuckett, "Synoptic Tradition in Some Nag Hammadi and Related Texts," *Vigiliae Christiane* 36, no. 2 (1982):184.

32. Robinson, 32.

33. Ibid.

34. Francis E. Williams, "Introduction: The Apocryphon of James," in *Nag Hammadi,* 30.

35. Blomberg, 213.

36. Robert Winterhalter, *The Fifth Gospel: A Verse-by-Verse New Age Commentary on the Gospel of Thomas* (San Francisco: Harper and Row, 1988), 13.

37. Although scholars differ on this, in my own reading of *Thomas* I noted that parts or all of 48 of the 114 sayings significantly resemble New Testament references. Saying 17 is very similar to Paul's statement in 2 Corinthians 2:9, Layton, 380–99, lists possible cross-references in his translation/annotation.

38. Summers, 24–32.

39. Robinson, 131. See Bruce, *Jesus and Christian,* 130–31, on the relation of this to the canonical Gospels. Compare this saying with Luke 12:10.

40. Robinson, 131.

41. Ibid., 132.

42. Layton, 377.

43. Gregory A. Boyd, *Cynic Sage or Son of God? Recovering the Real Jesus in an Age of Revisionist Replies* (Wheaton, IL: Victor Books, 1995), 134.

44. For technical treatments that see Thomas as dependent on the canonical Gospels, see Craig L. Blomberg, "Tradition and Reaction in the Parables of the Gospel of Thomas," *Gospel Perspectives,* vol. 5, 177–205; and Christopher Tuckett, "Thomas and the Synoptics," *Novum Testamentum* 30, no. 2 (1988):132–57.

45. Blomberg, *Historical Reliability,* 211.

46. Ibid., 212.

47. For a scholarly defense of the well-established position that the Oxyrhynchus fragments are earlier portions of *Thomas,* see Joseph A. Fitzmyer, "The Oxyrhynchus Logoie of Jesus and the Coptic Gospel According to Thomas," in Joseph Fitzmyer, *Essays on the*

Semitic Background of the New Testament (Missoula, MT: Scholars Press, 1974), 355–433.

48. James D.G. Dunn, *The Evidence for Jesus* (Philadelphia: Westminster Press, 1985), 101.

49. Ibid.

50. Ibid., 102.

51. Ibid. See also 96–98 for a more general discussion of the implausibility of a bona fide "Christian Gnosticism" in the first century.

52. Marvin W. Meyer, "Jesus in the Nag Hammadi Library," *Reformed Journal,* June 1979, 15.

53. Winterhalter, 4.

54. Interestingly, Winterhalter on page 14 notes that the Oxyrhynchus version of saying 2, mentioned by Dunn above, is more authentic than the Nag Hammadi version, but he does not speak of the later Gnostic influence. He affirms *Thomas's* overall authenticity as a historical record of Jesus' words.

55. Fitzmyer, "The Gnostic Gospels According to Pagels," 123.
Fitzmyer grants the existence of "protognostic tendencies at the end of the first century" but not the full-fledged Gnosticism of the Nag Hammadi documents (ibid.). On the issue of Gnostics as late comers see also Patrick Henry, *New Directions in New Testament Study* (Philadelphia: Westminster Press, 1979), 116–19.

56. James D.G. Dunn, *Unity and Diversity in the New Testament* (Philadelphia: Westminster Press, 1977), 287–88.

57. Ibid., 288. See also Blomberg, *Historical Reliability,* 219.

58. Patrick Henry, 282.

59. Dunn, *Evidence,* 97–98.

60. Raymond E. Brown, "The Gnostic Gospels," *The New York Times Book Review,* January 20, 1980, 3.

61. F.F. Bruce, *The Canon,* 278. See also Henry, 93–119.

62. Robert E. Speer, *The Finality of Jesus Christ* (Westwood, NJ: Fleming H. Revell Company, 1933), 108.

Chapter 7—The Lost Years of Jesus

1. Edgar J. Goodspeed, *Modern Apocrypha* (Boston: The Beacon Press, 1956), 7.

2. For a detailed comparison of Jesus and present-day Indian gurus see Vishal Mangalwadi, *The World of the Gurus,* rev. ed. (Chicago: Cornerstone Press, 1992).

3. The story of Elizabeth Caspari's supposed contact with the "Life of Saint Issa" uses this verse as a defense in Elizabeth Clare Prophet, *The Lost Years of Jesus* (Livingstone, MT: Summit University Press, 1984), 317. Janet Bock, *The Jesus Mystery* (Los Angeles: Aura Books, 1984), 116–17.

4. Janet Bock, *The Jesus Mystery* (Los Angeles: Aura Books, 1984), 116–17.

5. See Goodspeed, 3, and for exact bibliographic information on the French and American publications, Per Beskow, *Strange Tales about Jesus* (Philadelphia: Fortress Press, 1985), 121.

6. Nicholas Notovitch, *The Unknown Life of Jesus Christ,* translated by J.H. Connelly and L. Landsberg (New York: R.F. Fenno and Company, 1890), 7. (This stated publication date is in all likelihood mistaken, since the first editions did not come out until 1894.) I have chosen to cite this edition because it appears to be less condensed in translation than the edition translated by Virchand R. Gandhi and revised by G.L. Christie (Chicago: Progressive Thinker Publishing House, 1907). This edition includes some unusual spellings that I will not correct when quoting. I will, on some occasions, refer to Prophet's *Lost Years,* which reprints another edition of *The Unknown Life* (which appears to be the edition translated by Violet Crispe [London: Hutchinson and Co., 1895]; but this is never directly stated). This includes a preface added by Notovitch in response to his critics, which is not available in the editions to which I have direct access.

7. Notovitch, 8.

8. His exact reasoning for this is never spelled out.

9. Notovitch, 10.

10. Ibid., 10–11.

11. Ibid., 229–30.

12. The brief story diverges from the account in Exodus at many places that need not concern us.

13. If Buddhists worship anything, it is Buddha, not Brahma.

Chapter 8—Did Jesus Travel to India?

1. Edgar J. Goodspeed, *Modern Apocrypha* (Boston: The Beacon Press, 1956), 8.

2. Ibid.

3. Ibid.

4. Ibid.

5. Per Beskow, *Strange Tales About Jesus: A Survey of Unfamiliar Gospels* (Philadelphia: Fortress Press, 1985), 59.

6. For more on Jainism, see Walter Kaufmann, *Religion in Four Dimensions: Existential, Aesthetic, Historical, Comparative* (New York: Reader's Digest Press, 1976), 297–301. Kaufman does point out that the founder of Jainism is sometimes worshiped, but this goes against his stated teachings. Jainism is primarily known as atheistic, or at least as a nonworshiping agnosticism. God, if there be one, is not the prime focus of religious devotion. Therefore, the statement "the god of the Djaines" is not an accurate summary of their beliefs because the role of deity in Jainism is peripheral at best. It is not known as a monotheistic religion.

7. Later Buddhist sects such as Pure Land Buddhism appeal to a Buddha figure as savior, but this comes hundreds of years after the time period described in "The Life of Issa."

8. See Arid Romarheim, *Various Views of Jesus Christ in New Religious Movements—A Typological Outline* (unpublished manuscript), 12–13. This is available from Christian Research Institute, Box 500, San Juan Capistrano, CA 92693–0500.

9. Carl Jackson, *Oriental Religions and American Thought* (Westport, CN: Greenwood Press, 1981), 149–50.

10. We will discuss this in chapter 12.

11. See Beskow, 58.

12. See F. Max Muller, "The Alleged Sojourn of Christ in India," *The Nineteenth Century,* no. CCXII (October 1894), 518.

13. Ibid. Muller thought it very unlikely that the same "Jewish merchants who arrived in India immediately after the Crucifixion knew not only what had happened to Christ in Palestine, but also what happened to Jesus, or Issa, while he spent fifteen years of his life among the Brahman." Notovitch responded that the merchants were indigenous Indians who had returned from Palestine on business. See Nicholas Notovitch in Elizabeth Clare Prophet, *The Lost Years of Jesus* (Livingstone, MT: Summit University Press, 1984), 96.

14. As does Holger Kersten, *Jesus Lived in India* (Longmead, England: Element Book, Ltd., 1986), 36–37. Kersten's response is little more than an attack on Muller's character. He does not refute Muller's arguments.

15. Max Muller, *India, What Can it Teach Us?* (London, 1883), 279; quoted in Albert Schweitzer, *The Quest for the Historical Jesus* (New York: The Macmillan Company, 1973), 291.

16. Muller, "The Alleged Sojourn," 518. Muller did not adequately understand, it seems, the vast differences between Issa and Jesus; nevertheless, his comment shows that he was not predisposed to reject the document as spurious without giving it a fair chance.

17. Ibid.

18. Notovitch in Prophet, 94.

19. As an appendix to his article, Muller included a letter to him from an English woman familiar with the Himis monastery who wrote from Leh, Ladakh, on June 29, 1894. It claimed that Notovitch's story was a complete fabrication (Muller, "The Alleged Sojourn," 521–22). A more detailed case for fabrication will be made below.

20. Nicholas Notovitch, *The Unknown Life*, 226.

21. Goodspeed, 9.

22. Notovitch, 229.

23. Goodspeed, 10.

24. From a review of *The Unknown Life of Jesus Christ*, in *The Biblical World* 4, no. 2 (August 1894):147. No author is cited.

25. Notovitch, 244–45.

26. Beskow, 121.

27. J. Archibald Douglas, "The Chief Lama of Himis on the Alleged 'Unknown Life of Christ,'" *The Nineteenth Century* 230 (April 1896), 668–69.

28. Ibid., 669.

29. Ibid., 671.

30. Ibid., 672.

31. Ibid., 671.

32. Ibid., 671–72.

33. Ibid., 672.

34. Beskow, 59.

35. Douglas, 672.

36. Ibid., 669–70.

37. Ibid., 674.

38. Notovitch in Prophet, 91–92.

39. David L. Snellgrove and Tadeusz Skorupski, *The Cultural Heritage of Ladakh—Volume One: Central Ladakh* (Boulder, CO: Prajna Press, 1977), 127; quoted in Prophet, 37–38.

40. Snellgrove and Skorupski, 127.
41. Prophet, 35–36.
42. Notovitch in Prophet, 93.
43. Ibid., 94.
44. Notovitch, 151–52.
45. Beskow, 58.
46. Schweitzer, 328.
47. Beskow makes this comment about one of the supposed other witnesses of the manuscript: "Professor Nicholas Roerich, painter and amateur archaeologist, traveled in Ladakh in the 1920s and believed that he had found traces of *The Life of Saint Issa.* Unfortunately, his examples from living folk traditions lend no added reliability, for the first part of his account is taken literally from Notovitch's *Life of Saint Issa,* chapters 5–13 (only extracts, but with all the verses in the right order). It is followed by "another version" (93–94), taken from chapter 16 of Downing's *Aquarian Gospel.* There is a vague possibility that visiting enthusiasts from Europe had already spread these stories to Ladakh, and that they had taken root in popular belief. But Roerich's literal quotations rather suggest that he inserted them only because he found them attractive. He was of a romantic nature and seems not to have taken a great interest in more tangible facts (62–63).
48. Fida Hassnain, *A Search for the Historical Jesus: From Apocryphal, Buddhist, Islamic, and Sanskrit Sources* (Bath, UK: Gateway Books, 1994), 23.
49. For instance, the mostly Gnostic Nag Hammadi manuscripts have been photographically reproduced in scholarly volumes in the original Coptic language.
50. Prophet, 312.
51. Ron Rhodes, *The Counterfeit Christ of the New Age Movement* (Grand Rapids, MI: Baker Books, 1990), 55.
52. Richard Walters, "Christ, Christian, Krishna," *New Frontier,* December 1988, 5.
53. Ibid., 7.
54. Ibid.
55. Ibid.
56. Holger Kersten and Elmar R. Gruber, *The Jesus Conspiracy: The Turin Shroud and the Truth About the Resurrection* (Rockport, MA: Element Books, 1994). For two negative reviews of their claims, see Eugene O. Bowser's review in *Library Journal,* June 5, 1994, 72; and Gary Young's review in *Booklist,* June 1 and 15, 1994, 1732.

57. Michael Green, *The Empty Cross of Jesus* (Downers Grove, IL: InterVarsity Press, 1984), 93. On the speed of Jesus' death, see also James Charlesworth, *Jesus Within Judaism* (New York: Doubleday, 1988), 122–23.

58. William D. Edwards, Wesley J. Gabel, Floyd E. Hosmer, "On the Physical Death of Jesus Christ," *Journal of the American Medical Association* 255, no. 11 (March 21, 1986):1460.

59. Green, 93–94.

60. William Lane Craig, *Knowing the Truth about the Resurrection* (Ann Arbor, MI: Servant Books, 1988), 33.

61. Edwards, et al., 1463.

62. See Kenneth E. Stevenson and Gary R. Habermas, *The Shroud and the Controversy* (Nashville: Thomas Nelson Publishers, 1990).

63. Walters, 45; Kersten, *Jesus Died in India.* 179ff. For further criticism of this view, see Beskow, 63–64, 122–24.

64. Arguments for the resurrection of Jesus are presented in Chapter 14.

Chapter 9—Jesus and the Dead Sea Scrolls

1. See, for instance, H. Spencer Lewis, *The Mystical Life of Jesus* (San Jose, CA: Supreme Grand Lodge of AMORC, 1974), 23–42.
   He says some rather ominous things about Jesus and the Essenes being pure white Aryans.

2. Manly P. Hall, *The Mystical Christ* (Los Angeles: The Philosophical Research Society, Inc., 1951), 39.

3. Richard Walters, "Christ, Christian, Krishna," *New Frontier,* December. 1988, 7.

4. Shirley MacLaine, *Going Within* (New York: Bantam, 1989), 178–81.

5. Annie Besant, *Esoteric Christianity* (Wheaton, IL: The Theosophical Publishing House, 1953), 89.

6. Edgar Cayce, *Edgar Cayce's Story of Jesus,* Jeffrey Furst, ed. (New York: Berkley Books, 1968),130–58.

7. See James Charlesworth, *Jesus Within Judaism* (New York: Doubleday, 1988), 62–63; and F.F. Bruce, *New Testament History* (Garden City, NY: Doubleday, 1969), 115–21. Edward K. Cook presents the arguments for and against this view in his *Solving the Mystery of the Dead Sea Scrolls: New Light on the Bible* (Grand Rapids, MI: Zondervan Publishing House, 1994), 82–126.

8. See Charlesworth, 63.

9. G. Vermes, *The Dead Sea Scrolls in English,* third ed. (London: Penguin, 1988), xiv, comments on how the findings relate to the

reliability of the Old Testament: "With this newly discovered material at their disposal, experts concerned with the study of the text and transmission of the Scriptures are now able to achieve far greater accuracy in their deductions and can trace the process by which the text of the Bible attained its final shape. Moreover, they are in a position to prove that it has remained virtually unchanged for the last two thousand years."

10. A few fragments from horoscopes were also found. Vermes thinks that rather than indicate an astrological concern to predict the future, these fragments are probably "horoscope-like compositions" used as "literary devices." See ibid., 305.

11. Charles F. Pfeiffer, *The Dead Sea Scrolls and the Bible* (Grand Rapids, MI: Baker Book House, 1984), 112.

12. Ibid., 111.

13. Charlesworth, 71.

14. Quoted in Vermes, 79.

15. H. Spencer Lewis, 30. This Rosicrucian writer lists as the first of ten principles of Essenism: "God is principle. . . . God is not a person, nor does He appear to the outer man in any form of cloud or glory."

16. Vermes, 177.

17. Ibid., 80.

18. See ibid., 42–43.

19. On the Qumran Essene views of the afterlife, see ibid., 55–56; and John Hick, *Death and Eternal Life* (San Francisco: Harper and Row, 1980), 395.

20. Vermes, 65.

21. Ibid., 66.

22. William Sanford LaSor, *The Dead Sea Scrolls and the New Testament* (Grand Rapids, MI: William B. Eerdmans Publishing Company, 1972), 146.

23. Ibid., 148.

24. Ibid., 146.

25. Ibid., 147.

26. F.F. Bruce, *New Testament History,* 154.

27. LaSor, 150–51.

28. Josephus discusses John the Baptist and mentions nothing of an Essene connection, even though he was well acquainted with the Essenes. See *Antiquities of the Jews,* 18.5.2.

29. Charlesworth, 57.

30. See LaSor, 206–13; and Edwin M. Yamauchi, *The Stones and the Scriptures* (Philadelphia: J.B. Lippincott Company, 1972), 140–45; and Ron Rhodes, *The Counterfeit Christ of the New Age* (Grand Rapids, MI: Baker Books, 1991), 75–76. Vermes, xvi, makes this interesting comment on the Teacher of Righteousness in relation to Jesus: "And although the Teacher of Righteousness clearly sensed the deeper obligations implicit in the Mosaic Law, he was without the genius of Jesus who laid bare the inner core of spiritual truth and exposed the essence of religion as an existential relationship between man and man, and between man and God."

31. Josephus, *The Wars of the Jews*, 2.8.3.

32. Hans Kung, *On Being a Christian* (Garden City, NY: Doubleday, 1976), 198.

33. Vermes, 95.

34. Charlesworth, 72.

35. Vermes, 145.

36. F.F. Bruce, *Second Thoughts on the Dead Sea Scrolls* (Grand Rapids, MI: Wm. B. Eerdmans, 1964), 144.

37. See Charlesworth, 68–71, for a discussion of Jesus' statement "Blessed are the poor in spirit" (Matthew 5:3) as possibly having some reference to the Essenes. Although Charlesworth finds some possible positive influence by the Essenes on Jesus, he does not think Jesus was an Essene or that Essenism substantially contributed to Jesus' dynamic. For a different view of Jesus and the Essenes' understanding of "the poor," see Frank Moore Cross, Jr., *The Ancient Library of Qumran and Modern Biblical Studies*, rev. ed. (Grand Rapids, MI: Baker Book House, 1980), 241.

38. Charlesworth, 74.

Chapter 10—More Dead Sea Scroll Intrigue

1. Barbara Thiering, *Jesus and the Riddle of the Dead Sea Scrolls: Unlocking the Secrets of His Life Story* (San Francisco: HarperSanFrancisco, 1992), 4.

2. See N.T. Wright, *Who Was Jesus?* (Grand Rapids, MI: Wm. B. Eerdmans Publishing Co., 1992), 20–23.

3. Luke Timothy Johnson, *The Real Jesus: The Misguided Quest for the Historical Jesus and the Truth of the Traditional Gospels* (San Francisco: HarperSanFrancisco, 1996), 29.

4. Thiering, 90; emphasis added.

5. Ibid., 160.

6. Ibid., 117. For more on Gnosticism, see chapters 5 and 6.

7. Ibid., 3.

8. Wright, 23.

9. See Wright, 19, 25–26.

10. Ibid., 26.

11. Ibid.

12. Ibid., 27.

13. See David M. Paton, "An Evaluation of the Hypothesis of Barbara Thiering Concerning Jesus and the Dead Sea Scrolls," *The Qumran Chronicle* 5, no.1 (July 1995), 38.

14. See Wright, 30–31.

15. See ibid., 31–32; and Paton, 40–42.

16. Wright, 28.

17. See Paton, 42–44, against Thiering's thesis that Jesus was revived in the tomb by the application of aloes.

18. Johnson, 30–31.

19. Shirley MacLaine, *Going Within* (New York: Bantam, 1989), 179–80. The proper spelling is *Szekely,* not *Szekaly.*

20. Her undocumented comments seem to come straight from the introduction to *The Essene Gospel of Peace: Book Three* (San Diego: Academy Books, 1977), 11ff.

21. Fida Hassnain, *A Search for the Historical Jesus: From Apocryphal, Buddhist, Islamic, and Sanskrit Sources* (Bath: Gateway Books, 1994), 94–96. This book distinguished by its careless use of fraudulent and exotic materials on Jesus.

22. Edmond Bordeaux Szekely, *The Essene Gospel of Peace: Book One* (USA: International Biogenic Society, 1981), 9.

23. Ibid., 24.

24. Ibid., 13.

25. Ibid., 41.

26. Edmond Bordeaux Szekely, *The Essene Gospel of Peace: Book Two* (San Diego: Academy Books, 1977), 97.

27. This does not claim to be a translation from an ancient manuscript.

28. Edmond Bordeaux Szekely, *The Essene Jesus* (San Diego: Academy Books, 1977), 7.

29. Ibid., 34.

30. Ibid., 49.

31. Ibid., 50.

32. Ibid., 7.
33. See Edmond Bordeauẍ Szekely, *The Discovery of the Essene Gospel of Peace: The Essenes and the Vatican* (San Diego: Academy Publishers, 1975).
34. Per Beskow, *Strange Tales About Jesus: A Survey of Unfamiliar Gospels* (Philadelphia: Fortress Press, 1985), 84.
35. Ibid., 89.
36. Ibid., 129.
37. Szekely, *The Discovery,* 45.
38. Beskow, 88.
39. Ibid., 88–89.
40. For more on this, see Beskow, 85–86.
41. See Beskow, 90.
42. The first edition in 1937 of *The Essene Gospel of Peace* was titled *The Gospel of Peace by the Disciple John.* Curiously, references to authorship do not appear in the later editions. See Beskow, 83.
43. Beskow, 88.
44. See ibid., 81–91, for Beskow's entire fair, careful, and devastating critique.
45. Ibid., 89.
46. See Beskow, 50. On the Ahmadiyya movement, see Norman Anderson, *Jesus: the Witness of History* (Downers Grove, IL: InterVarsity Press, 1985), 84–85; and Irving Hexam, "Ahmadiya" (his spelling) in *Concise Dictionary of Religion* (Downers Grove, IL: InterVarsity Press, 1993), 14. Hassnain quotes from an Ahmadiyya source in his chapter on the crucifixion. See *A Search for the Historical Jesus,* 103.
47. Hassnain, 102–13.
48. Beskow, 44.
49. Ibid., 46.
50. Ibid., 48. See also Edgar J. Goodspeed, *Modern Apocrypha* (Boston: The Beacon Press, 1956), 26.
51. Elmar R. Gruber and Holger Kersten, *The Original Jesus: The Buddhist Sources of Christianity* (Rockport, MA: Element Books, 1995), 216.
52. Ibid., 224.
53. Ibid.
54. They attempt to make this case at length in Holger Kersten and Elmar R. Gruber, *The Jesus Conspiracy* (New York: Barnes and Noble, 1992). They claim that Jesus survived the crucifixion and died in India. This idea is criticized in chapter 8.

Chapter 11—Channels of Deception

1. *A Course in Miracles: Text* (Farmingdale, NY: Foundation for Inner Peace, 1981), "Introduction," n.p.
2. Dean C. Halverson, "A Course in Miracles: Seeing Yourself As Sinless," *Spiritual Counterfeits Journal* 7 (1987):18. I am indebted to this article for much of my analysis.
3. *A Course in Miracles: Manual* (Farmingdale, NY: Foundation for Inner Peace, 1981), 56.
4. *Course: Text,* 5.
5. *Course: Manual,* 84; emphasis in original.
6. *Course: Manual,* 83.
7. Ibid.
8. Marianne Williamson, *A Return to Love* (New York: HarperCollins, 1992), 29.
9. Ibid.
10. *Course: Manual,* 83.
11. Ibid.
12. Jon Klimo, *Channeling* (Los Angeles: J.P. Tarcher, 1987), 345.
13. For an elaboration of this, see Klimo, 185–201.
14. For a description of the various teachings, see Klimo, 146–67.
15. Ramtha (with Douglas James Mahr), *Voyage to the New World* (New York: Ballantine Books, 1987), 180–81; emphasis in text.
16. For a brief version of this story, see Robert Perry, *An Introduction to a Course in Miracles* (USA: Miracle Distribution Center, 1989), 8–16.
17. As of 1987, there were at least 300 groups in the United States studying the *Course.* See Halverson, 18.
18. *Course: Text,* 33.
19. Ibid.
20. *Course: Manual,* 81.
21. *Course: Text,* 46.
22. Ibid., 187.
23. Ibid., 13.
24. *A Course in Miracles: Workbook* (Farmingdale, NY: Foundation for Inner Peace, 1981), 119.
25. Williamson, 21.
26. Rama Jyoti Vernon, "Exploring a Course in Miracles," *Yoga Journal,* January/February 1983, 40.
27. Williamson, 61.

28. Perry, 4–5.
29. Quoted in Vernon, p. 40.
30. Ibid.
31. Referred to in Halverson, 23.
32. See "A Matter of Course: Conversation with Kenneth Wapnick," *Spiritual Counterfeits Journal* 7 (1987):8–17.
33. *Course: Text,* 53; emphasis added.
34. *Course: Workbook,* 70; emphasis added.
35. Halverson, 24; emphasis added.
36. Ibid., 26.
37. See Halverson, 27.
38. Williamson, 29.
39. Ibid., 45.
40. Ibid., 157
41. Ibid., 99.
42. I owe several of these insights to Dean Halverson's review of *A Return to Love* published in the *Christian Research Journal* (Summer 1992), 35–36.
43. See Francis A. Schaeffer, *The God Who Is There* (Downers Grove, IL: InterVarsity Press, 1968), 56–62.
44. Levi H. Downing, *The Aquarian Gospel of Jesus the Christ* (Marina Del Ray, CA: DeVorss & Co., Publishers, 1981), 110 (68:13).
45. It should be remembered that chapters and verses were only incorporated into the biblical books in the medieval period. Manuscripts before this time do not have them.
46. Downing, 14.
47. Ibid.
48. Ibid., 16–17.
49. Ibid., "Who Was Levi?" n.p.
50. Klimo, 344.
51. Downing, 13.
52. Per Beskow, *Strange Tales About Jesus: A Survey of Unfamiliar Gospels* (Philadelphia: Fortress Press, 1985), 79.
53. Downing, 76 (37:11–15).
54. Ibid., 96–97 (55:4–7).
55. Ibid., 265 (178:45,46); emphasis added.
56. Ibid., 64 (28:4).
57. Ibid., 255 (172:21).

58. Ibid., 260 (176:19).
59. Ibid., 33 (1:1).
60. Ibid., 74 (36:3).
61. Edgar J. Goodspeed, *Modern Apocrypha* (Boston: The Beacon Press, 1956), 18.
62. Downing, 76–77 (37:1ff).
63. Beskow, 76.
64. Downing, 261 (176:22).
65. Beskow, 80.
66. Goodspeed, 17.
67. For a detailed and well-documented treatment of Cayce's life history, see Gary North, *Unholy Spirits* (Fort Worth, TX: Dominion Press, 1986), 193–206.
68. Quoted in Thomas Sugrue, *There Is a River,* rev. ed (New York: Holt & Co., 1948), 247; cited in North, 204.
69. Jeffrey Furst, ed. *Edgar Cayce's Story of Jesus* (New York: Berkley Books, 1976), 39–40.
70. Ibid., 76–77.
71. Ibid., 47.
72. Ibid., 192.
73. Ibid., 192–93.
74. Ibid., 193.
75. Ibid., 194.
76. Ibid., 196.
77. Ibid., 76.
78. Ibid., 33.
79. Ibid., 73.
80. Ibid., 53.
81. Ibid., 51.
82. Hugh Lynn Cayce, *Edgar Cayce on Jesus and His Church* (New York: Paperback Library, 1970), 12.

Chapter 12—Channeling on Trial

1. Christ Kolham, illustrated by Robert Engman, *In Search of the New Age* (Rochester, VT: Destiny Books, 1988), 49.
2. Stewart C. Easton, *Man and World in Light of Anthroposophy* (USA: Anthroposophic Press, Inc., 1975), 199.
3. See Easton's chapter, "Anthroposophy and Christianity," 173–216, for a summary of Steiner's views on Jesus, the Christ, and Christianity.

4. For documentation of Cayce's false prophecies see Andrew Neher, *The Psychology of Transcendence* (Englewood Cliffs, NJ: Prentice-Hall, 1980), 159–61. Neher concludes, "In view of Cayce's extremely poor batting average for his prophecies that can be followed up, there seems little reason to regard him as a great prophet," 161.

5. See Karla Poewe-Hexham and Irving Hexham, "The 'Evidence' for Atlantis: Addressing New Age Apologetics," *Christian Research Journal*, Summer 1989, 16–19.

6. Brad Steiger, *Gods of Aquarius* (New York: Berkley, 1983), 115–16; quoted in William M. Alnor, *UFOs in the New Age: Extraterrestrial Messages and the Truth of Scripture* (Grand Rapids, MI: Baker Books, 1991), 31.

7. Raphael, *The Starseed Transmissions*, Kenneth X. Carey, ed. (Kansas City: Uni-Sun, 1987), 66; quoted in Alnor, 47.

8. *The Urantia Book* (Chicago, IL: The Urantia Foundation, 1955), 725.

9. Martin Gardner, *Urantia: The Great Cult Mystery* (New York: Prometheus Books, 1995), 24.

10. Quoted in Peter Stenshoel and Jay Kinney, "Audio Magicians: When Is a Cult Figure an Occult Artist?" *Gnosis*, Summer 1994, 42.

11. Gardner, 11.

12. *The Urantia Book*, 1341–42.

13. Ibid., 2091–93.

14. Ibid., 2002.

15. Ibid., 2016.

16. Ibid., 2023–24.

17. Ibid., 2021.

18. Ibid., 2059.

19. For a rich and learned discussion of the meaning of biblical inspiration, see Carl F.H. Henry, *God, Revelation, and Authority* (Waco, TX: Word Books, 1980) 3:129–493.

20. Michael Green, *I Believe in Satan's Downfall* (Grand Rapids, MI: Eerdmans, 1981), 28.

21. David Spangler, *Links With Space* (Marina Del Ray, CA: Devoss, 1978), 34.

22. For more on this, see Alnor, ibid., and Ron Rhodes, *The Culting of America* (Eugene, OR: Harvest House, 1994), 183–99; and Gary North, *Unholy Spirits: Occultism and New Age Humanism* (Fort Worth, TX: Dominion Press, 1986), 288–328.

23. John Ankerberg and John Weldon, *The Facts on Spirit Guides* (Eugene, OR: Harvest House, 1988), 34–35.

24. George Hackett with Pamela Abramson, "Ramtha, a Voice from Beyond," *Newsweek,* December 15, 1986, 42. This confession, if true, does not necessarily mean that every Ramtha session was a fraud, only that Knight was capable of producing the effect by herself. Another ex-follower I saw on a television program in 1987 said he believed Knight was legitimately in touch with Ramtha at first but later lost contact with him and relied on impersonation.

25. Sarah Grey Thomason, " 'Entities' in the Linguistic Minefield," *Skeptical Inquirer,* Summer 1989, 391–96. See also Marjory Roberts, "A Linguistic 'Nay' to Channeling," *Psychology Today,* October 1989, 64–65.

26. See Gardner, *Urantia.*

27. See Brooks Alexander, *Spirit Channeling* (Downers Grove, IL: InterVarsity Press, 1988), 16–19. For a more detailed treatment, see Graham Reed, "The Psychology of Channeling," *Skeptical Inquirer,* Summer 1989, 385–90.

28. For explanations of this sort, see Elliot Miller, *A Crash Course on the New Age* (Grand Rapids, MI: Baker, 1989), 167–69. His treatment of channeling is quite thorough and covers important aspects not covered in this chapter; see 141–82.

29. The Christ, *New Teachings for an Awakened Humanity* (Santa Clara, CA: Spiritual Education Endeavors Publishing Company, 1986), 50. For a redefinition of Jesus' life on earth, see the entire chapter, 45–60.

30. Alexander, 29.

Chapter 13—Jesus: What He Did, What He Said

1. Similarly, the resurrection brackets him off from all others relating to his destiny. This idea is discussed in Bernard Ramm, *An Evangelical Christology: Ecumenic and Historic* (Nashville: Thomas Nelson, 1985), 69.

2. C.S. Lewis, *Miracles* (New York: Macmillan, 1960), 59.

3. H. Spencer Lewis, *The Mystical Life of Jesus* (San Jose, CA: The Supreme Grand Lodge of AMORC, 1974), 74–75.

4. Lewis himself grants this, 74.

5. John Frame, "The Virgin Birth," in *Evangelical Dictionary of Theology,* Walter A. Elwell, ed. (Grand Rapids, MI: Baker, 1984), 1145, emphasis in the original.

6. Ibid. On the uniqueness of the biblical view of the virgin birth, see Norman Anderson, *Jesus Christ: The Witness of History* (Downers Grove, IL: InterVarsity Press, 1985), 74–75.

7. Elmar R. Gruber and Holger Kersten, *The Original Jesus: The Buddhist Sources of Christianity* (Rockport, MA: Element Books, 1995), 82–83.

8. Geoffrey Parrinder, *Avatar and Incarnation* (New York: Barnes and Noble, Inc., 1970), 135.

9. See J. Gresham Machen, *The Virgin Birth of Christ* (New York: Harper and Brothers, 1930), 339.

10. Ibid., 340.

11. Ibid., 342.

12. A.E. Vine, *Vine's Expository Dictionary of Old and New Testament Words* (Old Tappan, NJ: Fleming H. Revell Company, 1981), 2:274.

13. Ibid., 1:190.

14. "Christ," *Metaphysical Bible Dictionary* (Unity Village, MO: Unity School of Christianity, 1931), 150.

15. See the discussion of Carl Jung in chapter 5.

16. See Douglas Groothuis, "Myth and the Power of Joseph Campbell," in Douglas Groothuis, *Christianity That Counts* (Grand Rapids, MI: Baker Books, 1994), 150–62. See also Tom Snyder, *Myth Conceptions: Joseph Campbell and the New Age* (Grand Rapids, MI: Baker Books, 1995).

17. F.F Bruce, *New Testament History* (Garden City, NY: Doubleday, 1972), 173, emphasis in original.

18. Jean Houston, *Godseed* (Amity, NY: Amity House, 1988), 54.

19. Bruce, *New Testament History,* 172.

20. John White, "Jesus and the Idea of a New Age," *Quest,* Summer 1989, 17–18.

21. The Greek neuter case here indicates that Jesus is affirming that he is one *essence* with the Father, not one *person.* We thus find something of the Trinity entailed—both Jesus and the Father are equally divine.

22. See Gleason Archer, *Encyclopedia of Biblical Difficulties* (Grand Rapids, MI: Zondervan, 1982), 374.

23. On Jesus' view of Scripture, see John W. Wenham, *Christ and the Bible* (Grand Rapids, MI: Baker Book House, 1984).

24. For a helpful discussion of these verses in John, see Gary DeMar and Peter Leithart, *The Reduction of Christianity* (Fort Worth, TX: Dominion Press, 1987), 77–83.

25. White, 17.
26. The spiritual gifts given to the church are discussed in 1 Corinthians 12–14; Ephesians 4:11–16.
27. Vine, 2:207.
28. Houston, 21.
29. Joseph Campbell, *The Power of Myth* (New York: Doubleday, 1988), 66.
30. Ibid.

Chapter 14—Jesus the Christ: His Claims, His Credentials

1. John White, "Jesus and the Idea of a New Age," *Quest*, Summer 1989, 17; emphasis in the original.
2. Ibid.
3. See David Wells, *The Person of Christ* (Westchester, IL: Crossway Books, 1984), 41–42.
4. A.E. Harvey, *Jesus and the Constraints of History* (Philadelphia: Westminster, 1982), 110. See also Gary R. Habermas, "Did Jesus Perform Miracles?" in *Jesus Under Fire: Modern Scholarship Reinvents the Historical Jesus,* J.P. Moreland and Michael J. Wilkins, eds.(Grand Rapids, MI: Zondervan Publishers, 1995), 117–40. For a defense of the miraculous as philosophically and historically credible, see C.S. Lewis, *Miracles: A Preliminary Study* (New York: Macmillan Publishing Co., Inc., 1960); and Norman Geisler, *Miracles and the Modern Mind* (Grand Rapids, MI: Baker Books, 1992).
5. For other nature miracles, see Matthew 17:24–27; 21:18–22; Mark 11:12–14,20–25.
6. It is important to notice that while Jesus complimented the man on his faith in him, he did not correct his remark about being unworthy, as would be expected if Jesus believed the man were intrinsically divine. Jesus instead accepts his humility and responds accordingly.
7. On Jesus' prayer life, see Margaret Magdalen, *Jesus: Man of Prayer* (Downers Grove, IL: InterVarsity Press, 1987).
8. This is shown by a journal of recent origin called *The Shaman's Drum: A Journal of Experiential Shamanism.*
9. Michael Harner, *The Way of the Shaman* (New York: Bantam, 1982), 25–26.
10. The Gospels record a few cases where Jesus' healing involves spittle or mud. But the use of these elements is secondary to Jesus' personal power. They do not indicate ritual magic or ceremony. In

recent years, Morton Smith has written several controversial books arguing that Jesus should be viewed as a magician. For a critique of his claim that there was a "secret gospel of Mark" indicating Jesus as a magician, see F.F. Bruce, *The Canon of Scripture* (Downers Grove, IL: InterVarsity Press), 298–315; Joseph A. Fitzmyer, "How to Exploit a Secret Gospel," *America*, June 23, 1973, 570–72, and Ben Witherington, *The Jesus Quest: The Third Search for the Jew of Nazareth* (Downers Grove, IL: InterVarsity Press, 1995), 211–12. Concerning Smith's other claims, see Howard Clark Kee, *Miracle in the Early Christian World* (New Haven: Yale University Press, 1983), 211–12.

11. E. Stanley Jones, *The Christ of the Indian Road* (New York: Grosset and Dunlap, 1925), 191.

12. See John Stott, *Basic Christianity*, second edition (Downers Grove, IL: InterVarsity Press, 1971), 31.

13. For the theological significance of Jesus' title as "the Son of Man" and for his other titles, see Bernard Ramm, *An Evangelical Christology*, 107–16; and David Wells, *The Person of Christ* (Westchester, IL: Crossway, 1984), 67–81.

14. Statements such as this slam the door shut on reincarnation—a teaching often attributed to Jesus by reincarnationists. Jesus spoke of one final judgment, not of many incarnations, nor of any intervening lifetimes before the Last Day. This will be taken up in more detail in chapter 15.

15. B.B. Warfield's comments from *The Lord of Glory* are illuminating on this: "Speaking in the most solemn manner, he not only presents himself as the Son, as the sole source of knowledge of God . . . but places himself in a position, not of equality merely, but of absolute reciprocity and interpenetration of knowledge of the Father, as if the being of the Son were so immense that only God could know it thoroughly, and knowledge of the Son so unlimited that he could know God to perfection." Quoted in Herbert Lockyer, *Everything Jesus Taught* (San Francisco: Harper and Row, 1984), 20.

16. William Lane Craig, *Reasonable Faith: Christian Truth and Apologetics* (Wheaton, IL: Crossway Books, 1994), 246, emphasis in the original. See also Gordon Clark, *The Trinity* (Jefferson, MD: The Trinity Foundation, 1985), 14.

17. Thich Nhat Hanh, *Living Buddha, Living Christ* (New York: G.P. Putman's Sons, 1995), 55–56.

18. Ibid., 44.

19. On the idea of Jesus as "God in Focus," see J.B. Phillips, *Your God Is Too Small* (New York: Macmillan, 1979), 63–66.

20. It has been argued that Jesus' "I am" statements were spoken such that they were claims to deity as well. See Ethelbert Stauffer, *Jesus and His Story* (New York: Alfred A. Knopf, 1974), 174–95.

21. See R.C. Sproul, *Who Is Jesus?* (Wheaton, IL: Tyndale House, 1988), 23–32.

22. For a careful, developed treatment of this, see John Ankerberg, John Weldon, Walter Kaiser, *The Case for Jesus the Messiah* (Chattanooga, TN: The John Ankerberg Evangelistic Association, 1989) and Walter Kaiser, *The Messiah in the Old Testament* (Grand Rapids, MI: Zondervan Publishers, 1995).

23. B.B. Warfield, *The Person and Work of Christ* (USA: Presbyterian and Reformed Publishing Company, 1950), 17.

24. Lockyer, 27.

25. Mark L. Prophet and Elizabeth Clare Prophet, *The Lost Teachings of Jesus,* vol. 2 (Livingstone, MT: Summit University Press, 1986), 374.

26. Mark Prophet and Elizabeth Clare Prophet, *Science of the Spoken Word* (Livingstone, MT: Summit University Press, 1984), 86–87.

27. We will defend the historicity and explain the cosmic significance of the resurrection in chapter 15.

28. This is discussed at greater length in chapter 15.

29. For an excellent study of both the transcendence and condescension of Jesus Christ, see Jonathan Edwards, "The Excellency of Christ," in *The Puritan Sage* (New York: Library Publishers, 1953), 326–32.

Chapter 15—Jesus and the Cosmic Christ

1. David Spangler, *Reflections on the Christ* (Glasgow, Scotland: Findhorn, 1978), 107.

2. Ibid.

3. David Spangler, *Conversations with John* (Middleton, WI: Lorian Press, 1983), 5; quoted in Ron Rhodes, "The Christ of the New Age Movement," *Christian Research Journal,* Summer 1989, 12.

4. David Spangler, *Revelation: The Birth of a New Age* (San Francisco: The Rainbow Bridge, 1977), 141.

5. Sam Keen, "Original Blessing, Not Original Sin: A Conversation with Matthew Fox," *Psychology Today,* June 1989, 57.

6. Matthew Fox, *The Coming of the Cosmic Christ* (San Francisco: Harper and Row, 1988), 147.

7. Ibid., 154.

8. Ibid., 138.

9. Teilhard de Chardin, *Science and Christ* (New York: Harper and Row, 1965); quoted in Ron Rhodes, *The Counterfeit Christ of the New Age* (Grand Rapids, MI: Baker Books, 1991), 227.

10. For more on Teilhard de Chardin, see Tal Brooke, "Preparing for the Cosmic Millennium: and the Coming Global Church," *Spiritual Counterfeits Project Journal* 19, nos. 2–3 (1995), 4–17.

11. R.C. Sproul, *Who Is Jesus?* (Wheaton, IL: Tyndale House, 1988), 46.

12. Jaroslav Pelikan, *Jesus Through the Centuries* (San Francisco: Harper and Row, 1987), 62; emphasis in the original.

13. Carl F.H. Henry, *God, Revelation, and Authority* (Waco: TX: Word Books, 1979) 3:194.

14. Ibid., 195.

15. Fox calls his view *panentheism,* instead of pantheism, meaning "all things in God and God in all things" (*The Coming of the Cosmic Christ,* 57). This deifies the cosmos. This is to be distinguished from biblical *theism,* which affirms both the transcendence and immanence of God, yet without deifying the created and now-fallen world. See Romans 1:18–32.

16. See C.S. Lewis, *The Abolition of Man* (New York: Macmillan, 1947) on this.

17. Fox, 79.

18. Athanasius, *The Incarnation of the Word of God* (New York: The Macmillan Company, 1946), 79.

19. See John Ankerberg, John Weldon, and Walter Kaiser, *The Case for Jesus the Messiah* (Chattanooga, TN: The John Ankerberg Evangelistic Association, 1988); and Walter Kaiser, *The Messiah in the Old Testament* (Grand Rapids, MI: Zondervan Publishers, 1995).

20. Lawrence Waddy, *Pax Romana and World Peace* (London: Chapman and Hall Limited, n.d.), 122–23, cited in John Warwick Montgomery, *Faith Based on Fact* (Nashville: Thomas Nelson Inc., 1978), 192–93.

21. Ibid.

22. A.T. Robertson, *A Grammar of the Greek New Testament in the Light of Historical Research,* fourth ed. (London: Hodder & Stoughton; New York: George H. Doran, 1923), 54–55; cited in Montgomery, 197.

23. William James, *The Varieties of Religious Experience, The Works of William James.* Frederick Burkhardt, gen.ed., Fredson Bowers, text.ed. (Cambridge, MA: Harvard University Press, 1985), 400.

24. See Douglas Groothuis, *Are All Religions One?* (Downers Grove, IL: InterVarsity Press, 1996); and Harold Netland, *Dissonant Voices:*

Religious Pluralism and the Question of Truth (Grand Rapids, MI: Eerdmans, 1991).

25. John Warwick Montgomery, *Myth, Allegory and Gospel* (Minneapolis: Bethany Fellowship, Inc., 1974), 25–26.

26. C.S. Lewis, *God in the Dock* (Grand Rapids, MI: Eerdmans, 1979), 66–67. See the entire essay "Myth Becomes Fact," 63–67, for insightful comments.

27. For another Christian view of mythology as pointing toward something beyond itself, see G.K. Chesterton, *The Everlasting Man* (Garden City, NY: Image Books, 1955), 103–18.

28. For a discussion of how Christian historical claims differ from non-historical mythical ideas, see Carl Henry, *God, Revelation, and Authority* (Waco, TX: Word, 1976) 1:44–69.

29. Bernard Ramm, *Protestant Christian Evidence* (Chicago: Moody Press, 1967), 185.

30. C.S. Lewis, *Miracles* (New York: Macmillan, 1960), 143.

31. Edwin Yamauchi, "Easter—Myth, Hallucination, or History? Part Two," *Christianity Today*, March 29, 1974, 13.

32. Ibid., 15ff.

33. See William Lane Craig, *Knowing the Truth about the Resurrection* (Ann Arbor, MI: Servant Books, 1988), 21.

34. Pinchas Lapide, *The Resurrection of Jesus* (Minneapolis: Augsburg Publishing House, 1983), 98–99.

35. Gary Habermas and Anthony Flew, *Did Jesus Rise from the Dead?* Terry L. Miethe, ed. (San Francisco: Harper and Row, 1987), 23.

36. See Lapide, 95.

37. See Craig, 53–55.

38. On the alleged contradictions between the Gospel's accounts of the resurrection, see John Wenham, *Easter Enigma* (Grand Rapids, MI: Zondervan, 1984).

39. C.F.D. Moule, *The Phenomenon of the New Testament* (Naperville, IL: Alec R. Allenson, Inc., 1967), 13; emphasis his. See 1–20 for his entire argument.

40. Lapide, 46.

41. Michael Green, *The Empty Cross of Jesus* (Downers Grove, IL: Inter-Varsity Press, 1984), 94.

42. Ibid.

43. Craig, 109–10.

44. See Norman Anderson, *Jesus Christ: The Witness of History* (Downers Grove, IL: InterVarsity Press, 1985), 140–44; Craig, 109–13; and Green, 113–19.

45. Lapide, 126.

46. It can be argued that Lapide's refusal to recognize Jesus as the Messiah of all is quite inconsistent if he believes in Jesus' literal resurrection. As one letter to the editor in *Time* magazine commented, "Pinchas Lapide's logic escapes me. He believes it is possible that Jesus was resurrected by God. At the same time he does not accept Jesus as the Messiah. Why would God resurrect a liar?" *Time,* June 4, 1979, quoted in Norman Geisler, *False Gods of Our Time* (Eugene, OR: Harvest House, 1985), 165. See also Craig, 152.

47. Lapide, 92.

48. Blaise Pascal, *Pensees* (New York: Penguin Books, 1966), #310/801, p. 125.

49. Charles Colson, *Loving God* (Grand Rapids, MI: Zondervan Publishers, 1983), 67.

50. Ibid.

51. Ibid., 69.

52. Ramm argues that those who deny Jesus' resurrection face more difficulties than those who affirm it. See Ramm, 195–207.

53. For a much more detailed discussion of this, see Douglas Groothuis, *Confronting the New Age* (Downers Grove, IL: InterVarsity Press, 1988), 94–98.

54. Wilbur M. Smith, *Therefore Stand* (Boston: W.A. Wilde Co., 1945), 385. See also Gary R. Habermas, "Resurrection Claims in Non-Christian Religions," *Religious Studies,* 25 (June 1989): 167–77.

55. For an explanation of how Jesus used parables in ways that seemingly withheld information from people, see Gordon D. Fee and Douglas Stuart, *How to Read the Bible for All Its Worth* (Grand Rapids, MI: Zondervan Publishing House, 1982), 124–25.

56. See S. Moyter, "Mystery," *Evangelical Dictionary of Theology,* Walter Elwell, ed. (Grand Rapids, MI: Baker Book House, 1986), 741–42. On the differences between Christianity and the mystery religions of antiquity see R.C. Kroeger and C.C. Kroeger, "Mystery Religions," *Dictionary,* Elwell, ed.,742–44; and Ronald Nash, *Christianity and the Hellenistic World* (Grand Rapids, MI: Zondervan, 1984), 115–99.

57. On the fallacies of esoteric interpretation see Groothuis, *Confronting the New Age,* 87–91.

Chapter 16—Coming to Terms with Jesus

1. Stephen Mitchell, *The Gospel According to Jesus: A New Translation and Guide to His Essential Teachings for Believers and Unbelievers* (New York: HarperPerennnial, 1991), 9; emphasis added.

2. Thich Nhat Hanh, *Living Buddha, Living Christ* (New York: Riverhead Books, 1995), 193.

3. George Howe Colt, "In Search of Angels," *Life* (November 1995), 79.

4. Ibid., 65.

5. Ibid., 78.

6. Ibid., 72.

7. Terry Lynn Taylor, *Creating with the Angels: An Angel-Guided Journey into Creativity* (Tiburon: H.J. Kramer Inc., 1993), 54; quoted in Ron Rhodes, *Angels Among Us* (Eugene, OR: Harvest House, 1995), 49.

8. Randolf Price, *The Angels Within Us: A Spiritual Guide to the Twenty-two Angels that Govern Our Lives* (New York: Fawcett/Columbine/Ballantine, 1993), 7; quoted in Gary Kinnaman, *Angels: Dark and Light* (Ann Arbor, MI: Servant Publications, 1994), 176.

9. The work of Ring and Morse is theologically affected by their New Age orientation. Sabom is more objective.

10. For an analysis of her viewpoint see Doug Groothuis, *Deceived by the Light* (Eugene, OR: Harvest House, 1995), chapters 1 and 2.

11. Kenneth Ring, *Heading Toward Omega: In Search of the Meaning of the Near-Death Experience,* second ed. (New York: Quill, 1985), 151.

12. See Groothuis, chapter 6.

13. Lia Salciccia, "Christianity Fails to Honor Women," *Oregon Daily Emerald* (July 15, 1993), 2. My response was entitled, "Biblical questions on God, creation, sin and women," *Oregon Daily Emerald* (July 27, 1993), 3.

14. Salciccia.

15. See Douglas R. Groothuis, *Unmasking the New Age: Is There a New Religious Movement Trying to Transform Society?* (Downers Grove, IL: InterVarsity Press, 1986), 134–40.

16. Ibid.

17. For a biblical critique of goddess religion, see Aida Besancon Spencer, Donna F.G. Hailson, Catherine Clark Kroeger, and William David Spencer, *The Goddess Revival* (Grand Rapids, MI: Baker Books, 1995).

18. Alister McGrath, *Intellectuals Don't Need God and Other Modern Myths* (Grand Rapids, MI: Zondervan Publishing House, 1993), 174.

19. For an in-depth treatment of the issue of women in the church and society, see Rebecca Merrill Groothuis, *Women Caught in the Conflict: The Culture War Between Traditionalism and Feminism* (Grand Rapids, MI: Baker Books, 1994); and Rebecca Merrill Groothuis, *Good News for Women* (Grand Rapids, MI: Baker Books, forthcoming in 1996).

20. Alister McGrath, "In What Way Can Jesus Be a Moral Example for Christians?" *Journal of the Evangelical Theological Society* 34, no. 3 (September 1991): 295.

21. Blaise Pascal, *Pensees* (New York: Penguin Books, 1967), #417/548, p. 148.

22. Mitchell, 54–55.

23. Ibid., 179.

24. On this great biblical truth, see R.C. Sproul, *Faith Alone: The Evangelical Doctrine of Justification* (Grand Rapids, MI: Baker Books, 1995).

25. Pascal, #212/528, p. 98.

26. Ibid., #192/527, p. 87; see also #352/526, p. 133.

Appendix—The New Testament Canon

1. Willis Barnstone, ed., *The Other Bible* (San Francisco: Harper and Row, 1984), xvii.

2. J. Harold Greenlee, *An Introduction to New Testament Textual Criticism* (Grand Rapids, MI: Eerdmans, 1964), 54; cited in Norman L. Geisler and William E. Nix, *A General Introduction to the Bible* (Chicago: Moody Press, 1986), 430.

3. Justin Martyr, *The First Apology of Justin,* chapter 67.

4. Polycarp, *The Epistle of Polycarp to the Philippians,* chapter 12.

5. John Wenham, *Christ and the Bible* (Grand Rapids, MI: Baker Book House, 1984), 154.

6. Ibid.

7. *The Jung Codex,* F.L. Cross, ed. (London, 1955), 125, cited in Wenham, 154.

8. Wenham, 154–55.

9. Bruce thinks that Unnik's comments (from which Wenham elaborates) may be a bit overstated but grants that the *Gospel of Truth* alludes to and cites New Testament books "in terms which presuppose that they are authoritative." He also notes that the writer's allegorical method of interpreting the New Testament materials demonstrates his high view of the texts as authoritative and inspired to

some degree. See F.F. Bruce, *The Canon of Scripture* (Downers Grove, IL: InterVarsity Press, 1988), 147.

10. Irenaeus, *Against Heresies,* 3.11.7.
11. Geisler and Nix, 231.
12. Ibid., 278–82.
13. Ibid., 231.
14. Ibid.
15. See Bruce, *The Canon,* 255–69 for a treatment of the "criteria of canonicity." See also B.B. Warfield, "The Formation of the Canon of the New Testament," in *The Inspiration and Authority of the Bible* (U.S.A.: Presbyterian and Reformed, 1970), 411–16. For a more theological discussion of canonicity see Carl F.H. Henry, *God, Revelation, and Authority* (Waco, TX: Word Books, 1979), 4:403–49.
16. Bruce Metzger, *The New Testament: Its Background, Growth and Content* (New York: Abingdon Press, 1965), 276.

Index